Clippers and Whaling Ships

Tim McNeese

Crestwood House
New York

Maxwell Macmillan Canada
Toronto

Maxwell Macmillan International
New York   Oxford   Singapore   Sydney

Design and production: Deborah Fillion
Illustrations: © Chris Duke

Crestwood House
Macmillan Publishing Company
866 Third Avenue
New York, NY 10022

Maxwell Macmillan Canada, Inc.
1200 Eglinton Avenue East
Suite 200
Don Mills, Ontario M3C 3N1

Macmillan Publishing Company is part of the
Maxwell Communication Group of Companies.

First edition

Printed in the United States of America

10 9 8 7 6 5 4 3 2 1

Library of Congress Cataloging-in-Publication Data

McNeese, Tim.
    Clippers and whaling ships / by Tim McNeese. — 1st ed.
       p. cm. — (Americans on the move)
    Summary: Surveys the history of clippers and whaling ships and examines
their significance in America's growth as a nation.
    ISBN 0-89686-735-8
    1. Navigation—United States—History—19th century—Juvenile literature.
2. Clipper ships—United States—History—19th century—Juvenile literature.
3. Whaling—United States—History—19th century—Juvenile literature. 4. Whaling
ships—United States—History—19th century—Juvenile literature. [1. Clipper
ships—History. 2. Whaling ships—History. 3. Ships—History. 4. Navigation—
History. 5. Whaling—History.] I. Title. II. Series: McNeese, Tim. Americans on
the move.
VK23.M36   1993
387.2'2'097309034—dc20   91-27187

★

Contents

★

*During the mid-1800s, clipper ships were
the fastest sailing vessels in the world.*

Introduction

D uring the first half of the 1800s Americans became very involved in trade on the high seas. Many wooden ships were launched to work for the United States. The ships expanded the country's role in foreign trade and brought in new sources of income for the young nation.

Two types of ships were particularly important to Americans at that time. Clipper ships were tall, heavily masted vessels that could travel faster than any other sailing ship of the day. Whaling ships were used to hunt down whales for oil to be used as fuel in American homes and businesses.

Early American clippers enabled the young nation to play a major role in the world trade industry.

The Age of
the Clippers

The age of the clipper ship lasted only 20 or 30 years. It began in America in the mid-1840s. A small group of ship designers and builders had developed the early clippers for speed. These fast ships were needed because of the expansion in world trade at this time. Ships needed to sail great distances across the oceans in search of foreign goods.

The clippers were **rigged** with many different sails, which used the ocean winds to speed the ships along. At about the same time that the first clippers were being built, American geographers were charting the wind and water currents of the major oceans. The work of these scientists led to the mapping of new trade routes that allowed for shorter trips, which helped to make the new clipper ships the fastest sailing vessels in the world.

The word clipper comes from the word clip, meaning to travel or pass at a rapid speed. "To go at a fast clip" is another way of describing a quick rate of travel. The clippers' long and narrow wooden hulls enabled them to be such fast ships. The masts were tall and carried acres of canvas sails. In fact, clipper ships carried more sail than any other ships of the time. Because of their high masts, clippers were often described as "moonrakers," "skyscrapers" or "cloud cleaners." Actual ship names reminded people of just how fast these ships were: *Meteor, Flying Cloud, Lightning* and *Wings of the Morning* were a few such names.

Clipper ships were originally built for the new American trade with China. It was the tea trade, specifically, that encouraged ship designers to work up a plan that would shorten the time it took to travel from the United States to the **Orient** and back. Tea lost its flavor if it stayed too long in the holds of oceangoing ships. Getting the tea quickly to market became important to shipowners and builders. However, only a few American shipowners put up the money it took to build a new ship for the Chinese tea trade.

Another need caused an explosion in the clipper-ship industry. In 1848 gold was discovered in California. Soon gold fever spread across the United States and around the world. Tens of thousands of people suddenly wanted to get to California as quickly as they could. Dozens of new clipper ships that were being built for the tea trade were rushed to completion.

Clipper ships changed ocean travel dramatically. Before the days of the clippers, few ships could sail farther than 150 nautical miles in a single day. (A **nautical mile** measures 6,076 feet.) Those that could achieve this speed did not do so regularly. They often did not have enough sails to travel fast in low winds. But by the 1850s American clippers were sailing 250 nautical miles a day. Many clipper ships achieved greater speed records. For example, a clipper known as the *Champion of the Seas* could put in 465 nautical miles in 24 hours. No sailing ship had ever beaten this record.

Americans did not control the clipper ship trade for long, however. During the 1850s British shippers began to build clippers. They built their fast ships to bring Chinese goods, especially tea, to London. Some of these British clippers also carried bales of wool from Australia.

But for all their speed, clipper ships controlled world trade for only a generation. Within 30 years of the first sleek clippers, oceangoing steamers would be able to match their speeds. By the 1880s the age of the great clipper ships had come to an end. But the history of these sleek, swift ships is a fascinating story.

From Privateers to Clippers

Clipper ships were descendants of the ships of the Revolutionary War. Many of the larger and heavier American warships were sunk by the British during the war. But a group of smaller vessels called **privateers** was used to harass British ships. These ships were not part of the American Continental Navy. They were privately owned by individual shippers and captains. These ships were used effectively against slower British ships during the Revolutionary War and during the War of 1812 as well.

Some of the best of the privateers used during the War of 1812 were those called the Chesapeake Bay privateers. These smaller, two-masted boats were

designed after fast-sailing French fishing or coasting boats called **luggers**. The Chesapeake Bay privateers came to be known as Baltimore Clippers. They were technically called boats because they had only two masts. Seamen of the day considered only a vessel with three masts a ship.

Building the *Ann McKim*

Experts do not agree on when the first clipper ship was built or even which ship can be called the first. But there was a ship built in the early 1830s that many people feel was the first clipper. In 1832 a Baltimore merchant named Isaac McKim hired a Chesapeake shipbuilder to construct a newly designed ship. It was to be a three-masted, square-rigged ship that would be

Privateers were small vessels with two masts that were able to sail at tremendous speeds.

able to sail in the Chesapeake Bay area and all the way to China.

This long, narrow ship was 143 feet in length and had a V-shaped **hull**. Its bow was round but not sharp as were bows of later, true clippers. The ship was so narrow that it could carry only about half the cargo that ships of that length ordinarily carried. But that was not a problem for McKim. He preferred it that way. He wanted this ship to be fast—very fast.

McKim also wanted a fancy-looking ship. He spared no expense. The ship had a durable, live-oak frame. Its hull was covered with copper. The deck featured mahogany trimmings and brass **capstan** heads. A **figurehead** in the shape of a woman was attached to the ship's bow. McKim named the new ship the *Ann McKim*, after his wife.

★

Technically the design of the *Ann McKim* was not that of a true clipper ship. True clippers had flat keels for the entire length of the ship. The *Ann McKim* had a sloping **keel**.

But the *Ann McKim* was seen as a new kind of oceangoing vessel. It was very fast on the open seas. For several years it was the fastest trading ship in the world. But it had been an expensive ship to build. For this reason few other shipyards tried to copy its design. In 1837 McKim died. The *Ann McKim* was sold to another shipping company and was used in the growing China tea trade.

John Griffiths's *Rainbow*

By the 1840s John Willis Griffiths, an American ship-builder and designer, was studying the lines of the *Ann McKim* to try to determine why it was such a fast ship. Griffiths had been doing research on the shapes of ships as he worked on a new design of his own. For 200 years nearly all oceangoing ships had been built with rounded bows. This caused the ships to ride up and down over tossing sea waves. Such ships were safe and kept the decks mostly dry, because the hull pushed the ocean water away from the ship. But the rounded bow slowed down the ship. And no matter how big the ship was or how many sails it carried, such a design would never make for a fast ship.

Griffiths tested his design with ship models. His study of the *Ann McKim* caused him to completely re-think how a ship's hull should be constructed. Griffiths's new design would allow for a wider stern, which would let water run smoothly past the ship's hull. This design cut down on the ship's **drag**, the pull of the water on the ship, which robs the vessel of any real speed.

Many new clipper ships were built during the 1840s
and most of them were based on John Griffiths's design.

In February 1841, Griffiths went to New York City to display a scale model of the ship he wanted to see built. But no one wanted to build such a ship. A year later, however, things changed. In 1842 the British won the so-called **Opium War** in China. This opened China to foreign trade.

Suddenly American businessmen wanted to have fast ships that could make the 30,000-mile voyage to and from China. American consumers already wanted Chinese trade goods such as spices, silk, firecrackers and, of course, tea. New York and New England shipbuilders were desperate for a new ship design that would offer the needed speed.

In 1843 a New York company commissioned the building of a new ship based on Griffiths's designs. The new ship, to be called the *Rainbow*, received a lot of attention in its New York shipyard. So many old sea captains and ocean veterans laughed at the new design that the company nearly stopped construction of the *Rainbow*.

Others Join In

But others were coming up with designs similar to Griffiths's. One important ship designer, Captain Nathaniel B. Palmer, whittled a model from a block of white oak. The model resembled Griffiths's ship. A notable difference, however, was that the Palmer hull had a flatter bottom.

Palmer convinced William H. Low of the New York merchant company, A. A. Low & Bros., that his design would make a fast merchant ship. Low commissioned a New York shipbuilder to construct such a vessel. This ship was built just a mile away from where construction on the *Rainbow* had stopped. Named the

Houqua, after a well-known Chinese merchant who had recently died, it was launched in May 1844.

The *Houqua's* first captain was, of course, Palmer himself. He set sail for Canton, China, on May 31, 1844. The *Houqua's* first China run was a success. The ship arrived in Canton in 95 days and the return trip took only 90 days, 23 days shorter than any previous China voyage Palmer had made.

Launching the *Rainbow*

With the success of the *Houqua*, construction began again on the *Rainbow*. It was launched on February 22, 1845. Despite serious problems with its rigging and masts breaking, the *Rainbow* made the China run in 102 days. It returned loaded with a cargo of pekoe tea. In that one voyage the ship earned more than twice the cost of its construction.

The *Rainbow's* second trip was even more successful. Its captain brought the ship into Hong Kong in 99 days and loaded it with tea. Then he sailed it back to New York in only 84 days. In fact the *Rainbow* arrived back in New York before any other returning ship could report on its arrival in China.

The *Sea Witch*

Sailing records were made to be broken. The owners of the *Rainbow* ordered another ship to be built. They asked Griffiths to design it. The new ship was called the *Sea Witch*. The *Sea Witch* was probably the first true clipper ship. It was built with a sharper bow than the *Rainbow*. This would allow it to glide swiftly through the water. It was 170 feet long and about 34 feet wide. (Most true clipper ships were about five times as long as they were wide.) Griffiths built the ship with a nearly flat bottom.

The *Sea Witch* looked beautiful in the water. It was painted black with a gold stripe around its side. Its figurehead was a Chinese dragon. The ship was launched on December 8, 1846.

And what a majestic ship it was! With the help of an expert sea captain, Griffiths had built tall masts on the *Sea Witch*. The mainmast, the tallest of all, towered over the water 140 feet, as high as a 14-story building. The *Sea Witch* boasted many large sails, each to help it move quickly along.

The captain, Robert "Bully" Waterman, set sail for China on the *Sea Witch* on December 23, 1846. Slowed by bad weather, the ship arrived in China in 104 days. But it made it back to New York in only 81 days. On its second voyage to China the *Sea Witch* made the trip back to the United States in 77 days. But it was its third voyage that made the *Sea Witch's* reputation permanent. On that trip Waterman sailed to China by a different route. Most sailing ships made the China trip by sailing east and around Africa. But this time Waterman sailed around Cape Horn at the southern tip of South America. Then he took his ship across the wide Pacific Ocean. He made the trip in 121 sailing days. In fact the *Sea Witch* arrived in China before the tea crop was even ready to ship out!

Sailing back to New York around Africa, the *Sea Witch* sped across the oceans. On many sailing days it logged nearly 300 nautical miles each day. On its fastest day the mighty clipper put in 308 nautical miles. On March 25, Captain Waterman completed his voyage. He sailed into New York harbor after only 74 days and 14 hours on the seas from Hong Kong. The *Sea Witch* set a new sailing record on this voyage.

The Sea Witch was one of the most famous clipper ships ever built.

It was a record that would never be broken by any other clipper ship.

Gold Fever in California

Early clippers like the *Sea Witch* were built for one reason: to get Chinese trade goods from China to the customers of the world as quickly as possible. But by 1849 there was another assignment for the first clippers.

In 1848 gold was discovered in California. News of the find spread around the world quickly. By 1849 tens of thousands of men were looking for a way to get to the California gold camps as fast as they could. Some of these early gold seekers decided to go to California by traveling across the West in wagon trains. But many decided to take passage on any ship that

During the late 1840s and early 1850s many clipper ships brought people to San Francisco to take part in the California gold rush.

looked as if it could make the trip around South America to California, a distance of about 15,000 miles.

Throughout 1849 approximately 800 ships sailed from the East Coast to California. But only one clipper, the *Memnon*, delivered would-be miners to California. (This was because the other eleven clippers were sailing to and from Hong Kong.) However, the *Memnon's* voyage took only 122 days. Most other ships took over 200 days.

Clippers also became involved in the California gold rush in another way. By the end of 1849, 20,000 people had found their way to San Francisco. Merchants soon realized that all those thousands of prospectors in California needed supplies. Trade goods could be sold at very high profits. A barrel of flour that cost five dollars back East could be sold in California for ten times that amount. And the miners needed lots more than flour. But the key would be, as usual, speed. A ship that could make the most voyages could make the most money.

The first clipper to bring a large cargo to California was, in fact, the *Sea Witch*. It made the trip from New York in 97 days. Merchants had loaded the clipper with about $85,000 worth of merchandise. So desperate were the gold miners for nearly everything from flour to playing cards to old newspapers that the goods were sold for $275,000. This amount was four times what it had cost to build the *Sea Witch*.

With the arrival of the 1850s and the California gold rush, new clipper ships were built. In the shipyards of New York, many new clippers were under construction. Soon, so many were being built that 10,000 men were at work on them.

The 1850s were the golden age of the clipper ship. Hundreds of the sleek ships were launched. Many of the new ships were larger than the earlier models.

One of the outstanding clipper-ship builders of the decade was Donald McKay. He built the best of the 1850s clippers. He designed 13 clippers and 12 of them were capable of sailing at speeds above 400 nautical miles an hour!

Donald McKay

Donald McKay was born in Tennessee, far from any ocean. But he grew up with 16 brothers and sisters in the Canadian province of Nova Scotia. Here he built small boats for himself and a younger brother to sail on a nearby river. At age 16 McKay took passage on a coastal schooner and arrived in New York. He got a job as a laborer in a shipyard, working for the famous ship-builder Isaac Webb.

McKay agreed to work for Webb for $2.50 a week, plus $40 a year to pay for the boy's food, lodging and clothing expenses. McKay was to be an **apprentice**, a person who works for someone else to learn a trade or skill, for 4½ years.

But McKay did not finish his apprenticeship with Webb. After four years, McKay was offered a job as a **shipwright**. This was McKay's dream: to be a full-fledged shipbuilder. He asked Webb if he would release him from his apprenticeship, and Webb agreed.

McKay went to work for Jacob Bell, a New York shipbuilder. Soon McKay was married to the daughter of another shipbuilder. The marriage helped McKay's shipbuilding skills. His wife, Albenia, was well versed in algebra and trigonometry. She taught McKay many things he did not know about the subjects, and he used these skills in designing new ships.

While working in New York shipyards, McKay met John Griffiths, then a draftsman in the Smith & Dimon shipyard. Griffiths would not build his great ships, the *Rainbow* and the *Sea Witch*, for many years. He and McKay talked together often about plans each had for building new and faster ships. In 1839 McKay was chosen to serve as foreman of the Brooklyn Navy Yard, an important position. When the job did not work out, he went to New England and found work in a Massachusetts shipyard. In 1841 McKay was offered a partnership with a shipbuilder named William Currier. By 1844 McKay had been put in charge of a new shipyard in Boston, Massachusetts. Soon he would put his designs to use and build his first clipper ship. This was the *Stag Hound*, which was launched in 1850. It was the largest merchant ship built at that time. The ship was so successful that, in one voyage to California and China, the *Stag Hound* recovered the cost of its construction.

Soon Donald McKay was known as the builder of the best and fastest clipper ships in the world. McKay asked five of his brothers to come down from Nova Scotia to help him build his ships. He even designed and built new shipbuilding equipment, such as a steam-powered saw, to speed up the building of his clippers. He used a steam hoist to lift heavy beams and **spars** into place on his ships.

In April 1851 McKay launched his second clipper, the *Flying Cloud*. This ship was grand, indeed. It was larger than the *Stag Hound*. It measured 229 feet long, 41 feet wide and nearly 22 feet deep. It was twice the tonnage of the already famed *Sea Witch*. In the month following its launch tall masts and the rigging and sails were added. The great ship towered as high as a 20-story building.

By early June the *Flying Cloud* was ready for the trip to California. This first voyage was difficult. The ship sailed through a gale and had many problems with its masts and sails. But after an exciting voyage it arrived in San Francisco in 89 days, beating the standing record of 96 days held by the clipper *Surprise*.

The ship's cargo of butter, cheese and other merchandise was sold for a handsome profit. Then the ship set sail immediately for China. There it took on a load of fresh tea and headed west, around Africa, for New York. In this one successful voyage the *Flying Cloud* paid for itself.

During the 1850s Donald McKay had other clipper ships built. Perhaps his best was the *Great Republic*, which for many years would be the largest wooden sailing vessel in the world. Originally this ship weighed 4,555 tons, twice the weight of any previously built wooden ship. It was 325 feet long, as long as a city block. One-and-a-half million board feet of yellow pine and over 4 million pounds of white oak were used in its construction. The great ship used 336 tons of iron and 56 tons of copper. Its mainmast rose 200 feet into the sky, the height of a 20-story building. It became the first clipper ever to carry four masts. Its sails measured out to 15,653 square yards of canvas.

On October 4, 1853, McKay launched the *Great Republic*. Fifty thousand people lined Boston harbor to watch the great new clipper slip into the water. Church bells rang and cannons boomed.

The ship was then towed to New York. By Christmas the ship was completely rigged and ready for sailing. It had been loaded with a cargo of wheat bound for England. But tragedy struck. On the night of December 26 a fire broke out in a dockside bakery. Flames and sparks fell on the *Great Republic's* sails. The great ship caught fire. Cut from its mooring in the harbor, the largest wooden ship afloat burned for two days. Water poured into the ship's hold soaking the grain cargo. The wheat swelled, splitting the seams of the hull. When the tragedy was over, the *Great Republic* had sunk into the mud of New York harbor.

The loss of the *Great Republic* was difficult for Donald McKay to accept. He had spent endless hours planning, designing and watching his great vision being built. And now it was gone. McKay signed the charred hull of the *Great Republic* over to the insurance company. The company in turn paid him what he had invested in the ship.

McKay would never again attempt to build a ship as large as the *Great Republic*. He had 38 more smaller

★

*The Great Republic burned afloat for two days
before sinking to the bottom of the harbor.*

ships built before his death in 1880. But he built fewer and fewer clippers. McKay supervised the construction of barks, schooners and navy gunboats, as well as clippers. These later clippers would be well built and very seaworthy. But they would set very few sailing records.

End of the Age

In fact the golden age of the clipper ship did not last beyond the beginning of the American Civil War. Events in the United States and around the world made clipper-ship construction difficult and nearly unnecessary. By 1857 the United States was in a difficult economic **depression** that hit the shipping industry hard. From 1855 to 1860 American cargo tonnage on oceangoing ships dropped from 65,000 tons to 17,000. This was a 75 percent drop in only five years. Clippers were no longer important in getting goods quickly to California. The western states were manufacturing their own goods and raising their own food. At about the same time the railroads were growing. With 30,000 miles of track in America, the rails were carrying more freight and mail. The role played by oceangoing ships like the large and speedy clippers was becoming less and less important.

To add to the troubles of American clippers, English merchants were beginning to have their own clipper ships built. They had decided not to rely on American clippers to deliver Chinese tea to London. Then came the Civil War, which cut off ocean trade for many parts of the country for four years.

During the war a small fleet of Confederate steam cruisers roamed the high seas, searching for Northern merchant ships. When they spotted a cargo ship, the

The destruction of clippers during the Civil War led to the
end of the age of these swift-sailing American ships.

heavily armed cruisers would fire a warning shot. If the ship was a Northern trading vessel, the Confederates would take off the crew. Then they would empty the trader of all the cargo the cruiser could carry. Finally they would set fire to the enemy ship. Fourteen clipper ships were destroyed this way during the war. This was a small fraction of the total number of ships (about 150) burned by the South, but such threats caused insurance on the clippers to soar.

Many American clipper ship owners sold their vessels to foreign traders. By 1865 nearly all of America's clipper ships had been sold off. This brought an end to the glory days of the great American clipper ships. When the war ended, British clippers had a **monopoly** on the China trade. Americans played a very small role in such trade in the years to follow.

American Whaling Around the World

In the 18th and 19th centuries American ships sailed from sea to sea hunting for whales. The whalers' legacy is one filled with stories of great whale hunts and dangerous harpooning adventures. Whaling tales have even found their way into American literature. The 19th-century novel *Moby Dick* is today considered one of the best adventure books ever written. Its author, Herman Melville, had sailed around the world and had many experiences on whaling ships.

Where It All Began

American colonists began whaling during the early 1600s. New Englanders from Massachusetts, Rhode Island, Maine and other states hunted whales in and

During the early 1600s, American colonists began to hunt whales.

near American waters. At least 125 New England whaling ships worked the whale fisheries in the waters off the New England and Canadian coasts. The most important fisheries were found off Davis's Strait, the Gulf of St. Lawrence and the Strait of Belle Isle.

Why did these men hunt whales? The answer is simple. Whales provided three valuable products that Americans and others wanted. They were sperm oil, **spermaceti** and **ambergris**. Sperm oil was found in the sperm whale's head and in its blubber or body fat. In those days, people used this in oil-burning lamps. Spermaceti is another kind of whale oil found in the whale's head. When the whale was killed, this oil became a solid, waxy substance after it was exposed to air. The spermaceti was used to make candles. These candles

*Sperm whales provided products that were very valuable
to the American people and to their trading industry.*

were some of the finest of the day, burning for a long
time and giving off little smoke.

Ambergris was another substance for which
whalers looked. This rare material was found in the
intestines of some sperm whales. It was formed when
the whale could not digest something it had eaten.
What collected in the whale's 1,000 feet of intestines
was a squishy, black, bad-smelling mass. But as with
whale oil, ambergris hardened when exposed to air and
began to have a pleasant odor. It became very prized
because it was used in expensive perfumes to make
their scent last longer. In the Orient it was a valued
spice. One whaling captain, in 1858, sold an 800-pound
block of ambergris for $10,000.

Nantucketers Lead the Way

The hunting of the great sperm whale helped the New England whaling industry expand during the last half of the 1700s. For most of the century crews on the whaling ships of Nantucket had hunted whales. As a result, by 1750 most of the local whale population was extinct. Forced to search elsewhere for whales, Nantucket whaling ships set out for the open seas. As early as 1740, Nantucketers sailed far from New England shores to discover whales in faraway places. Approximately 50 boats were returning to Nantucket annually with 5,000 barrels of whale oil, carrying a value of $25,000. By 1750 the Nantucket fleet had grown to 60 vessels and was bringing home a whale bounty valued at nearly $100,000. When the Revolutionary War began, in the mid-1770s, Nantucket whalers numbered their ships at 150 and the whale harvest was coming in at half a million dollars per year.

Searching for Whales

Between 1770 and 1775 the New England whaling industry expanded much more than it previously had. Sailors on Nantucket whaling ships were venturing away from familiar waters and discovering whales in far-off places: the Gulf of Mexico, the Caribbean and South American waters.

Before the Revolutionary War began the British Parliament tried to limit the American whaling industry. The English government did this by declaring certain hunting grounds off limits to colonial whaling ships. But most New England captains ignored the laws. And many found new whaling grounds that were not covered by parliamentary restrictions. When the War of

Nantucket was a chief American
whaling port during the 1700s.

Independence was over, the laws mattered to the New England whalers even less. But new problems for American whalers lay over the horizon.

Challenges to American Whaling

Even though the colonists won the War of Independence, the British Parliament made matters difficult for American whalers after the war. In 1784 Parliament passed a law that put a heavy tax on American whale oil brought into England. This move greatly disabled the American whaling industry. Many Nantucket whalers were encouraged to leave New England to find steady work on British whaling ships. By the 1790s 150 American whaling captains and 500 whalers had gone over to the British whaling fleet. There were four times as many English whaling ships by then as there had been in 1775.

At the same time the demand for whale oil was rising. People everywhere wanted it to light their homes and businesses. Whale oil was selling for nearly $500 per ton. With prices like that the New England whaling industry was able to rebuild. Nantucket whaling ships were soon found on the high seas in even larger numbers. By 1820 Nantucket was the most popular American whaling port. It was called home by more than 70 whaling ships. These ships brought in 30,000 barrels of sperm whale oil annually.

In the decades that followed, Nantucket became less important as a whaling port. A natural sandbar formed at the mouth of the harbor. This meant large whaling vessels could not dock. Whalers moved to another deep-water harbor at the town of New Bedford. By the 1850s 80 percent of American whaling ships docked in New Bedford. The number of vessels there,

★

approximately 400, was half of all the whaling ships in the world!

Searching for New Fisheries

Whether the whaling ships were American or British, the old sperm whale fisheries were on the decline. By 1790 the waters off New England and eastern Canada held fewer and fewer whales. As a result, whalers were forced to look elsewhere. They sailed farther from home and stayed at sea longer.

By 1789, for example, the first whales discovered in the Pacific Ocean by American whalers were harpooned. These whales were found off the coast of Chile in South America. The ship was the *Emilia*, and its captain was James Shields.

Although the *Emilia* was a British ship, most of its crew were Americans. Many of them were from Nantucket. After sailing the Atlantic down the east coast of South America, members of the crew decided to take the ship around Cape Horn to look for whales in the Pacific Ocean. There the crew caught many fish. Dolphins followed the ship. The water seemed alive with sea life.

Finally, in early March, the crew of the *Emilia* spotted a large herd of whales. As quickly as they could move, the men took to the whaleboats. And on March 3, 1789, a Nantucket harpooner killed the first sperm whale in the Pacific Ocean.

Life on a Whaling Ship

By 1820 the number of Nantucket whaling ships roaming the oceans was growing. Many of the ships by that time were larger than earlier vessels. They had three

The crew of the Emilia found that they were often
followed by dolphins during their search for whales.

masts and carried six or seven whaleboats. Earlier ships had carried only one or two. Often the ships were manned by crews of at least 40 men.

The golden age of whaling had arrived. Ships were larger and voyages were longer. Many trips lasted two, three and even four years. The ships did not return home until they were loaded with whale oil. Often a ship stayed out of ports along the way because many crew members would desert if allowed to go ashore. The food and water onboard were often bad, since a ship took on provisions only at the beginning of a voyage. Over time food would spoil.

Whaling ships were not known for their comfort. Crews were not paid well. Even as late as 1860 a regular seaman on a whaling ship was paid only about 20 cents a day. An unskilled worker on land could receive nearly a dollar a day. Many whaling ships carried crews who were taken from the lower classes. But among the crews, those who were harpooners were seen as important. Often they had sleeping quarters near the ships officers rather than with the rest of the crew.

Killing a Whale

Whale killing usually began with the sighting of a whale from high atop the ship's **crow's nest**. The crow's nest was a platform on top of a mast, where a sailor would look for whales on the horizon. When he sighted a whale's spout, the lookout would shout down to the crew, "Thar she blows!"

At this warning the whaleboats were lowered. Most whaleboats were about 25 feet long and easy to maneuver. A whaleboat crew numbered six men: an officer, who sat in the stern and steered the boat; a harpooner, who sat in the bow and helped row; and four other rowers. The two rowers on the **port** side had 15-foot oars. The two on the **starboard** side had smaller oars. These oarsmen rowed as close to the whale as possible.

Once in position near the whale, the officer ordered the harpooner to drop his oar and take up his killing tool. The harpooner moved to the side of the boat and threw his **harpoon**. He tried to aim the harpoon to strike the whale close to the eyes.

Next came a long fight between men and whale. When a whale was hit, it either dove or began to swim very fast. The harpoon was tied to a coil of rope held in a basket. If the animal dove too deep the sailors had to cut the rope so that the boat would not be pulled under. Whales often traveled as fast as 15 knots, pulling the small whaleboat behind them. Sometimes the whale would turn and attack the boat. Whaling was often very dangerous work.

But the worst was yet to come. Now the harpooner and officer switched places in the whaleboat. Each had to crawl past the other with the boat moving wildly. The harpooner moved to the stern. The officer took over the position at the boat's bow.

The common practice was for the officer to deliver the death blow to the wounded whale. When the whale tired, the boat was brought in close to it. The officer was armed with a very sharp five-foot-long spear. His job was to wound the whale a second time by sticking the spear into the animal's head. Once this was done, he would attempt to twist the spear, making the wound bigger.

Then the boat crew waited for the whale's response. The whale could do anything. It might capsize the boat with its tail. It could even try to grab the boat in its mouth. Frequently, though, the whale's two

When a sailor spotted a whale, he would stand on the ship's crow's nest and shout "Thar she blows" to alert the rest of the ship's crew.

★

Cutting up a whale was difficult
work for crew members.

wounds would be enough for the great animal. Blood would spurt from the blowhole. "Flurry! Flurry!" the men would shout. This meant that the whale was dying and the battle would soon be over.

Carving up the Catch

Once their captive was dead, the men rowed back to their ship, towing the whale. Often they had been pulled so far that they were miles away. The whale was rowed to the ship's starboard side, tail first. Men came off the ship with great cutting hooks and knives. Standing on the back of the huge beast, the men began cutting off the blubber. They then passed the slabs of flesh onto the ship. This step often took at least five hours. The work was difficult. The men had to be careful and keep their balance on the bobbing carcass. Often sharks would be present, taking great bites off the sides of the dead whale.

The crew peeled off the blubber in a single spiral of fat, rolling the dead body over in the water as they worked. When the whale's intestines were exposed, the crew examined them carefully for ambergris. This hardened substance was separated out. It would be sold for perfume making and for use in medicines. The blubber spiral was then hoisted onboard the ship. Cutters went to work cutting it into pieces called **blanket strips**. The blubber was then cut into blocks. The blocks were then sliced like bacon strips into what sailors called **bible leaves**. These strips were **tried out**, or cooked, to remove the precious oil. This process took many hours.

Blubber was generally kept in the cooking pots for more than a day. The smell was awful, and the men found it difficult to stand the odor.

Shipboard Difficulties

Rendering the blubber made deck life difficult for sailors, and not only because of the smell. The oil coated the deck, making walking hard. Oil fires sometimes occurred, setting oil-soaked decks ablaze.

Then there were the rats and roaches. Whale oil and blood attracted them. Cats were brought onboard to kill the rats. Nothing could be done to combat the cockroaches. The freezing temperatures of the waters around Cape Horn killed some of them. But in the Pacific they bred wildly. And they grew— some of them were 1½ inches long! Their most annoying habit was to crawl into sleeping sailors' beards in search of food particles.

Great Days for American Whaling

The most productive period for American whaling began in the 1830s and lasted until the outbreak of the Civil War. America was the leading whaling country and would be until the 1880s. During the 1840s there were 750 American whaling ships at sea, the largest number ever. Nearly all of them called New England home and came to port in New Bedford, Boston and Nantucket, all in Massachusetts. New London, Connecticut, and Sag Harbor, New York, were two other noted whaling ports. On the Pacific Coast, San Francisco became the largest whaling port.

New Sources of Oil

The decline of the whaling industry was brought on by two developments. The first was the discovery of oil in America. In 1859 Edwin Drake drilled an oil well in

As with the clippers, many whaling ships were sunk during the Civil War, causing a great decline in the whaling industry. ★

western Pennsylvania, giving birth to the American oil industry. Oil produced on land became cheaper than whale oil. By 1862 the price of a barrel of American-produced oil had dropped from $20 to ten cents. Americans began using **kerosene**, which was very cheap, replacing whale oil almost entirely.

The Civil War was instrumental in bringing the crushing blow to American whaling. Just as with clipper ships, Confederate cruisers stopped whaling ships off American waters and sank them. Almost half of the American whaling fleet was destroyed during the war.

The whaling industry continued for the remainder of the 1800s. But it would never be as important to the nation's economy as it had been between the years 1830 and 1860.

Glory Days

The age of the American clipper ships and whaling ships covered the same basic period in American history. In fact the 1850s were the peak times for both industries. In far-off nations speedy clippers could be found tying up in exotic ports of call: Canton, Hong Kong and others. These great tall ships carried American trading interests around the world. Whaling ships have added equal color to maritime history, filling books with legends and tales of whaling expeditions from the warm Pacific Ocean to the icy waters off Cape Horn. Clippers and whaling ships both made their marks on the history of American sailing ships, and they helped America grow.

For Further Reading

Adkins, Jan. *Wooden Ships*. New York: Grosset & Dunlap, 1978.

Graham, Ada and Frank. *Whale Watch*. New York: Delacorte Press, 1978.

Kalman, Bobbie. *Arctic Whales and Whaling*. New York: Crabtree Publishers, 1988.

Stein, R. Conrad. *The Story of the Clipper Ships*. Chicago: Children's Press, 1981.

Stein, R. Conrad. *The Story of the New England Whalers*. Chicago: Children's Press, 1982.

Whipple, A.B.C. *The Clipper Ships*. Alexandria: Time-Life Books, 1979.

Glossary

ambergris—A rare substance found in the intestines of some sperm whales. It was used to make expensive perfumes.

apprentice—A person who learns an art or trade through training under a skilled worker and practical experience.

bible leaves—Bacon-like strips of whale blubber that were cut and put into cooking pots to remove the oil.

blanket strips—Rectangular pieces of cut whale blubber.

capstan—A machine that raises up heavy objects, tied to a cable or rope, by a rotating, vertical drum.

crow's nest—A platform high on a ship's mast where sailors serve as lookouts.

depression—A period of low economic activity.

drag—The natural force that slows ships moving through water.

figurehead—The carved figure on the bow of a ship.

harpoon—A large spear or javelin used in hunting whales.

hull—The frame or body of a ship.

keel—A timber running the length of a ship's hull.

kerosene—A flammable product distilled from natural oil, often used in oil lamps.

lugger—A small fishing boat.

monopoly—A situation where one or a few people have exclusive possession or control of something, especially a business.

nautical—Having to do with navigation, ships or seamen.

nautical mile—During the age of clipper ships, a British measurement of 6,076 feet (1853.2 meters).

Opium War—Trade war between Great Britain and China from 1839-1842 for the control of the opium trade in China.

Orient—The countries that make up the Far East, including China and Japan.

port—The left side of a ship.

privateers—An armed ship paid for by an individual and used against the warships of an enemy.

rigging—A network of lines used on a ship that works the sails and supporting masts.

shipwright—A carpenter skilled in shipbuilding.

spar—A rounded piece of wood used on a ship to support the ship's rigging and masts.

spermaceti—A kind of sperm whale oil found in the head of the animal. Spermaceti became solid and waxy when exposed to air. It was used to make such things as candles.

starboard—The right side of a ship.

tried out—To cook whale blubber.

Index

Migration, Minorities and Citizenship

General Editors: **Zig Layton-Henry**, Professor of Politics, University of Warwick; and **Danièle Joly**, Director, Centre for Research in Ethnic Relations, University of Warwick

Titles include:

Muhammad Anwar, Patrick Roach and Ranjit Sondhi (*editors*)
FROM LEGISLATION TO INTEGRATION?
Race Relations in Britain

Naomi Carmon (*editor*)
IMMIGRATION AND INTEGRATION IN POST-INDUSTRIAL SOCIETIES
Theoretical Analysis and Policy-Related Research

Adrian Favell
PHILOSOPHIES OF INTEGRATION
Immigration and the Idea of Citizenship in France and Britain

Sophie Body-Gendrot and Marco Martiniello (*editors*)
MINORITIES IN EUROPEAN CITIES
The Dynamics of Social Integration and Social Exclusion at the
Neighbourhood Level

Simon Holdaway and Anne-Marie Barron
RESIGNERS? THE EXPERIENCE OF BLACK AND ASIAN POLICE OFFICERS

Atsushi Kondo (*editor*)
CITIZENSHIP IN A GLOBAL WORLD
Comparing Citizenship Rights for Aliens

Danièle Joly
HAVEN OR HELL?
Asylum Policies and Refugees in Europe

SCAPEGOATS AND SOCIAL ACTORS
The Exclusion and Integration of Minorities in Western and Eastern Europe

Jørgen S. Nielsen
TOWARDS A EUROPEAN ISLAM

Jan Rath (*editor*)
IMMIGRANT BUSINESSES
The Economic, Political and Social Environment

Peter Ratcliffe (*editor*)
THE POLITICS OF SOCIAL SCIENCE RESEARCH
'Race', Ethnicity and Social Change

John Rex
ETHNIC MINORITIES IN THE MODERN NATION STATE
Working Papers in the Theory of Multiculturalism and Political Integration

Carl-Ulrik Schierup (*editor*)
SCRAMBLE FOR THE BALKANS
Nationalism, Globalism and the Political Economy of Reconstruction

Steven Vertovec and Ceri Peach (*editors*)
ISLAM IN EUROPE
The Politics of Religion and Community

Östen Wahlbeck
KURDISH DIASPORAS
A Comparative Study of Kurdish Refugee Communities

John Wrench, Andrea Rea and Nouria Ouali (*editors*)
MIGRANTS, ETHNIC MINORITIES AND THE LABOUR MARKET
Integration and Exclusion in Europe

Migration, Minorities and Citizenship
Series Standing Order ISBN 0–333–71047–9
(*outside North America only*)

You can receive future titles in this series as they are published by placing a standing order. Please contact your bookseller or, in case of difficulty, write to us at the address below with your name and address, the title of the series and the ISBN quoted above.

Customer Services Department, Macmillan Distribution Ltd, Houndmills, Basingstoke, Hampshire RG21 6XS, England

The Politics of Social Science Research

'Race', Ethnicity and Social Change

Edited by

Peter Ratcliffe
Reader in Sociology
University of Warwick

in association with
Centre for Research in
Ethnic Relations,
University of Warwick

First published 2001 by
PALGRAVE
Houndmills, Basingstoke, Hampshire RG21 6XS and
175 Fifth Avenue, New York, N. Y. 10010
Companies and representatives throughout the world

PALGRAVE is the new global academic imprint of
St. Martin's Press LLC Scholarly and Reference Division and
Palgrave Publishers Ltd (formerly Macmillan Press Ltd).

ISBN 0–333–72247–7

This book is printed on paper suitable for recycling and
made from fully managed and sustained forest sources.

A catalogue record for this book is available
from the British Library.

Library of Congress Cataloging-in-Publication Data
The politics of social science research : 'race', ethnicity, and
social change / edited by Peter Ratcliffe.
        p. cm. — (Migration, minorities, and citizenship)
    Includes bibliographical references and index.
    ISBN 0–333–72247–7
    1. Racism—Research—Political aspects. 2. Ethnicity—Research–
–Political aspects. 3. Social change—Research—Political aspects.
    I. Ratcliffe, Peter. II. Series.

    HT1521 .P576 2001
    305.8'007'2—dc21

                                                    2001021028

10   9   8   7   6   5   4   3   2   1
10   09 08 07 06 05 04 03 02 01

Printed and bound in Great Britain by
Antony Rowe Ltd, Chippenham, Wiltshire

To the memory of Valerie Karn and Barry Troyna

Contents

Preface

This book represents the culmination of a project which I see as raising central issues for sociology as a discipline. It also explains in large part why I chose my particular career path. Although I derive immense satisfaction from theoretical debates, and of course recognise that these as integral to an understanding of the empirical world, my fundamental commitment to the discipline comes from its ability to question and challenge existing social formations, and thereby promote change. The current volume focuses on particular aspects of social division and inequality, but the centrality accorded to 'race', ethnicity and nation should not be allowed to obscure the more general issues for the profession globally.

In many ways, the project was conceived at a three-day workshop which I convened at the World Congress of Sociology in Madrid in July 1990. Focusing on the politics and ethics of international research on 'race' and ethnicity, it attracted a distinguished panel of academics from North and South America, Europe and Australia. The contributors deserve special thanks here both for the quality of their work, and for enduring a gruelling programme of presentations and debates at the height of the Spanish summer. Many thanks must then go to the University of Warwick and the International Sociological Association for providing financial support for the workshop: the former via its Research and Innovations Fund, the latter through its Research Committee on Ethnic, Race and Minority Relations.

In my view, the issues raised here have become more, not less, important, over the past decade. Events unfolding in the 1990s also convinced me that this volume should reflect the experiences of the widest possible range of societies and of researchers working within them. I extend my warmest thanks to my (in some cases) long suffering contributors, and to my close friends and colleagues, all of whom have been compelled to endure my obsession with this project, in particular my desire to take the time to 'get it right'.

This book is dedicated to the memory of two friends and colleagues, Barry Troyna and Valerie Karn. Both, in very different ways and in different substantive arenas, devoted their lives to the study and exposure of social divisions and, more significantly, to redressing the resulting inequalities. I share their concerns, and vow to continue their mission.

PETER RATCLIFFE
Kenilworth

Notes on the Contributors

Walter R. Allen is Professor of Sociology at the University of California, Los Angeles. He has held teaching appointments at the University of Michigan (1979–89) and the University of North Carolina (1974–79). Dr Allen's research and teaching focus on family patterns, socialization and personality development, race and ethnic relations, social inequality and higher education. He is co-director of *CHOICES*, a longitudinal study of college attendance among African American and Latino high school graduates in California. Dr Allen's more than eighty publications include 'The Color Line and the Quality of Life in America' (1987), 'Enacting Diverse Learning Environments: Improving the Climate for Racial/Ethnic Diversity in Higher Education Institutions' (1999), 'College in Black and White' (1991) and 'Black American Families, 1965–84' (1986). Dr Allen has also been a consultant to industry, government and the courts on issues related to race, education and equity.

Dipannita Basu is an Assistant Professor of Sociology and Black Studies at Pitzer College, Claremont, USA. Her research interests include black cultural entrepreneurship within hip hop culture, and the sociology of popular music. Research for her doctorate concerned itself with black entrepreneurship in Manchester (UK). It examined how small business ownership can provide insights into the political economy of the Black British, and explored the policy implications for black inner city entrepreneurship in the context of the economic rejuvenation of inner city areas. Her work on rap music and hip hop culture focuses on the way in which the post-Fordist structure of the cultural industries, in particular music, has facilitated an upsurge of entrepreneurial activity by blacks in the field of rap music and hip hop culture. She is currently working with Pnina Werbner on the implicit racialization of scholarly discourses in the literature on ethnic entrepreneurship.

Hassan Bousetta is a Research Associate in the Faculty of Political and Social Science at the Katholieke Universiteit Brussel. He is currently completing doctoral research on the socio-political mobilisation of Moroccans in four European cities. His research interest and publications cover the field of ethnic and migration studies, and extend to the field of Mediterranean politics. He has published several articles in, for example, the *Journal of Ethnic and Migration Studies* (Formerly *New Community*), *Migrantenstudies, Revue Européenne des Migrations Internationales, Migrations-Société*, and *Courrier Hebdomadaire du CRISP.*

Milena Davidovic trained as a sociologist at the University of Belgrade, gaining her MA and PhD. She is now based at the Institute of Social Sciences, Centre for Sociological Research in Belgrade, where she has undertaken sociological research for over twenty years. This extensive research and field work experience spans the following areas: labour migration (and especially the contemporary emigration of Yugoslav workers and their children to developed West-European countries); social strata of Yugoslav society; The Yugoslav War 1991: nationalism and the role of intellectuals. She was formerly active in the Professional Association of Sociologists in former Yugoslavia and Serbia. For the past three years she has been guest researcher in the Department of Media and Communication at Umeå University (Sweden), working on a project financed by *SIDA*: 'Media and Democracy in a post-Communist Society: The Case of Serbia'.

Vicki L. Hesli is Associate Professor of Political Science and Director of Graduate Studies at The University of Iowa. She has authored, and co-authored, articles about voting behavior, women and politics, political party development, religion, separatism, and regional autonomy. These studies generally have an area focus on Russia and Ukraine. Publications have appeared in several journals including *Electoral Studies, Slavic Review, Comparative Political Studies, American Political Science Review, British Journal of Political Science* and *Europe-Asia Studies.* She is also co-author, or co-editor, of four books; most recently, *Medical Issues and Health Care Reform in Russia from Edwin* (1999).

Christine Inglis is Director of the Multicultural Research Centre in the Faculty of Education at the University of Sydney. She is also Vice-President (Publications) of the International Sociological Association. Her research has been particularly concerned with migration and ethnic relations in the Asia Pacific Region and Australia. The effects of the growing importance of highly skilled immigrants and the blurring of distinctions between 'permanent' and 'temporary' immigrants are being explored in her current study of British and Chinese immigrant professionals in Sydney. Among recent publications is *Multiculturalism: New Policy Responses to Diversity* (1996).

Brian Kessel teaches, and serves as the Undergraduate Advisor, in the Department of Political Science at Western Illinois University. Prior to coming to Western, he was a Visiting Professor at Kalamazoo College. He received his PhD from the University of Iowa in 1998 with the dissertation *Party Activism in Unconventional Parties: the Case of the German Greens*. His reserach has been supported by the National Science Foundation and the German Academic Exchange Service (DAAD). He enjoys teaching and has taught courses on West European Politics, Russian Politics, Environmental Politics and American Government.

Marco Martiniello is a senior Research Associate at the National Fund for Scientific Research (FNRS) and Lecturer in Politics at the University of Liège. He earned a BA in Sociology from the University of Liège, and PhD in Political Science from the European University Institute, Florence (Italy). He is the Director of the Centre d'Études de l'Ethnicité et des Migrations (*CEDEM*). He is the vice-chair of the Belgian Association of Political Science. His latest books include *Migration, Citizenship and Identities in the European Union*, 1995, edited, *Sortir des ghettos culturels*, 1997; *Où la la Belgique?* (1998; co-edited); *Multicultural Policies and the State* (1998); and *Minorities in European Cities* (2000; co-edited).

Mark Orkin is President of the Human Sciences Research Council, Pretoria. He was previously Head of Statistics South Africa, the government department that produces South Africa's statistics, Professor of Social Research Methodology in the Faculty of Management at the University of the Witwatersand, and the founder-Director of the Community Agency for Social Enquiry, which handles large-scale research for government and civil-society organisations. His PhD in sociology examined the socio-political attitudes of black South African students. His recent publications include 'The Politics and Problematics of Survey Research: Political Attitude Studies during the Transition to Democracy in South Africa', *American Behavioral Scientist*, 42(2), 1998, pp. 201–22.

Peter Ratcliffe is Reader in Sociology at the University of Warwick, UK. A statistician by training, he has published widely in, and at the interface between, the disciplines of Sociology, Social Statistics, Social Policy and Social Geography. His books include: *Colonial Immigrants in a British City: a class analysis* (1979; co-authored), *Racism and Reaction: a profile of Handsworth* (1981); *Ethnic Discrimination: comparative perspectives* (1992; (co-edited); 'Race', Ethnicity and Nation: international perspectives on social* *conflict* (1994; edited); and, *Ethnicity in the 1991 Census, volume 3* (1996; edited).

Jan Rath received his MA degree in cultural anthropology and urban studies and a PhD from Utrecht University, and has also been active in political science, sociology of law, economics and economic sociology. He is now Associate Professor and co-director in the Institute for Migration and Ethnic Studies (*IMES*) at the University of Amsterdam, and manager of a research programme on the immigrant economy. For an overview of his current activities, check the internet at http://home.-pscw.uva.nl/rath. The author wishes to thank the Institute for Sociology of Law at the Catholic University of Nijmegen for their support in relation to his chapter in the current volume.

Rupert Taylor is an associate professor in the Department of Political Studies, University of the Witwatersrand, Johannesburg. His fields of interest include: 'race', 'ethnicity' and nationalism in South Africa; political violence in South Africa; and the Northern Ireland conflict. He has recently completed directing a major research project on 'Peace and Conflict Resolution Organizations in the South African Transition' and is currently editor of *Politikon* (South African Journal of Political Studies) and *Voluntas: International Journal of Voluntary and Nonprofit Organizations*. Publications include articles in *The Economic and Social Review, The Round Table, Telos, Race and Class, Ethnic and Racial Studies, Transformation* and *Peace and Change.*

Part I

Towards a Sociology of the Sociology of 'Race', Ethnicity and Nation

1
Sociology, the State and Social Change: Theoretical Considerations

Peter Ratcliffe

This book is concerned with some of the key issues facing contemporary societies in the new millennium. More than ever, identity in respect of 'race', ethnicity and nation is embedded in the very fabric of social relations. It defines not only who we are but also how we are likely to be perceived, and treated, by others. At the same time, there is a sense in which its various elements are inherently intangible and fluid. Thus, the postmodern 'turn' focuses on 'difference' and a total rejection of essentialism. The conjuncture of historical imaginings and contemporary material experiences engender a sense of hybridity, an ever-changing difference. But however contemporary sociologists conceptualize these issues, they are, I would argue, compelled to confront some harsh realities. Identity is not simply an interesting 'problem' for dissection and analysis: it also constitutes the basis on which hundreds of thousands of people have been murdered, raped and driven from their homes: a genocidal process often euphemistically labelled 'ethnic cleansing'.

Inequality, exclusion and conflict: the problem stated

This brief introduction has expressed the central concerns addressed in this volume. The world faces an ever more complex problem: the reconciling of difference, and in particular the desire to assert 'difference claims' where those claims inevitably impact on the (counter) claims of others. Whether or not these claims appeal to a form of primordial essence, the result can be the same. Ethnic mobilization, grounded in notions of territoriality and based simultaneously on claims of sameness and difference ('we' and 'the other'), is a pivotal element in any attempt to understand the dynamics of social change in the contemporary world. The 'grand narrative' returns to centre stage in the guise of 'true' narrative, in the sense of invented or 'imagined' notions of community (Anderson, 1983). 'Mobilization', as conceived here, is broad and multifaceted. It refers not only to overt appeals to national identity or to 'race'/ethnic pride, as a means of galvanizing support for policies of mass expulsion and genocide (so-called 'ethnic cleansing'), but also to more subtle forms of 'racialization' which provide justification for continuing material inequalities and processes of 'social exclusion' (Ratcliffe, 1998; 1999).

An individual's concept of self-identity, insofar as this is understood reflexively, is modified from without. Some would argue that the central task of the sociologist is to understand the nature of these shifts of identity, and in particular the impact of the discursive forces of mobilization on the construction of identity. This book, while acknowledging the importance of this agenda for the development of cultural theory formation, asks a number of rather different types of question, namely what (and who) constitute the sources of the mobilization process, and what are the underlying objectives of the project (both explicit and implicit)? Is its locus in 'state' policy, interpreted in the broadest sense, or is it 'community based'? Where this mobilization project is not explicitly territorial; for example where it simply represents the struggle for recognition in a multicultural or polyethnic society, we wish to interrogate the form, content and context of these 'recognition claims'. As will be discussed in the next section of the chapter, we wish in particular to ask what role the sociologist might, even should, adopt in relation to these forces and change processes.

In exploring this agenda, the current volume unambiguously espouses a materialist perspective. It is concerned with social inequalities and the means by which they might be addressed. This means that it inevitably addresses core aspects of the structure–agency debate. It is about the role of individual actors, and groups of actors, in promoting meaningful social change through their work. It is about the willingness of 'the state' to sanction, and support, research which may be highly critical of its actions. It is also, more significantly, concerned with the issue of political will; the will to support radical policy shifts, which may go far beyond the purely 'practical' to redress years of prejudice, maltreatment and 'racial' hostility towards minorities.

The role of sociology and sociologists

Why do research, empirical or otherwise, on 'race' and ethnicity? One answer would be that these are extremely interesting concepts which tax the sociological imagination because of their sheer elusiveness and complexity. Another would be that much contemporary debate is cast in these terms; one can even 'see' their effects worldwide in terms of social conflict. In other words, they appear to have a contemporary salience as 'meaningful' social divisions (to be 'added' to the core concepts of class and gender). This inevitably leads, or should lead, to a questioning of their ontological status, but the important question for the current volume is whether the sociologist opts to remain within the confines of such theoretical debates or explicitly pursues a wider agenda.

This clearly invokes classic debates in the discipline both about value orientation and about the sociologist as detached observer/commentator/scientist, reformer or revolutionary. The first of these positions is clearly untenable in the current context. To undertake research in this field, even at the level of highly conceptual, macro (non-substantive) 'theory', implies a value commitment which negates claims to 'value freedom'. It would be difficult to sustain a claim for 'value neutrality' either. To justify this view, one can always resort to the popular rhetorical statement that 'all research is political': here, it is abundantly clear that one cannot acknowledge, and 'discount', one's understandings of culture, ethnicity and 'race' – if only because they are deeply embedded in one's own identity.

The key issue is that of the 'political' as well as the intellectual role of the sociologist. The value commitment invoked by research on 'race'/ethnic inequalities and racism appears to demand a rejection of any attempt to adhere to the tenets of value-freedom, or even value-neutrality. Racism can be conceived of as a value system which in a very fundamental sense negates the basic human rights of sizeable sections of humanity. As such, it constitutes a departure from most common-sense understandings of what counts as an acceptable code of ethics and morality. Indeed, the International Sociological Association's Research Committee on Ethnic, Race and Minority Relations, in its articles of membership (drawn up during the period of Apartheid South Africa), imposes on its signatories an unambiguous obligation to oppose the system of apartheid and racism wherever they occur.

The question is whether this is in reality taken on board as a canon on which 'our' research is based or whether it simply represents a convenient self-justification. Some, no doubt, would regard it as no more binding, or prescriptive, than a vague commitment to the notion of 'equal opportunity'. There is also, of course, the general point that sociologists are not strictly bound by a code of ethics in the way that other professional groups, such as doctors and lawyers, are. Nor could they be, even if this was felt to be desirable. As a consequence, national sociological associations simply provide guidelines on what is regarded as 'best practice'. It is also clear that there has been increasing evidence of a 'radical individualism' amongst sociologists, something which by definition rejects external regulation. This led the current author, a little over a decade ago, to parody a statement made in 1987 by the UK's Prime Minister, Margaret Thatcher, outlining her view of contemporary Britain as being without 'society':

> it may be that there is no such thing as a community of sociologists, simply individual male sociologists, individual female sociologists and (individual) sociology departments (and research units).
>
> (Ratcliffe, 1988: 1)

The truth, or falsity, of this vision of the profession has important implications for the sociological agenda, as will be seen later. From the various accounts presented in this volume, however, it will become clear that research on matters of 'race', ethnicity and nation usually falls into either the reformist or revolutionary model, and occasionally into both at one and the same time. The 'revolutionary paradigm' tends to focus on empowerment and the by-passing of state institutions. Thus, state funding for research is not an issue: social change is conceptualized as essentially 'bottom-up' not 'top-down'. Even so, there are major variations within the 'paradigm'. Community mobilization and empowerment at a local level represent rather different forms of 'revolutionary' mission from one which asserts the need for global changes in the balance of power between major social blocs.

In most of what follows we see the image of sociologist as social reformer or 'social engineer', often in a distinctly Durkheimian sense. By the very demand to raise research funds they are typically required, or at least expected, to undertake projects which are in some way 'relevant' to the contemporary social world. This can, and usually does, mean that sociologists are following agendas set by others. The implications are clear. Our autonomy is deeply compromised: indeed it would be somewhat naive to expect otherwise given our role (in the main) as state employees. Departments of State at a national level, along with local authorities and major bodies involved (say) in the provision of health and education services, sponsor projects the remit for which is usually fixed, if only in broad terms. Research Councils provide alternative sources of funding but, as will be seen, these too are invariably required by government to support projects which are deemed 'socially relevant', meaning that they fit into current (state) thinking about key social problems.

The central question to be asked then is 'where exactly does the agenda come from?'. In the same way that it is naive to see 'the profession' as untainted by core elements of an externally imposed agenda, it is also wrong to suggest that the agenda is unaffected by the work of sociologists. This element of reflexivity is important in the context of many of the societies considered in this book. It is undoubtedly true also that much sociology remains committed to a critical assessment, and re-assessment, of social policy and the state's role therein. More theoretical work, in a substantive sense, clearly co-exists with the more directly policy-relevant approach.

Perhaps the most important insight comes from an assessment of the 'radical individualism' model hinted at earlier. This is that no clear, coherent 'sociological agenda' has emerged in any of the societies covered in the current volume. This is both unremarkable, given the contentious nature of the subject, and desirable in the sense of reflecting a certain intellectual pluralism. It also undoubtedly ensures that the state's agenda (insofar as such a thing can be said to exist) does not hold sway unequivocally. There is, however, a down-side to the individualist (non-)agenda. Irrespective of whether state policy challenges, or does not challenge, racism(s) and ethnic/'racial' inequalities, that is, whether or not it follows an egalitarian agenda, sociology itself, as a 'broad church', is not without its ungodly elements. Indeed, it has sometimes been seen as presenting a direct threat to 'the black cause it seeks to espouse' (Bourne with Sivanandan, 1980, p. 331); a threat therefore all the more insidious because the sociologist (typically) comes in the guise of a friend. But, what precisely are these dangers?

It seems rather trite to argue that we need to be aware of the implications of what we write; and certainly one cannot predict/control for all possible uses (and misuses) of our work. On the other hand, there seems at times to be little awareness of the potential dangers of the sorts of cultural essentialisms and stereotypes to which many sociologists, even if unwittingly, are prone. Obvious examples here are Pryce's (1979) association of 'West Indian culture' with drug-taking and pimping; repeated research *on* black communities (usually by White researchers) as if *they* were the 'problem' (Lawrence, 1982; James and Harris, 1993, introduction); and theorizations which, though apparently remote from action at street level, have an negative impact nonetheless, in the sense of (further) disempowering minority communities.

A rather obvious example of the latter is sociobiological theory, strongly defended by writers such as Pierre van den Berghe (1978; 1986). Although it is perhaps rather invidious to select one theorist from the many who might be deemed to be 'guilty parties' in this respect, he openly argues in the introduction to the 1978 edition of *Race and Racism* that researchers are culpable for failing to test socio-biological theorizations because they are afraid of what they might find. This is not only naive and mischievous, it also contains a fatal flaw. The theorizations to which he refers are not testable in a scientific sense, and therefore the only result of leaving them on the agenda is to fuel debates (say) about alleged 'race' differences; thereby leaving open the door to dubious, even racist, speculation passing as respectable 'theory'.

The authors in this present volume would generally ascribe to the view that sociological research on 'race', ethnicity and nation, whether predominantly theoretical or empirical, should ultimately be grounded in the values of social emancipation. This means accepting and adopting research practice which conforms to a number of basic canons:

- A rejection of the view that 'races' exist in any 'real', scientific sense.
- A rejection of cultural or ethnic essentialism.
- A commitment to research which empowers, or at least avoids the dis-empowering, of minorities.
- A cautious approach to funders of research to ensure a commitment to redressing inequalities and a concomitant rejection of racism, prejudice and discriminatory processes. [This implies a need on the part of sociologists to assess the degree of political will on the part of funders to *act* on the research findings.]
- A rejection of eurocentric notions of culture and ethnicity and the commitment to 'equality of opportunity' in the research process itself (in such matters as the recruitment of staff and the subsequent relations between members of the research team).
- In policy terms, an acceptance of the salience of 'difference' (equivalent in 'practical', empirical terms to the rejection of essentialism). Thus, 'equality of opportunity' is replaced by ethnicity-sensitive policy-making, with differential outcome assessments made prior to implementation.

This is not to preclude 'pure', basic research, that is, theoretical research with no obvious pay-off in practical terms. If for no other reason, it is needed to ensure effective theory-driven empirical research. Furthermore, it is of course the height of arrogance, and even patronizing, to suggest that the role of sociologists is simply to undertake research to improve the lot of minorities. For one thing, they are usually simply not in a position to deliver meaningful change (hence the above injunction to take on research where the political will to act is present). In any case, they should refrain from promising that they can. Secondly, minorities are perfectly capable of changing things for themselves, and are, in an obvious sense, in the best position to make judgements as to the most appropriate course of action at a particular juncture and in a particular social milieu: hence, the importance of empowerment.

Despite the problems inherent in the public–private dualism, it is useful to recognize the wider role of sociologist as both researcher and private citizen. The efficacy of agency in both spheres should be recognized. It is often argued that one's identity is important not only in methodological terms but also in terms of the power to promote effective social change. For this reason, we now turn to consider these matters.

The identity of sociologists: the salience of 'race'/ethnicity, gender and class differences?

There has been a long running debate in the UK literature about the precise identity of those who routinely conduct research into 'racial'/ethnic inequalities. This began in earnest as far back as 1980, when the journal *Race and Class* published an article entitled 'Cheerleaders and Ombudsmen: the sociology of race relations in Britain'. Jenny Bourne and Anil Sivanandan argued that 'the race industry' (of which academe was seen as an integral part) was betraying the very people whose interests it was supposed to defend and promote. It is worth following up these points in some detail here since the underlying issues transcend national boundaries.

These writers argued that, although sociologists often display an overt value position identifying with the concerns of oppressed minorities, in practice they have damaged, and continue to damage, their interests in a number of ways. For one thing, they tend to treat their communities as 'zoos', an historical displacement of the anthropological gaze from the colonial periphery to the metropolitan core. The accusation contains elements of both (middle)-class voyeurism and an ethnocentrism (even racism) rooted in pathogized images of 'ethnic minorities'. Hence, there is a strain of cultural deficit theory distancing 'we' from 'the other'. At its crudest, it is suggested that the problem stems from the imposition of white, middle-class, male values. The sociologist stands accused of building his (*sic*) career on, and in the process earning a good living off, the backs of the oppressed.

The crux of the argument appears to be that rather than challenging structures of inequality, researchers merely reproduce, or re-package, them. In this view, research does nothing to redress historical imbalances in material well-being and distorts or conceals the everyday experiences of minorities. But, in what sense does this relate to identity? Both Bourne (1980) and James and Harris (1993) appear to suggest that the problems can be laid at the door of white academics (in the guise of a 'white perspective').

In other societies, this might emerge as a more explicitly 'ethnic' issue: for example, a Serbian perspective in present-day Yugoslavia, or a (Jewish) Israeli perspective in contemporary Israel. The obvious question, however, is whether such 'race'/ethnically-based perspectives can be identified. For example, is there such a thing as (say) *a* 'black perspective'? The papers contained in this volume question this essentialist notion of (researcher) identity based on phenotype, arguing that such crude forms of perspectivism are misguided, unhelpful and even dangerous (cf Chapter 2 in this volume).

To build a research team comprising men and women from a variety of ethnocultural heritages is clearly good research practice, as was implied earlier. So is the career development, and increased employment of, 'Black researchers'. But it is theoretically naive, patronizing (some would even argue racist) to suggest that phenotype and 'perspective' are inevitably correlated. One cannot infer from the presence of a 'black' researcher that the resulting product will be non-oppressive; one work cited earlier (Pryce, 1979) being an obvious case in point. Here, a 'West Indian' researcher used his identity as a way of gaining access to 'fellow West Indians' in Bristol. Indeed, he acknowledges that he used his identity to facilitate a depth of access which would have been denied to others. But a moment's reflection suggests that his claim of 'common identity' is distinctly spurious: he was a middle-class, university-educated Jamaican (born and brought up in the Caribbean) studying largely working-class black Bristolians, many of whom had either been born in the city or arrived as very young migrants with their families in the 1950s and early 1960s.

His 'outsider' persona comes across very clearly in the methodology chapter of his book. Even more pertinently in the current context, he indulges in a myriad of stereotypes which mirror those of white racist 'common-sense'. He talks of social situations where he shared drinks with an informant '... and, *of course*, smoked [*took drugs*]' (ibid.,

p. 280, my emphasis). He also talks at length about black male 'hustlers' exploiting their female partners and acquaintances through pimping activities and, by describing others as 'law-abiding', suggests that this is somewhat unusual (rather than the norm). It hardly needs to be said that other black researchers would have adopted a very different research 'perspective' and produced a very different account of the St Pauls area of Bristol as, I would suggest, would most white researchers.

The published account could be, and was, read as providing a justification for the use of 'hard' policing methods. In angering large sections of the local black population it also, not surprisingly, made it considerably more difficult for future researchers (indeed, most outsiders) to gain their confidence. Pryce had betrayed both his subjects and his professional colleagues. The obvious conclusion here is that having (and/or using) a particular identity to gain enhanced access may impose a heightened responsibility on the sociologist in that subjects drop their guard and thereby become more vulnerable. In this particular case, one cannot imagine (say) a white researcher being privy to some of the social settings reported in *Endless Pressure*.

While clearly not an argument against using researchers of minority origin, it does heighten the problems, as well as the possibilities, associated with an identity which appears to be congruent with the subjects of a study. Pryce's research also raises, as was implied above, important questions about the salience of other aspects of identity. On his own admission, he presented an essentially male view of Bristol's 'West Indian' community. It is unlikely – though of course entirely possible – that a female researcher of Caribbean origin would have presented an analysis of male/female relationships similar to Pryce's. Mirza (1992), in her study of young black women growing up in London, makes a point of stressing how her identity permitted particular insights into the lives of her subjects. Unlike Pryce, who despite his caveats, attempted to talk about the community as a whole, she focused specifically on other young women with geographical and educational roots which mirrored her own. In commenting on her research, she stresses the importance of sharing a common culture with her subjects. This is, however, highly debatable as a statement of 'fact' in the sense that one could question the degree of commonality. It once again essentializes and 'freezes' culture; and, more importantly, it leads ultimately to a recipe for research practice which is clearly absurd: that of multidimensional identity matching. Others, following Oakley (1981), may wish to go even further by attempting to prescribe differential *methodologies*, invoking the use of different methods/techniques, on the basis of (say) gender identity.

The implications of these debates for the current volume are twofold. First, the identity of the researcher (both subjectively constructed and externally ascribed) has implications for the nature, and quality, of the data generated in a study. Secondly, this identity bears ethical and political implications. As we have seen, some writers (predominantly of minority origin) have argued that this implies that white/majority researchers have no useful role to play in this substantive area; that their work is methodologically flawed (both because of a lack of direct cognitive experience, and because of their ascribed identity – as 'oppressor'), and is (partly as a result of this) politically dangerous.

The position adopted by the contributors to this book is somewhat different. While accepting that researchers are not, and cannot be, invisible, and that their values are intimately linked to the research process, we would argue that there is a very important place for practitioners of majority origin. As already argued, our principal focus is on material inequalities. Attacks on white researchers have tended to focus on their paternalistic treatment of black communities and 'their problems'; poverty, poor housing, high levels of unemployment, and so on. The implication, even if only implicit, that the 'problems' are located within these communities, underscores the process of pathologization (Lawrence, 1982). The elevation of researcher to the status of 'white expert' only makes matters worse – in the sense of further disempowering those whose 'problems' are being investigated (Ratcliffe, 1992).

The key to this dilemma lies in the location of the 'problem'. Minority communities experience the *effects* of 'the problem' rather that 'owning' it; the 'problem' being racism and the associated panoply of discriminatory forces. Insofar as the 'problem' is in reality a white/majority problem and is located within majority communities and the institutions they dominate, there is a rather obvious role for white/majority researchers. This is particularly the case where institutional racism is the focus of research, as is argued by Ratcliffe in Chapter 6. In the context of societies where ethnocentrism and racism are historically embedded/endemic, the white/majority researcher is assumed to concur with the dominant ethos of an institution or social group. In a very obvious sense, therefore, they are more likely to be privy to the sorts of data which may otherwise be concealed.

Sociology, the state and social change: some key terms defined

This book is concerned with a whole series of complex issues: in some ways it raises *the* key issues for the discipline of sociology. At the simplest level, it is about the role of the sociologist, and sociological research, in effecting social change given the intrinsic contraints imposed (amongst other things) by state institutions. At the broadest, macro-level, it requires an elucidation of the structure–agency dualism in the context not only of individual, sovereign nation-states but of a global system comprising a myriad of putative 'races', 'ethnic groups' and 'nations'. It attempts to explore these issues via a number of case studies chosen so as to exemplify the widest possible range of disciplinary contexts in societies with radically different (though often interlinked) historical trajectories.

The first thing to note is that there is nothing self-evident about the three terms in the chapter's title. As we have already observed, sociologists are neither a clearly defined profession with a homogeneous training programme such as is the case with doctors and lawyers; nor, even using a fairly wide definition of the term, are they the only people involved in research on 'race and ethnic relations'. For the purposes of this book, the term 'sociologists' will be used in a generic sense to encompass all those within (or sometimes outside) the world of academe who write about or research issues of 'race', 'ethnicity' and 'nation'. Where appropriate, we shall refer to disjunctures between 'sociologists' so defined and the formal professional bodies operating in the society concerned.

It will quickly become clear that both the nature of 'social change' and the factors bringing it about are frequently elusive. Such change also occurs without conscious intervention – for example, via state policy, whether or not influenced by 'us' (sociologists). It is taken as axiomatic that both the nature of research and its likely impact will depend on a number of things. A society's economic, political and cultural heritage provide the context within which intellectual traditions develop. All of the former affect the way in which issues are problematized (or not, as the case may be) and the likelihood of meaningful social change in the relative material conditions of superordinate and subordinate groups. But this is only one, rather narrow, interpretation of 'social change'.

In many ways, the term is a much more elusive one. As with many 'common-sense' notions, most social commentators would probably claim to comprehend/apprehend its meaning; with rather fewer able to define it convincingly. In an obvious sense 'it's going on all the time', in that no society is, or could be, totally static (even in the most trivial sense). Power relations between groups change over time, the political economy of a given society is constantly in a state of flux, and ideological forces and material conditions might best be seen as constituting an ongoing dialectical relationship (Genovese, 1976). For the most part here, 'social change' will be taken to refer to tangible, measurable shifts in the relative economic and political position of groups locally defined on the basis of 'race', 'ethnicity' and 'nation', bearing in mind intersections with class, gender and social status.

Although in many cases the roots of these shifts will be located principally in intrasocietal factors, they will often represent only the surface appearance of more far reaching, even global, shifts in power relations. During the 1980s, both the US and UK witnessed discernable shifts to the political right with, as we shall see in Chapters 2, 3 and 6, direct effects on the position of minorities and also indirect effects through broader changes in the institutional structure of society. In Eastern Europe, political changes over the past decade have taken the form of major paradigm shifts. In the former USSR in the late-1980s (cf Chapter 10), *perestroika* under the Gorbachev presidency was accompanied by a massive growth in ethnic conflict and rising nationalism associated with demands for sessession. The ultimate break-up of the Soviet Union, and independence for the Baltic states, were accompanied by widespread (internal and external) 'nation(al)' conflicts from the Ukraine and Georgia to Azerbhajan to Chechnya. The wars in the Balkans during the 1990s, most notably in Bosnia-Herzogovina and Kosovo, revealed the true horror of 'ethnic cleansing' and left an abiding legacy of hatred between, for example, Muslim/Albanian and Serb and Serb and Croat (cf Chapter 9). The freeing of Nelson Mandela and the 'unbanning' of the ANC in South Africa materially affected the ground rules for future struggles towards the ultimate elimination of apartheid (cf Chapter 4). Set against these momentous historical events, it may appear that academics and others concerned with serious social commentary, have a relatively insignificant role to play as prime movers and catalysts for change. But this may well be to seriously underestimate the potential of this group.

The term 'the state' is another which has been subject to much sloganeering and sloppy thinking, even in the social science literature. In the general desire to avoid such glib rhetoric, and the constant need to debate different conceptualizations of 'the state', in this volume the term will be used sparingly. This risks the atomization of hegemonic power relations, but we would argue that social change and shifts in power and ideology can usually be understood more clearly without resorting to the concept of state. We shall tend to talk instead about institutional interests such as those of central and local government, the judiciary and the police, the media, major (international) capital, academe (and, more generally, the educational system). Insofar as the concept of 'state' rears its head it will be seen to encompass most of the elements within the classic Poulantzian model (but without the rigid structuralist interpretation).

The role of case studies

The key issues for our analysis relate to the location of the discipline within the polity of a given society. In exploring these issues in the context of very different types of society, a highly complex picture emerges. Some would argue that its multidimensionality defies theoretically-driven categorization: the organizational schema for case studies employed here is one firmly grounded in broad forms of sociohistorical trajectory. The latter is central to our analysis as it relates to the evolution of the state, the nature of internal social divisions (and prospects for meaningful change), and the nature and development of academe and the position of sociology within it.

Before presenting these analyses, however, we begin with an exploration of one of the key issues raised in the current chapter, the politics of identity. Although primarily focusing on US debates, the issues which Basu tackles in Chapter 2 are salient to all case studies in that substantive struggles for equality outside academe are invariably mirrored by internal struggles for equity and control of the research agenda. She argues that exclusionary forces present in the wider society are often mirrored within academe, within resultant (negative) effects on the discipline, its agenda, and its influence on the wider polity.

Prior to the exploration of a number of European case studies, we look at three very different industrialized economies: one rooted in slavery; the second recently emerging from an era of rigid 'racial' segregation; the third (also a product of European settlement but involving the virtual elimination of the indigenous population), having a history of nation-building based on immigration. Allen's analysis of the US, in Chapter 3, is in some ways a substantive corollary of the previous chapter, demonstrating how the African–American agenda has been subverted. It also demonstrates the rigidity of perceptions of 'race' difference rooted in slavery. Post-apartheid South Africa is a very important case study (Chapter 4) in that it locates the struggles of a internally divided discipline in a changing political context. Taylor and Orkin suggest a role for academe in the promotion of a non-racial society. The case of Australia, discussed by Inglis in Chapter 5, illustrates the difficulties faced by sociologists attempting to influence the political agenda in a largely hostile environment (and with research continually under threat).

Part III of the book looks at three European societies with a colonial history and a legacy of hatred, xenophobia and racism towards immigrants from former colonies. It opens with Ratcliffe's account of the UK (Chapter 6). It illustrates how the relationship between academe and the 'state' shifts significantly at different historical/political junctures. The plurality of UK approaches to 'race'/ethnic inequalities and racialization processes appears to be largely absent in The Netherlands. Rath, in Chapter 7, argues that mainstream sociology has precipitated the marginalization of Marxian approaches to the sub-discipline. Martiniello and Bousetta, in Chapter 8, suggest that in Belgium it is the *sub-discipline* which is marginalized, inevitably leading to a failure to influence the political agenda. Importantly, reflecting on the issue of researcher identity, they argue that this undervalued area of academe is dominated by those of minority origin.

The final part of the book takes a close look at two case studies of socialist, and former-socialist, societies of Eastern Europe, where the focal point of analysis shifts to 'nation'. Yugoslavia, the focus of Chapter 9, was an obvious choice. Davidovic demonstrates the ebbs and flows in the embattled history of the discipline, ranging from its rejection as 'bourgeois science' to a partial acceptance in a highly circumscribed form. It shows how sociologists failed to foresee, and even comprehend, the violent conflict and 'ethnic cleansing' which engulfed the Balkans during the 1990s. Many, indeed, simply adopted the nationalist rhetoric of their political masters. In the final chapter, Hesli and Kessel appraise the state of the discipline in Russia. Marked shifts in the sociological agenda mean the increased audibility of the people's voice, if not (or not yet) control over the motor of change.

References

Anderson, B. (1983) *Imagined Communities*, London, Verso.
van den Berghe, P. (1978) *Race and Racism*, New York, Wiley.
van den Berghe, P. (1986) Ethnicity and the Sociobiology Debate, in J. Rex and D. Mason (eds) *Theories of Race and Ethnic Relations*, Cambridge, Cambridge University Press.
Bourne, J.(with A. Sivanandan) (1980) Cheerleaders and Ombudsmen: the Sociology of Race Relations in Britain, *Race and Class*, XXI(4), pp. 331–51.

Genovese, E. (1976) Materialism and Idealism in the History of Negro Slavery in the Americas, in G. Bowker and J. Carrier (eds) *Race and Ethnic Relations: Sociological Readings*, London, Hutchinson.

James, W. and Harris, C. (eds) (1993) *Inside Babylon: the Caribbean diaspora in Britain*, London, Verso.

Lawrence, E. (1982) 'Just plain common sense: the roots of racism' and 'In the abundance of water the fool is thirsty: sociology and black pathology', in CCCS, *The Empire Strikes Back*, London, Hutchinson, pp. 47–94.

Mirza, H. (1992) *Young, Female and Black*, London, Routledge.

Oakley, A. (1981) Interviewing Women: a Contradiction in Terms?, in H. Roberts (ed.) *Doing Feminist Research*, London, Routledge and Kegan Paul.

Pryce, K. (1979) *Endless Pressure*, Harmondsworth, Penguin.

Ratcliffe, P. (1988) Race and the Sociologist: the Case for a Research Agenda, paper presented at the ISA/CRES Seminar on *New Frontiers in Social Research*, University of Amsterdam.

Ratcliffe, P. (1992) Renewal, Regeneration and 'Race': Issues in Urban Policy, *New Community*, 18 (3), 387–400.

Ratcliffe, P. (1998) 'Race', Housing and Social Exclusion, *Housing Studies*, 13 (6), 807–18.

Ratcliffe, P. (1999) Housing Inequality and 'Race': Some Critical Reflections on the Concept of Social Exclusion, *Ethnic and Racial Studies*, 22 (1), 1–22.

2
The Colour Line and Sociology

Dipannita Basu

Introduction

'The problem of the twentieth century would be the problem of the colour line – the relation of the darker to the lighter races of men in Africa, in America and the islands of the sea', wrote W. E. B. Du Bois in 1903. This article traces the 'problem of the color line' through the experiences of African–American sociologists (and other cultural workers) within the institutions and practices of the academy.[1] My concern is not so much with the individual merits of researchers, white and black, within the academy, but how the power relations inscribed within white American academia can selectively silence, sanction and marginalize those who are black, and spurn the sociological insights they bring to the analysis of 'race'. There are, of course, effective white researchers, scholars and other cultural workers who have been able to evoke deep sympathy, understanding and intellectual fortitude in their analysis of black people (Liebow, 1967; Valentine, 1968).

I do not claim that there exists a single black perspective, or that simply by virtue of being black, observations and theories are more valid. Nonetheless, it is more than plausible that blacks approach discussions, evaluations and observations of race differently from those who have no experience of its exclusionary powers, except at the level of the 'scientific method'. The latter exigency enables whites to write about blacks and their communities, when they have little first-hand knowledge of them, and to exclude other viewpoints that are based on experiences closer to the people studied. My focus, therefore, is the way in which the assertion and ascription of racialized identities inflect the experiences and work of black scholars and cultural workers. How is their work and presence within academic life, and its impact outside, tolerated or contingent upon the current political climate on issues of 'race', interwined as it is by internal class divisions, gender and sexuality?

Walls of exclusion and silence: Du Bois and Mydral

> Like it or not, and know it or not, sociologists will organize their research in terms of their prior assumptions; the character of sociology will depend upon and will change when they change.
>
> (Gouldner, 1970, p. 28)

> Research in the social sciences will remain stunted and inadequate until it includes the search for knowledge on power relations among men and the means for generating the will and the capacity for action directed toward the achievement of a good society.
>
> (Louis Wirth, 1947, quoted in Cox, 1970, xi)

The canonization of Robert Park's work together with Mydral's *The American Dilemma* impacted heavily on both the direction of American sociology and on social policy debates. But how did these revered scholarly works come to underlay a hierarchy of knowledge whose exclusionary powers have led to a 'white' sociology that often neglects or berates insights from African–Americans themselves, unless they conform to the established viewpoints and paradigms?

In America, during the first few decades of the twentieth century, urban sociology and the University of Chicago were virtually synonymous. The leading figures of Robert Park and Ernest Burgess were canonized within the urban sociology discipline. In contrast, W. E. B. Du Bois's sociological works were rendered comparatively invisible. Park's theories continued to provide models for the study of race and ethnicity as recently as the 1960s.

Du Bois was one of the first social scientists to combine methods of data collection and description with a spatial analysis of economic and social processes in his classic *The Philadelphia Negro* (the first holistic account of urban black America). He eschewed social Darwinism, recognizing that it provided a justification for the oppression of black people.[2] Unlike Park, who emphasized the role of communication and empathy in mitigating racial subordination, Du Bois recognized how racism structured residential patterns, the existence of housing submarkets, job discrimination and the importance of public opinion, which he recognized as sanctioning institutional racism.[3] By drawing on his own experience as a black American, he was more open to a hermeneutic or interpretative approach to race issues, that accommodated fundamental chasms of race, gender and class conflict – unlike the natural science models so exalted in his day. Despite his profound insights, and despite being in the same university as Burgess and Park, their work on 'race'made little reference to his. His work was routinely neglected by major journals such as *The American Journal of Sociology,* and he was unable to work in influential institutions (Sibley, 1995).

This is not to say that black sociologists' voices were not registered, but visibility meant that their research and scholarship conformed to Park's view of urban society. Black scholars under the apprenticeship or influence of Park's theoretical orientation gave little importance to the power relations of racism, and collaborated in problematizing the sociology of black communities as the 'Negro problem'. The black sociologist, E. Franklin Frazier, applied Park's thesis on social disorganization to the black family.[4] His doctoral dissertation at the University of Chicago was published in 1931 as *The Negro Family in Chicago,* and his *The Negro Family in the United States,* published in 1939, received the Ainsfield Award as the most important race relations book of the year. But, adopting a more radical stance on the 1935 Harlem riots in *The Negro in Harlem: a Report on Social and Economic Conditions Responsible for the Outbreak of March 19, 1935,* Frazier's work was rendered relatively invisible. The report's findings of institutionalized racism in New York and the role of economic institutions in maintaining blacks in perpetual dependency was too controversial for Fiorello La Guardia, Major of New York, to release.

Myrdal's *An American Dilemma,* consisting of 45 chapters spanning over 1300 pages, was written in the same period. Raised to the pantheon of classic 'race relations' texts, it was authored by a foreign-born white liberal Swedish economist. The Carnegie Corporation, which sponsored it, was not only racially exclusive but strongly supported white supremacy in apartheid societies (Stansfield, 1985). They were responding to the sea change in race relations and politics during that period – initiated by fear rather than philanthropy. It was a time when the 'Negro Problem'was moving north, where black votes were plentiful, but black militancy was increasing. The trustees of the Foundation were assured that Mydral's elite credentials and immersion in the world of government grants, foundations and corporations would result in a work that would not be politically contentious (Stansfield, 1985; Steinberg, 1995). They were not mistaken. Mydral did not challenge any major political or economic institution: had he done so the book would probably have disappeared without trace. One of his most vehement critics, Oliver Cox, argued that he failed to illuminate the social determinants of the well-known 'dilemma', that he merely recognizes it and rails against it.

The contention amongst his critics was that he reduced the disenfranchisement of blacks – their economic and geographical restriction, their exclusion from juries, the segregation of schools and public accommodation – to the beliefs that whites had about blacks. He failed to recognize the structural basis and material sources of racism. He failed to mention how the state might act to redress the wrongs he described. In short, his failure was not of recording racism in an erudite and extensive manner, but the failure to commit himself to the rights of full citizenship for black Americans.

Ironically, when the (white) director of the University of North Carolina Press, W. T. Couch, commissioned the report *What the Negroes Wants* to find out what the Negro *really* wants, he was disturbed by the virtual unanimity of opinion amongst the 14 black contributors. What emerged was what they *really* wanted was equal rights for blacks. The introduction to the book subsequently contained an introduction by Couch which repeatedly invokes the *American Dilemma*, thereby distancing himself from the book's contributors (including Langston Hughes, A. Philip Randolph, Mary McLeod Bethune and Frederick Patterson). As Steinberg (1995, pp. 48–9) incisively concludes:

> The juxtapositioning of the contents of *What the Negro Wants* and *An American Dilemma* points to Mydral's most stunning failure: despite his apotheosis of American democracy and the American creed, and despite his repudiation of American racism and second class citizenship, he was unwilling to commit himself. Mydral's genius was to dispense only as much medicine as the patient was willing to swallow, and his book was perfectly tailored to the political and racial climate of the post-war decade – Mydral's opus served as an epitaph to the old racial order and as an intellectual baptism for a new racial status quo ... that would persist until it came under challenge from grassroots protest movement.

So, while white scholarship within the field of race relations progressed from social Darwinism (that held that blacks were inherently inferior) to Mydral's assumption that racism was rooted in a pre-rational belief system, the view that society as a whole was racist was marginalized. White, middle-class men were in a position racially (and in terms of class) to wait patiently for social change and to base their sociology on theories wedded to the existing racial hierarchy. History, however, has shown how summoning the forces of reason and science to counter retrograde racial attitudes and hostilities based on a pre-rational and pre-democratic logoism obscured the racist nature of society as a whole: a view not lost on many black scholars, but nonetheless marginalized by the academy. For example, the collaborative work of the activist, Stokely Carmichael, and Charles Hamilton, a black political scientist, postulated a colonial model of race relations that challenged the tendency of social scientists to abstract racist ideologies from the political and economic context. Their theoretical analysis was not welcomed by the social science fraternity of the time. Similarly, Robert Blauner's *Racial Oppression in America* was by his own account well received by minority scholars and by students but not by mainstream sociologists, particularly his own colleagues whose dismissal of its merits resulted in his being turned down twice for promotion to full professor (Blauner, 1972).[5]

In contrast, Nathan Glazer's *Beyond the Melting Pot* received the *Saturday Review of Literature*'s Ansfield-World Award for its contribution to intergroup relations. The book's influence in blaming America's race problem on blacks themselves, while simultaneously accepting blame for the origins of 'the problem', set the *leitmotif* for much of sociological research in the next couple of generations. The Moynihan report (1967, p. 47) on the black family argued the culture of poverty to be 'capable of perpetuating itself, without assistance from the white world'. His report, despite invoking criticism and sparking a national political debate, provided the basis for a presidential speech establishing new federal policy goals.

> The white family has achieved a high degree of stability and is maintaining that stability. By contrast, the family structure of lower class Negroes is highly unstable, and in many urban centers is approaching complete breakdown.
>
> (Glazer and Moynihan, 1965, p. 5)

Such pronouncements reflect a dominant white scholarship that argues that the principal cause of the plight of black communities is to be found in their *own* cultural deficiencies. Such a view belies an unexamined and strong moralistic tone that makes implicit and explicit value judgements about the culture of lower class blacks, often juxtapositioned against the values of white Middle America. In turn, self-help and self-examination became the prescription for the ills of lower class blacks. Yet, many of the communities are not studied in their own right in terms of their *own* social order, cultural idiom, or lifestyle. Instead they tend to be compared to everything in America that is non-black and non-ghettoized, and are subsequently seen to deviate from an ethnocentric norm.

Of course, some scholars have been astute in meeting the need for recording and interrogating what might be described as the lower-class life of ordinary people, on their own grounds and on their own terms.[6] Elliot Liebow, in his study of lower-class Negro men *Tally's Corner*, was quite aware of his methodological biases, such as the exclusive focus on people on the street corner, not those at work, home or elsewhere. Phillipe Bourgois' (1995) acclaimed analysis of a Puerto Rican community recognizes the overly moralizing critiques of poor communities of colour that inadequately comprehend that structural transformations are integral to the lived experiences of the poor young. Yet his study continues to be informed by the culture-of-poverty thesis.

In the 1960s, a paradigm crisis in the sociology of race was voiced (Pettigrew, 1980). While sociologists were unequipped, and unprepared, to recognize the upheavals and conflicts over race and class, black activists were not. A number of 'black movement' books found an audience,[7] and sociology yielded to the examination of racism as a system of discrimination and institutionalized disadvantage. However, scholarship on race continued to obscure the privileged side of the colour line to examine the ways in which white people are socialized to be colourblind, and how their not 'seeing' both constitutes their identity formation and sustains the privilege of 'whiteness' (Frankenberg, 1993). Such an absence in mainstream studies of 'race'resulted in a general failure of the dominant both to reflect on their dominance and to erase or mythologize the historical power relations between blacks and whites (Hall, 1992). In a white-dominated society, 'truths' about crime, welfare, immigration and the nature of the American creed are often informed by the tutelage of pedagogical and institutional racism and sexism, as well as by a social science which equates 'blackness' and 'Femaleness' to exotica, invisibility, danger and savagery, and 'whiteness'and 'maleness' to the norm.[8] While black writers such as Du Bois, Ralph Ellison and James Baldwin began to unravel the privilege of whiteness in the early part of the century, it was not until the late-1980s and early-1990s that mainstream American academia, led in large part by black scholars, turned the gaze of 'race relations' onto whiteness (increasingly viewed as a symbol of racial identity, displacing it as an unnamed, universal moral referent).[9]

The 1980s and 1990s also witnessed a renaissance in black cultural workers, intellectuals and artists. Through critical analysis in areas such as cultural studies, legal studies, film theory and literary theory (as well as sociology), black intellectuals challenged the demise of the black essential subject, and questioned the tensions within the signifiers of blackness. These black intellectuals forged a new cultural politics of difference that deconstructed the signs of blackness in relation to pre-vailing power dynamics. Additionally, they presented important ways in which the stability and power of grand theory, the unified subject, disinterested knowledge and the authority of positivist epistemologies were challenged (Collins, 1990).[10]

They debated the analytical study and location of race, class, gender, sexuality within the signs of blackness, calling attention to the way in which blackness is a force for political change and cultural identity, and how this is played out in its complex tropes of affirmation, opposition, menace and authenticity. As a result, political claims on blackness be-came problemitized because of the complex interplay and intersections of forms of difference (Crenshaw, 1991). Angela Davis, Michelle Wallace, Audre Lourde, Patricia Williams, bell hooks, Toni Morrison, Tricia Rose, and Kimberly Crenshaw also challenge the assumed masculinist and heterosexual power of blackness, by speaking to the silence and margin-alization of black gay men and women, and black feminists.

Politics of whiteness, sociology and scholarship in the 1980s

> We'll soon be able to celebrate Martin Lucifer Coon's birthday.
> Bell, 1988[11]

In the 1980s, Reaganism was marked by its re-energized conservatism. The moral panics generated by right-wing attacks on race preferential programmes, immigration laws and the failure of the welfare state, was propped up by diverse conservative and right-wing groups as well as scholars. Whiteness became a signifier for white middle-class resistance to 'taxation, to the expansion of state-furnished rights of sorts, and to integration' (Winant, 1992, p. 166). The threat of minority rights – the rewriting of history from the bottom up by previously silenced or appro-priated voices – were viewed as attacks on the sensibilities and collective consciousness of America and its institutions. These concerns seeped into the ivory tower through attacks on affirmative action and multi-culturalism. At affirmative action's inception, Barnes (1973) claimed: 'We are now entering a new era of discrimination on the basis of race, creed and color. Large numbers of qualified scholars will pay with their careers simply because they are male and white'. Despite the historic, and ongoing, under-representation of minorities, Barnes sparked off calls for 'equal rights'and the cessation of 'reverse discrimination'. He aired the (subsequently popular) view that European males are being disadvantaged by affirmative action while European – American women, as well as minority women and minority men, benefited.

Within academia, African – American males were, until the 1960s, mostly limited to jobs in historically black colleges. In the 1970s, aggressive hiring increased their representation in white institutions. In 1972, 3.4 per cent of all sociology positions were filled by African–Americans (Harris, 1975: 4). In the field of sociology, between 1985 and 1989, 24.4 per cent of doctorates (the pool for assistant professors) were earned by minorities as were 14.6 per cent of the doctorates between 1975 and 1984 (the pool for associate and full professors), yet there continued to be an under-representation of minorities employed in the profession. In the 1980s, 12 per cent of the sociology faculty was made up of minorities. In 1992, their representation rose slightly to 13.5 per cent (National Center for Educational Statistics, 1996, Table 227). Black women are particularly under-represented in sociology. In 1984, 5.2 per cent of African–American men and 3.2 per cent of African–American women were assistant professors. At the level of full professor the numbers were 4.6 per cent and 0.1 per cent respectively (Saunders, 1990; Menges and Exum, 1983; Misra, Kennelly and Karides, 1999). In 1995, the American Sociological Association (ASA) passed a number of resolutions encouraging diversity, appealing to various ASA editors to increase the representation of women and people of colour, in journals such as the *American Sociological Review, Sociological Theory*, and *Sociological Methods*, charging that they did not adequately represent the diverse interests, methodologies or the racial/gender make-up of the discipline.

Black scholars also interrogated their own experiences in the academy, to examine expressions of whiteness in the perceptions of 'difference'in hiring practices, interactions of white colleges with blacks, and expectations of job performance. In response to the under-representation of blacks and other minorities in sociology, the charge that there is simply a limited supply of minority sociologists is countered by claims that this argument masks entrenched racism and sexism. There is, for example, a tendency towards hiring practices that focus on hiring PhD's from 'elite' departments, where minorities and women are less likely to be found (Mickelson and Oliver, 1991) Others argue that covert forms of racism mask the adherence to a notion of meritocracy regarding professional qualifications that subtly favour whites (Anderson, 1988). The individualistic value orientation of western cultures, and especially the biases in academia towards white men (who primarily occupy the high status roles), are identifiable in a number of ways: evaluations of intellectual endeavours, credentials, allocation of resources and criteria for success and failure (in relation to promotion, tenure and hiring and firing of faculty). Gender, race and class influence the entry, and opportunities, of black faculty and students, the funding and value of research undertaken, tenure decisions and the institutional appropriation of critical and interdisciplinary departments such as ethnic studies.

The historical cross-over of black thinkers and activists (in the black community) coupled with collectivisitic and collaborative ways of learning and doing research are invariably seen as insufficient evidence of 'serious scholarship', thereby failing the 'objective'criteria for promotion/tenure reviews. These activities include service-learning, action-orientated projects and experimental teaching methods that are often encouraged at one stage (notably in the 'PR of diversity', found in the marketing materials of universities and colleges) then discounted later (during promotion and tenure decisions). Black scholars routinely find their research judged by colleagues as thinly veiled racial/gender crusades rather than 'objective research'. Their activism and challenge to the *status quo* are construed as displaying outright hostility to established paradigms of scholarship and the protocols of ascendancy in the academy. In her study of black women academics, Donaldo Cook further suggests, that within the academy:

> The system of institutionalized whiteness will not change until white faculty recognize the ways in which they impose their cultural values on black faculty, and value what black faculty can offer their departments. Inclusive is not just about 'being nice' to blacks by giving them positions in white departments; rather it is about respecting the intellect of blacks and including them in their frame of reference to enhance the offerings of the department and advancement in the discipline. The perspectives of White academia will not be broadened and redefined until Whites confront Whites on their White supremacist attitudes and behaviors.
>
> (Cook, 1997, p. 108)[12]

Another source of vituperative attack on multiculturalism in college campuses during the late-1980s, were critiques of 'Afrocentricism' viewed as part of a wide-ranging assault on academic freedom, imposed by so-called political correctness. Arthur Schlesinger's book, *The Disuniting of America*, is instructive in this regard. This notable liberal historian claims the disuniting of America by the 'cult of ethnicity' among non-whites results in challenging the idea of 'one people', rejects the notion of the melting pot, and results in a 'multiethnic dogma which abandons historic purposes, replacing assimilation by fragmentation, integration by separatism' (Schlesinger, 1992, p. 17). But his analysis ignores the workings of a European-centred base of power and privilege. Although accusing Afrocentrism of being 'bad history' and 'history as therapy', Schlesinger himself subscribes to a view of history that is simply another variant of nationalist myth-making. Thus:

> the key question becomes not so much the teaching of bad or therapeutic history but whose history one wants to teach: a question which, in turn highlights the central issue of hegemonic power relations.
>
> (May, 1999, p. 19)

Often that power is tied up with the funding of research: for example, conservative think-tanks seeking to justify white racial privilege and Euro-American cultural hegemony. Prominent cases include Peter Skerry's *Mexican Americans: the Ambivalent Minority*, funded by the American Free Enterprise Institute, and the sponsoring by the Hoover Institute of Peter J. Duignan's *Hispanics in the United States*. The latter supports an ideology that essentially blames Latinos for the decay of American social and cultural values, working hard:

> at deconstructing and then exploiting the language of the Civil Rights Movement as part of an attack on the entire concept of equity. Though access to the media, they control the debate on class and race exploitation by delegitimising discussion of the struggle of the oppressed for equity, and dismissing it as an effort to impose 'political correctness'.
>
> (Acuna, 1996, xiv)

Groups such as the National Association of Scholars (NAS) use phrases such as 'equality versus quality'in education to mask their opposition to more inclusionary practices and pedagogy. They claim that tenured radicals politicize the university system by their demands for greater diversity and the silencing of dissenting voices through political correctness.[13] The NAS convention in San Francisco was reported for the

National Review (1993, p. 18), an ultra-conservative journal under the heading 'The Latin-Americanization of the Universities'.[14] Again, their claims were based on criticizing the left for politicizing knowledge and imposing their own. They never questioned how their own epistemological base and assumptions are also politicized, defining what, and what are not, permissible paths, histories and tools to unpack knowledge. Nor are those who opposed multicultural education and 'political correctness' lonely, besieged, defenceless scholars.[15]

Conservative think-tanks such as the Hoover Institution and the Heritage Foundation, whose scholarship is produced in concert with the public policy initiates of the right, are well endowed and well publicized. The Heritage Foundation Fellow, Charles Murray, wrote *Losing Ground*, which essentially argued that the social programmes of the 1960s and 1970s worsened trends in ghetto poverty. His book became the rallying cry for the conservative assault on the welfare state, and provided support to the growing white backlash against racial integration of neighbourhoods, school busing, undocumented workers and 'lax' immigration laws. Opposing affirmative action only added to the trope of discontent reflected in a declining suburban, and white, commitment to the welfare state (made all the more palatable by the presence of scholars of colour: especially black).

Public policy and black voices: checkerboard politics

> In order to to get beyond racism we must first take account of race. There is no other way. And in order to treat some persons equally, we must treat them differently.[16]

Under the Reagan/Bush administrations, conservative policies gathered momentum with both black and white commentators. Black conservatives such as Walter William, Stephen Carter, Glen Loury, Thomas Sowell, Robert Woodson, Clarence Thomas and Shelby Steele were embraced by conservatives as adding legitimacy to challenges to the liberal 'Great Society' initiatives, and to federal civil rights policies on black and poor communities (Marable, 1991; Reed, 1991).[17] Reagan's symbolic embodiment of the 'good old days' and his appeal to 'traditional values' turned on the complex post-civil rights discourse of race in general, and blacks in particular.[18]

Rather than resting on notions of white supremacy, Reagan repositioned whites as victims, by the putative unfairness of social policies such as quotas and affirmative action. Black voices were no hindrance in this endeavour. Black neo-conservatives, thrust into the role of 'model minorities', were vocal in their general opposition to redistributive programmes, and affirmative action. Blackness was more an accident of birth than a category requiring structural realignments for historic – and systematic – inequalities. In highlighting the voices of black conservatives in the debate on affirmative action, the tempting conclusion is that it must be bad for blacks.[19]

This is not to suggest that black Americans are a monolithic group, something that is often envisioned by white America, and used by some black leadership to stifle the voices of dissent both within the black public sphere and black politics. A conservative stratum has always existed in the black community, but it was in the 1980s that it became most significant in exerting an influence over society. Abandonment and betrayal are nothing new to the black middle-class, nor is their complicity in white power structures. Both Frazier and Du Bois wrote articulately about their presence, in dissenting ways. Du Bois argued that the Talented Tenth should be the thinkers, leaders and analysts for their community. Frazier presented a more cynical view of the 'black bourgeoisie', as failing to be a responsible elite. In the 1930s, George S. Schuler displayed a loathing for black leaders such as Du Bois and Garvey.[20] Charles Kiel, the black anthropologist and the author of *Urban Blues*, took issue with Ralph Ellison, the black artist and critic as to the subcultural status of black Americans. Kiel was averse to the melting pot tone of Ellison, which he felt echoed the assimilatory values of middle-class blacks.[21]

The rise of black neo-conservatism in the 1980s and 1990s is evident in both political and academic circles. Arguably, the three most influential African–Americans in the country at present are General Colen Powell, Clarence Thomas, the Supreme Court Associate Judge, and Ronald Brown, the Commerce Secretary. Within the Republican Party, black conservatives include Congressmen J. C. Watts and Gary Franks of Connecticut, and in the Democratic Party, Mayor Michael White of Cleveland, Ohio, all of whom openly subscribe to 'colour-blind' policies. Within academia, black conservatives such as Thomas Sowell and Walter Williams argue that the role of racial discrimination is small enough as to be insignificant in accounting for the stagnation of black economic life. Sowell holds that the support for affirmative action by civil rights leaders was misguided because it hurts the disadvantaged. He argues that the occupational gains made by women and minority groups were the result of economic upswings, strong labour demands and improved educational attainments rather than civil rights legislation and affirmative action policy. Political demands on the part of minority groups encourage a culture of dependency rather than self-help because, historically, ethnic groups that have sought advancement through political channels have ended up economically worse off than those who have eschewed politics. Accordingly, government affirmative action programmes reduce both choice and the incentive to self-help. 'Discrimination thus becomes an interest, a means to pursue political career ends' (Sowell, 1981, p. 103). Concessions to minority political demands are seen as a favour rather than a right.

Glen Loury and Shelby Steele were especially vocal in their criticism of the black underclass as being in a state of moral and social decline. Great Society welfare programmes and entitlements for the poor, they argue, simply create a culture of dependency, out-of-wedlock births, violence and unemployment. But the visibility of black conservatives is not a measure of their ability to speak for the majority of black people, differentiated as it is by class, place, gender and sexuality. Their political allegiance to a 'colour-blind' society is made all the more salient by their racialized identity. Their close ties and dependence upon the government, universities and foundations enable them to be the black spokesmen for the White House, where they enjoy the notoriety rather than their capacity to speak for the vast majority of 'their black communities'. At a time when America's 'colour-blind' society continues to produce scholarly works attributing black poverty to motivations (Murray, 1984; Kaus, 1992), family structure (Gordon, 1994), and intelligence (Herrnstein and Murray, 1994), and continues to blame blacks (amongst others, such as low-income women) for a society in which opportunity structures for blacks are heavily circumscribed (Hacker, 1992, Massey and Denton, 1993), the political implications are self-evident. It was Reagan who appointed conservative Clarence Thomas to the Supreme Court. Thomas once famously used his own sister as an example of the typical 'welfare'queen, sponging off and cheating the state. While building his professional life on his championing of individual achievement and race-blind policies, he nonetheless played the racial card of black victimization in the Congress Hearings in the Clarence Thomas/Anita Hill hearings.[22]

Prior to Reagans' administration, the Commission on Civil Rights enjoyed substantial independence from presidential interference, and was bipartisan. In his first year of office, Reagan replaced the chairman of 24 years, with a conservative black Republican, Clarence Pendleton.

In 1978, *The Declining Significance of Race*, by William Julius Wilson, and *The Truly Disadvantaged* in 1987, articulated what was essentially

Moynihan's position – that class rather than 'race' (which had been addressed through the civil rights movement) was responsible for the condition of many African Americans.[23] The emphasis on class, rather than being radical and challenging the structures of racial inequality, was taken to mean that lower-class blacks needed the education and skills that were necessary for economic mobility. Wilson gained widespread attention because he was projected as a black liberal advocating race-blind policies. He subscribed to the view that affirmative action only benefited the least disadvantaged in the black community. While he advocated group-not race-specific policies, he wrote in his chapter 'hidden agenda' that race-blind policies would be the only way in which race-conscious programmes would be tolerated; an ironic twist when one considers that the principal message drawn from his work appeared to be that race matters little in economic terms.

The fact that he was black, provided both a stamp of legitimacy and a shield against charges of racism. It is no surprise that when Bill Clinton talks of how *The Truly Disadvantaged* deeply influenced him, he 'raced' the author by referring to him as 'the famous *African American* sociologist William Julius Wilson'.[24] Nathan Glazer, commenting on Wilson's *The Declining Significance of Race*, argued that the book did not say things which had not been said before, but it was 'the first time that a black social scientist has said them with such strength' The book was judged by the American Sociological Association as worthy of the Spivak Award in intergroup relations in 1978. Wilson also won the prestigious Frank Seidman distinguished Award in Political Economy. As one of the selection committee members stated, 'if anyone is a successor to Gunnar Mydral in the study of black society in the US, it's Bill Wilson'. While his 'retreat from race' provided Wilson with accolades and national attention, it did so because as a black scholar he provided a respectable ('coloured') gloss to the notion that race no longer matters. The Association of Black Sociologists, on the other hand, passed a resolution stating that Wilson's book ignored the persistent oppression of blacks.

While black neo-conservatives and (some) liberals claimed that racism is no longer a significant factor in accounting for the current structures of inequality, their ideas and assumptions do not go uncontested or unproblemitized, particularly within the black community itself. Fortunately, black scholars in various professions and disciplines have published books that highlight the everyday racial demons they encounter in the corridors and classrooms of the white ivory tower. Black feminists have raised questions of conflicting allegiances or identities around race, class and gender. In opposition to white feminist critiques of family, which signalled a site of oppression, Hazel Carby and Pratibha Parmar in Britain, and bell hooks and Angela Davis in the US, have challenged traditional feminism on the basis of three concerns.

First, they view families as institutions that provide a means of collective support in the face of racism (though acknowledging the contradictory aspects of black motherhood); secondly, black feminists have argued that reproductive rights have distinct meanings for black women. For white women, the demand for 'voluntary motherhood' was rigidly bound to lifestyles enjoyed by white middle-class women. For many poor and working-class women, there were more pressing (such as economic inequality) needs than the issue of embryonic birth control. In black, Chicana, Latina and Native American communities, community revelations and experiences of forced sterilization and sterilization abuse put a different inflection on the debate about reproductive rights and the control of the body. Finally, black lesbians and gays experience homophobia within and outside of the black community.

Conclusion

Some 97 years after Du Bois prophesized about the problem of the twentieth century being about the 'colour line', 60 years after the intellectual triad of Alain Locke, Charles Johnson and Du Bois were emphatically denied access to mainstream academia, and 25 years after the emblems of segregated life eroded from the ivory tower, a battle ensues where 'colour' casts a 'line' in the hallowed sanctums of academic institutions, be it visible or invisible. The recent decision by the ASA Council to deny editorship of the prestigious journal *American Sociological Review* to a team of black sociologists led by Walter R. Allen (author of Chapter 3 in this volume) resulted in a public debate where accusations of institutional racism are denied by the ASA and the ASR Council. A statement by the ASA Section on Racial and Ethnic Minorities charged that the whole incident smacked of institutional discrimination by those who wished to maintain the *status quo*, including prominent white scholars who had insightfully written about race in America in the past.

For a significant number of black sociologists, the spectre of race should at least be considered a possibility: for many it was central to the hiring politics of the journal. For those defending their right to deny the editorialship, the central issue was not of race but of 'quality' and 'merit', even though 'qualified' is often a code word for elitism, indistinguishable from white privilege (Feagin and Vera, 1995). These divergent readings of the same incident bring to the fore once again the impact of the colour line, where the persistence of white supremacy continues to possess the power to produce and prohibit, to develop and delimit, criteria for legitimization, scientificicity, and objectivity. This, in turn, sets parameters and draws boundaries for the visibility, availability and the legitimacy of ideas on race: from the exclusionary practices Du Bois experienced in the production and control of sociological knowledge, to the hiring and hyping of blacks as merely symbolic representations of the black community, to the current accusations of racism within the field of sociology.

This enduring white American value system extends beyond the study of sociological subjects. Expressions of whiteness include hiring practices, interactions of white colleges with blacks, expectations of job performance, and the arbitrary and subjective criteria by which whites evaluate blacks within an institutional setting like the academy. They also affect the entry and opportunities of black faculty and students, criteria for research funding and publications, tenure decisions and institutional appropriation of critical and interdisciplinary departments such as ethnic studies (Cose, 1994; Nelson, 1993; Bell, 1994). The common theme, from a white perspective, continues to be a 'Negro Problem', whereas the continuing problem actually appears to be that which whites took upon themselves to have with blacks.[25] And it remains to be seen, as we enter the twenty-first century, whether:

> The (*continuing*) tragedy of race relations in the United States is that there is no American dilemma. White Americans are not torn and tortured by the conflict between their devotion to the American creed and their actual behaviour. They are upset by the current state of race relations, to be sure. But what troubles them is not that justice is being denied, but that their peace is being shattered and their business interrupted.
>
> (Silberman, 1968, p. 10)

Notes

1 I am not suggesting a singular coding for the 'colour' line, whereby only the racialized relations of African–Americans result in exclusion and oppression. However, for the purposes of this chapter, I have concentrated primarily on African–Americans – who have particularly galvanized America's attention – and inattention toward questions of 'race'. I have not confined intellectual work on 'race' to the purely academic. Within black society, writers, playwrights, and activists have frequently been role-models, motivators and

referents for generations of black scholars. Writers like Ralph Ellison, Gwendolyn Brooks and Richard Wright were intellectuals who existed outside the black academy and mainstream public life. Wright was highly sceptical of traditional black scholars, particularly those still fixated on the rural South. He and his contemporaries informed the young, often urban-based intellectuals of the 1960s such as Sonia Sanchez and Amiri Bakaka. Their basic beliefs and ideas were at loggerheads with the largely middle-class and Southern leadership of the Civil Rights Movement. Like the nineteenth century scholars Frances Ellen Watkins, Martin Delany, Anna Cooper and Alexander Crummell before them, they were not produced from the historic sites of black intellectual breeding.

2   The racial logic that promotes the notion that race awareness causes racial strife and divisions is used by black conservatives such as Thomas Sowell and Walter Williams. Both are committed to the Milton Friedman free-market school of economics, thus substantiating their claims to be scientific, rational and non-partisan. Both argue that the role of racial discrimination is small enough to be insignificant in accounting for the stagnation of black economic life. Shelby Steele's tactic of employing the jargon of clinical psychology ensures his representation as 'the perfect voice of reason in a sea of hate'. In *Reflections of an Affirmative Action Baby* (1991) law professor Stephen Carter describes his mission as 'to describe history with a sort of certainty that natural scientists bring to the task of describing the physical world'.

3   It was clear to Du Bois that the dynamics of racism, and its ensuing inequality and oppression, could only be understood fully within a larger critque of capital and class. He also dealt with the question of privilege and white supremacist ideology by postulating that the plight of the white working-class throughout the world today is directly traceable to Negro slavery in America, on which modern commerce and industry were founded. He also argued that white labour prevented its self-emancipation because of its privileged position, ranging from their access to land to their relative class mobility.

4   The work of black sociologist Franklin Frazier paved the way for the pathologization of the black poor as socially and pathologically disorganized, to the extent that community institutions and social control had been eroded. 'Broken families', 'family desertion', 'illegitimacy' are all value-laden terms that do not behove the language of a scientific observer, but are persistently used to describe the lives of poor blacks. Without any direct observation of the dwellers he studied, rather by using filtered case histories and statistical abstractions, Valentine (1968) claims that black illegitimacy rates are five to ten times those of whites. This is despite in-built biases in the statistics (which the author admits!) as information is collected by social agencies, workers, police and the courts. A generation later, prescriptions for the ills of lower class blacks are also steeped in patronizing and pejorative terms, with disorganization and criminality often imputed to black communities.

5   Blauner (1972, p. 87) writes: 'My own framework probably owes more to the social movements of the oppressed than standard sociology'. He goes on to cite four fallacies within traditional sociology. Firstly, that racial and ethnic groups were neither central nor persistent elements of modern society. Secondly, that 'race and racial oppression are not independent dynamic forces

but are ultimately reducible to other casual determinants, usually economic or psychological'. Thirdly, the position that the most important aspects of racism are the attitudes of white Americans and lastly 'the so-called immigrant analogy, the assumption, critical in contemporary thought, that there are no essential long-term differences – in relation to the larger society – between the third world or racial minorities and the European ethnic groups'.

6 See also Valentine (1968), Gutman (1976) and Stack (1974).

7 For example, Martin Luther King, Jr. *Stride toward Freedom: the Montgomery Story* (Harper and Row, 1958), Angela Davis *Angela Davis – An Autobiography* (Random House, 1974), H. Rap Brown *Die Niger Die* (Dial Press, 1978).

8 In a study of racism in the Netherlands and the US, Philomena Essed (1990) studied 'racism' from the perspective of women of colour. The main forms of everyday 'racism' concern not only the experiences of women of color, but their experiences of whiteness. She suggests that 'Everyday racism implies that people of color can, potentially, experience racism everyday. As a result, people of color learn to observe the behavior of whites systematically. They develop expertise in judging how whites behave towards them. They also gain insights into the white delusion of superiority and the ideology which defines people of color as inferior. (Essed, 1990, p. 258).

9 While whiteness may have been invisible in the 1980s, white youths have since been shown as being particularly sensitive to their white status (Dyer, 1998; hooks, 1992). For whiteness as enacted historically at both national and local levels, see Frankenberg (1993), Carby (1993) and Roediger (1994).

10 Within the realms of education, science and rational knowledge, the presence of the (savage) non-white creates a scale in which white men are at the helm of humanity, by being rational, logical, unemotional and restrained.

11 Comments made by members of the President's staff in the presence of Terrel Bell, the secretary of the Department of Education during the Reagan administration, with reference to establishing a national holiday to honour Martin Luther King, Jr.

12 For further reading on dilemmas and contributions of African American women struggling with Eurocentric disciplines, faculty and administrations see Joy James and Ruth Farmer *Spirit, Space and Survival* (Routledge, 1993). See also Cherrie Moraga and Gloria Anzaldua (eds) *This Bridge Called My Back* (New York, Kitchen Table Press, 1983). The anthology includes writings by radical women of colour touching on the harsh realities of racism.

13 Founded in 1982, the Coalition for Democracy later gave rise to groups such as the National Association of Scholars (NAS). NAS received funding from conservative organizations such as The Olin and Smith-Richardson Foundations and the Heritage Foundation.

14 In America, immigration and its elision with 'Mexican' immigration represents a resurgent form of nativisim, which gains legitimacy through scholarly insights and interventions. Roy Beck, editor of the conservative quarterly journal *Social Contract*, and a Santa Barbara history professor, Otis Graham, who is also a member of FAIR (Federation for American Immigrant Reform, an anti-immigrant group), blamed undocumented immigrants for the Rodney King 'riots'. In blaming mass immigration for widening the gap between rich and poor, and creating a diminished life for African–Americans, they fail

to appreciate the particularly adverse effects social and economic restructuring has had on black and Latino communities. Princeton physicist Harry Kendall and Garret Hardin, Emeritus Professor at the University of California Santa Barbara, along with FAIR, argued that immigration would cost dearly. D'Antonio (1993) claimed the increase of the Mexican population from its present 80 million to an estimated 125 million in 15 years would mean a clamour from the south to the north. Alan C. Nelson, Commissioner of the Immigration and Naturalization Services from 1982–89, as well as being a consultant to FAIR, popularized, through well-financed campaigns, the idea that immigration (read Mexican) was a liability to the country. Conservative think-tanks like Empower America and the Heritage Foundation have also become major players in the shaping of public policy, leading to anti-immigration legislation, especially in California (Acuna, 1996).

15   Links to the media resulted in articles in both broadsheets and mainstream academic publications. For example, Daniel Reichs in the *Los Angeles Times* and John L. Rossenfield in the *California Academic Review*.

16   Supreme Court Justice Harry Blackmun in the *Bakke* case, where Allan Bakke filed a suit against the University of California, claiming that affirmative action discriminated against him as a white person.

17   The workings of white hegemony often pits marginalized groups against each other: such that claims to the moral ground of 'most oppressed' by various marginalized groups render invisible white supremacy, resulting, in for instance the pitting of the 'model minority' against the 'immoral minority'. [A current example would be the case of Dinesh D'Souza, of Asian descent, who continues to subscribe to 'The Negro Problem'.]

18   For insightful analyses of 'race' and 'racism' in America at the century's end see Wahneema Lubiano (ed.) (1997) *The House That Race Built: Black Americans, US Terrain*, New York, Pantheon Books.

19   In the American social formation, formal leadership tends to come from the wealthy and powerful: even grassroots representatives are pressurized by the interests of capital, political representation, colleagues, and so on. The same criticism has been applied to black intellectuals, whose politics and critical voices are often muted in their rise as 'public intellectuals'. More recently, Cornel West, a self-proclaimed socialist, with a high public profile, proclaims race matters, but sees the nihilism within the black community as the chief source of the problems that beset black communities. While he claims to escape from the retrograde implications of conservatives, the political outcome of his position, the 'politics of conversion', fails to translate into practical solutions, ultimately ignoring the broader structures of racialized oppressions and stratifications. See Steinberg (1995).

20   In such publications as *Black and Conservative* (New Rochelle, NY, Arlington House, 1966) and *Black No More* (Boston, North Eastern University, 1931).

21   Issues of class were also highlighted by Malcolm X's popularity, Martin Luther King's shift to the concerns of the working classes and poor, and the Marxist class analyses of the League of Revolutionary Black Workers, C. L. R. James and James Boggs.

22   The black conservatism of Clarence Thomas provides an example of the reinforcement of black male power over black women, in the context of

white attacks. This is also prevalent in Black Nationalism. Louis Farrakhan's Nation of Islam supported Thomas' appointment, despite Farrakhan's criticisms of the Republican Party's racist and conservative politics.

23 The *Moynihan Report* popularized the view that slavery created a black subculture that is pathological and matriarchal. In *The Truly Disadvantaged*, the prevalence of pathology among the black urban poor was a consequence of deindustrialization, not slavery. It was the loss of manufacturing jobs for high-school educated men that was economically devastating.

24 Omi and Winant's *Racial Formation in the US* provides an acute criticism of Clinton's handling of race issues.

25 The 'race relations' literature has tended to focus on black Americans, to the relative neglect of Native Americans, Asians and Latino Americans. In a review of the three 'major' sociology journals from 1900–74, Lavender and Forsyth (1976) found that 71 percent of articles focused on blacks, 13 per cent on white ethnic groups, 7 per cent on Asian Americans and 5 per cent on native Americans.

References

Acuna, R. (1996) *Anything But Mexican*, London, Verso.

Anderson, T. (1988) Black Encounters of Racism and Elitism in White Academe: a Critique of the System, *Journal of Black Studies*, 18, 259–72.

Barnes, B. (1973) Backlash Mounts for Women and Minorities: Reverse Bias Alleged in College Hiring, *Footnotes*, Washington, DC, ASA.

Bell, T. (1988) *The Thirteenth Man: a Reagan Cabinet Memoir*, New York, The Free Press.

Blauner, R. (1972) Race and Radicalism in My Life and Work, in J. H. Stanfield II (ed.) *A History of Race Relations Research*, New York, Harper and Row.

Bourgois, P. (1995) *In Search of Respect: Selling Crack in El Barrio*, New York, Cambridge University Press.

Carby, H. (1992) Encoding White Resentment, in W. McCarthy and W. Crichlow (eds.) *Race, Identity and Representation in Education*, New York, Routledge.

Carmichael, S. and Hamilton, C. (1967) *Black Power: the Politics of Liberation in America*, New York, Vintage Books.

Crenshaw, K. (1991) Mapping the Margins: Intersectionality, Identity Politics, and Violence Against Women of Color, *Stanford Law Review*, 43, 1241–99.

Collins, P. W. (1990) *Black Feminist Thought*, London, Harper Collins.

Cose, E. (1994) *The Rage of the Privileged Class: Why Are Middle Class Blacks Angry? Why Should America Care?*, New York, Harper Collins Publishers.

Cook, D. (1997) 'The Act of Survival in White Academia', in M. Fine, L. Powell and L. L. Wong, (eds) *Off White: Readings on Race, Power, and Society*, New York, Routledge.

Cox, O. C. (1970) *Caste, Class and Race*, New York, First Monthly Review.

D'Antonio, M. (1993) Apocalypse Soon, *Los Angeles Times*, 29 August.

Davis, A. (1981) *Women, Race and Class*, London, Routledge.

Du Bois, W. E. B. (1903) *The Souls of Black Folk*, New York, Bantam Books, 1989.

Du Bois, W. E. B. (1992, first published in 1935) *Black Reconstruction in America, 1860–1880*, New York, Athenaeum.

Du Bois, W. E. B. (1967, first published in 1899) *The Philadelphia Negro*, University of Pennsylvania Series, Benjamin Bloom, New York.

Dyer, R. (1988) 'White' *Screen*, 29(4), Autumn.

Einstein, Z. R. (1982) The Sexual Politics of the New Right: Understanding the 'Crisis of Liberalism' for the 1980s, *Sign* 7 (3), 567–88.

Ellis, J. (1991) Political Correctedness and Reason, *California Academic Review* (Fall).

Feagin, J. R., and Hernan V. (1995) *White Racism*, New York, Routledge.

Frankenburg, R. (1993) *White Women, Race Matters: the Social Construction of Whiteness*, Minneapolis, MN, University of Minnesota.

Frantz, D. (1996) Influential Group Brought Into Campaign by Kemp, *New York Times*, September 1, sec.1, p. 15.

Frazier, E. F. (1968) *The Negro in Harlem: a report on Social and Economic Conditions Responsible for the Outbreak of March 19, 1935*, New York, Arnos Press.

Glazer, N. and Moynihan, D. (1963) *Beyond the Melting Pot*, Cambridge, Mass, MIT Press.

Gordon, L. (1994) Pitied but Not Entitled: Single Mothers and the History of Welfare, New York, Free Press.

Gouldner, A. (1995) *The Coming Crisis of Western Sociology*, New York, Basic Books.

Gutman, H. (1976) *The Black Family in Slavery and Freedom*, New York, Pantheon Books.

Hacker, A. (1992) *Two Nations: Black and White, Separate, Hostile and Unequal*, Charles Scribner's Sons, New York.

Harris, J. R. (1975) *Women and Minorities in Sociology: Findings from Annual ASA Audit*, Washington DC, Footnotes, ASA.

Herrnstein, R. and Murray, C. (1994) *The Bell Curve: Intelligence and Class Structure in American Life*, New York, Free Press.

hooks, bell (1992) *Black Looks: Race, and Representation*, New York, Routledge.

James, J. and Farmer, R. (1993) *Spirit, Space and Survival*, New York, Routledge.

Katches, M. (1993) Immigrants Pay Their Way, *Daily News*, 28 July.

Kaus, M. (1992) *The End of Equality*, New York, Basic Books.

Lavender, A. D. and Forsyth, J. M. (1976) The Sociological Study of Minority Groups as Reflected by Leading Sociological Journals, *Ethnicity*, 3, 388–98.

Lusane, C. (1991) *Pipe Dream Blues: Racism and the War on Drugs* Boston, South End Press.

Liebow, E. (1967) *Tally's Corner*, Boston, Little, Brown.

May, S. (1999) Critical Multiculturalism and Cultural difference: Avoiding Essentialism, in S. May (ed.) *Critical Multiculturalism; Rethinking Multicultural and Antiracist Education*, Falmer Press, London.

Marable, M. (1991) *Race, Reform and Rebellion: the Second Reconstruction in Black America, 1945–1990*, Jackson, University of Mississippi Press.

Massey, D. S. and Denton, S. (1993) *American Apartheid: Segregation and the Making of the Underclass*, Cambridge, MA, Harvard University Press.

Menges, R. J. and Exum, W. (1983) Barriers to the Progress of Women and Minority Faculty, *Journal of Higher Education*, 54, 123–44.

Mickelson, R. A., and Oliver, M. (1991) Making the Short List: Black Candidates and the Faculty Recruitment Process, in P. G. Altbach and K. Lomotey (eds) *The Racial Crisis in American Higher Education*, Albany, State University of New York Press.

Misra, J. Kennelly, I. and Karides, M. (1999) Employment Chances in the Academic Job Market in Sociology: Do Race and Gender Matter?, *Sociological Perspectives*, 42 (2), 215–47.

Morrison, T. (ed.) (1992a) *Race-ing Justice, En-gendering Power: Essays on Anita Hill, Clarence Thomas, and other Constructions of Social Reality*, New York, Pantheon Books.

Morrison, T. (1992b) *Playing in the Dark: Whiteness and the Literary Imagination*, Cambridge, Harvard University Press.

Moynihan, D. P. (1967) The Negro Family: the Case for National Action, in L. Rainwater and W. L. Yancey (eds) *The Moynihan Report and the Politics of Controversy*, Cambridge, Mass, MIT Press.

Murray, C. (1984) *Losing Ground: American Social Policy, 1950–1980*. New York, Basic Books.

Mydral, G. (1944) *An American Dilemma: the Negro Problem and Modern Democracy*, New York, Harper & Row.

National Center for Educational Statistics (1996) *Survey of Earned Doctorates*, Washington, DC, US Government Printing Office.

National Review (1993) The Latin-Americanisation of the Universities, 24 May.

Nelson, J. (1993) *Volunteer Slavery: My Authentic Negro Experience*, New York, Penguin Books.

Pettigrew, T. F. (1980) *The Sociology of Race Relations*, New York, Free Press.

Reich, D. (1991) The Overlooked Problem of Multi-Culturalism in the Classroom, *California Academic Review*, Fall.

Reed, A. (1991) The Underclass as a Myth and Symbol: the Poverty of Discourses about Poverty, *Radical America*, 24 (1), 21–43.

Roediger, D. (1994) *The Wages of Whiteness: Race and the Making of the American Working Class*, London, Verso.

Saunders, D. (1990) Tenure for Black Faculty: an Illusion in the White Academy, in *Black Issues in Higher Education*, April 12.

Schlesinger, A. Jr. (1992) *The Disuniting of America*, New York, Norton.

Silberman, C. E. (1968) *Crisis in Black and White*, New York, Random House.

Sibley, D. (1995) *Geographies of Exclusion*, New York, Routledge.

Skerry, P. (1993) *Mexican Americans: the Ambivalent Minorities*, New York, Free Press.

Sowell, T. (1981) *Markets and Minorities*, Oxford, Blackwell.

Sowell, T. (1984) *Civil Rights: Rhetoric or Reality*, New York, William Morrow.

Sowell, T. (1987) *Compassion Versus Guilt and Other Essays*, New York, West Morrow.

Stack, C. (1974) *All Our Kin*, New York, Harper & Row.

Stansfield, J. (1985) *Philanthropy and the Jim Crow in American Social Science*, Westport, Conn., Greenwood Press.

Steinberg, S. (1995) *Turning Back: the Retreat from Racial Justice in American Thought and Policy*, Beacon Press, Boston.

Valentine, C. (1968) *Culture and Poverty*, Chicago, The University of Chicago Press.

West, C. (1993a) The Postmodern Crisis of the Black Intellectual in L. Grossberg (ed.) *Out There: Marginalization and Contemporary Cultures*, Cambridge, MIT Press, pp. 689–706.

West, C. (1993b) *Race Matters*, Boston, Beacon Press.

Wilson, W. J. (1978) *The Declining Significance of Race*, Chicago, University of Chicago Press.

Wilson, W. J. (1987) *The Truly Disadvantaged*, Chicago, University of Chicago Press.

William, W. (1982) *The State Against Blacks*, New York, McGraw-Hill.

Part II

Non-European Societies: Histories Rooted in Slavery, Apartheid and Genocide

3
Whatever Tomorrow Brings: African-American Families and Government Social Policy

Walter R. Allen

> Sometimes I feel like a motherless child. Sometimes I feel like a motherless child. A long, long way from home.
>
> From a negro spiritual

Since our involuntary arrival in this country, African-Americans have lived an existence fraught with hardship and uncertainty; yet in tribute to their character, this existence has been marked by determination and accomplishment. Historically, the relationship of blacks with the United States government has been paradoxical, to say the least. At one point this government provided the legal basis for, and military enforcement of, our slavery. Later, the government declared our emancipation, while at the same time sanctioning institutional arrangements calculated to ensure our continued social, economic and political subjugation. More recently, the government waged a 'Holy War' on the social, economic and political inequities that had come to symbolize the black experience in this country – only to retreat from the battle just as significant gains were being won. This chapter explores the relationship between empirical research, state policy and processes of social change by examining the vexed relationship between United States government social policy and the status of black families and their children.

At the dawn of a new century – nearly 400 years after African slaves were first brought to this country – it is appropriate that we examine the current situations of African-Americans and what the future seems to promise. Some findings from recent research give cause for celebration: we see evidence that many of the barriers that once prevented blacks from achieving the full realization of their potential have been cast aside. We are shown evidence of an emerging middle class, increased educational access for our young, and the opening of occupational opportunities in areas that previously excluded blacks (Toliver, 1998). This is the good news from the current research record, providing evidence of progress, prosperity and promise. Unfortunately, the bad news conveyed in the research record also exists in great abundance. We are told of the worsening situation as regards female-headed households. Over one-half of our children now grow up in such homes – homes, handicapped by poverty and all its attendant difficulties, by virtue of the society's economic and social welfare practices which consign black, single, female heads of household (and by definition, their children) to lives dimmed by economic deprivation and social degradation (Allen and James, 1998; Allen, 1995). We are reminded of the incredible numbers of black males snatched from productive roles in the community through premature death by homicide, imprisonment, retreat into drugs and chronic unemployment. In the midst of these statistical indicators, we find cause for great concern, if not alarm, over the very future of African-American family life.

A concern over the future of black American families and their children is the central motivating theme of this chapter. To this extent, it is necessary to begin by acknowledging the critical importance of government social policy as a potential determinant of whether black family futures are positive or negative. In this connection, we examine how government social policy affects black family life. Next, we examine the contributions of black families to the maintenance of positive mental health in African–American communities. Over the years, black families have demonstrated a remarkable ability to engender and cultivate positive mental health among members often exposed to the most negative and horrendous of circumstances. The ability of black families to produce sane, productive individuals in the midst of circumstances that would seem to guarantee insanity and destructive behaviour is taken here as problematic, and is systematically explored. Lastly, this chapter elevates the various social policy, theoretical and research issues examined to a call for new values. It examines the place of values in scientific ideology, public policy and professional roles. The chapter then suggests how changes in these values might assist in the creation of positive futures for black families.

The history of family policy in the United States

Due to fundamental changes in the structure of our society, family and individual dependence on government has become more pronounced than ever before (Hill, 1997). The forces of urbanization, industrialization and economic restructuring created an immensely complex, impersonal and insecure environment. Consequently, individual and nuclear family needs for supportive relationships intensified as societal pressures became more abundant and increasingly difficult to manage. Yet the effectiveness of extended-family networks in the provision of such supportive services has declined due to changes in family structure, norms and geographic patterns. Government and proxy public institutions are thus increasingly called upon to fill the void left by these receding extended family and support networks (Edin and Lein, 1997).

Awareness that vital system maintenance functions were becoming problematic for extended families to perform – and the perceived consequence of this fact – combined to prompt many concerned people to call for the creation of a national family policy. [In the context of this chapter, 'family policy' refers to consensus on a core set of family goals, towards which the government deliberately shapes policies, actions and programmes.] Although many, if not all, governmental policy decisions at the national level influence families, the task of bringing about the adoption of a conscious, planned national family policy has proven difficult. Several historical traditions and conditions in this country represent obstacles to the development of a well-articulated national family policy (Hill *et al.*, 1993; Takaki, 1990; Chilman, 1973; Schorr, 1962; Sussman, 1971; Laing, 1971; Ball, 1972). Among the more important are:

1. The national commitment to individualism

From the very beginning, our society has been inclined to deal with individuals rather than families. Families have been viewed as secondary in importance to individuals; they essentially represented vehicles for the satisfaction of individual needs. This distinction has been preserved in the formal organization of federal government activities where one finds agencies working on the problems of retired, young, aged, poor female and handicapped individuals. However, nowhere does there exist a single agency concerned with the family unit in its entirety.

2. The mechanics of the free enterprise system

As long as family goals are in concert with the goals of private industry and business, the system functions to ensure their well-being. In instances where these interests conflict, however, families suffer because they, unlike industry or business, are without the protection of professional, full-time advocates. Families lack the resources to ensure that their interests are effectively represented. Consequently, family goals are often subordinated to the more organized, better funded, corporate interests in the society.

3.   The mechanics of the democratic system

By its very nature, the political process in the United States is antagonistic to monolithic statements of family goals. Such statements are bound to run counter to the variety of cultural, religious and economic family variants reflected in US society. Instead, the tendency is to allow the majority or most powerful group to prevail. For this reason, one sees at the national level policies that reflect the expectations of white, protestant, middle-class families.

4.   National ethic of non-interference in families

Unlike any other groups or associations, families in US society are invested with unique privileges of privacy. The historical division of church and state has granted the family a special immunity from interference by the government (since families were defined as falling within the realm of the church). Families also derive their 'sacred' quality, to an extent, from the US national ethic that advocates for and protects private property. As numerous authors have pointed out, family relationships have often been perceived as property relationships after a fashion. Historically, laws granted husbands *de facto* ownership rights over wives, while parents were accorded the same privileges with regard to their children. Government efforts to intervene in families are thus doubly hampered. Such rights are seen as interference with their rights of privacy (i.e. religious choice) and self-determination of personal 'property'.

5.   Limitations in family research and theory

As a relatively young area of scientific inquiry, 'family studies' is characterized by conceptual and methodological problems that hamper the development of solid evidence on which to base national policy. The status of fundamental research (which we know informs policy research) is somewhat rudimentary. Researchers in the area fail to display consensus over what constitutes the most appropriate conceptual and methodological perspectives in the analysis of family phenomena. By the same token, little agreement exists over the most useful data, or data collection strategies. Indeed, researchers commonly disagree over the interpretation/implications of the 'facts'. We find, therefore, that the development of national family policies has also been retarded by dissensus amongst 'opinion formers' and the historic scarcity of systematic, dependable, empirical data that can be used to guide decisions.

Despite these problems, numerous pieces of family legislation have been enacted. In cases where efforts to enact family policies have been successful, the policy-making machinery has functioned in a more or less predictable fashion. Most often, proposed family policies have been favourably received when they conformed to one or a combination of the following standards:

1. *Standard of congruence*: family policy legislation fares best when it can be shown to be *congruent* with the perceived needs of individuals. The greater the degree of consistency between family and individual necessities, the more likely that legislation focused on family is to be enacted.
2. *Standard of coincidence*: family legislation also occurs frequently as a coincidental outcome of other planned social policy legislation. Often other societal problems and/or issues of concern prompt the development of laws and regulations that happen, by coincidence, to contain provisions relevant to family welfare.
3. *Standard of correction*: in the rare instances where family legislation develops explicitly, it is generally intended to correct a narrowly defined problem in American family systems. The focus of such 'crisis-oriented' legislation tends to be solely on the facet(s) of family life deemed to require emergency intervention.

The development of national family policies in the United States has therefore faced numerous problems. Social norms and principles of operation have combined to militate against the emergence of cogent, coordinated government programs *vis-à-vis* families. Where explicit governmental family policies and programmes were formulated, these generally failed to be systematic and thorough responses to the needs of families. Rather, such programmes were compromised by a combination of legislative expediency and limited information (on families). Predictably, these problems associated with national family policy are amplified many times over when we talk about black family policy at the national level. The historically unique social, economic and political position of blacks in this society further complicates the already difficult equation linking research, government and family (Omi and Winant, 1994).

Black family and national social policy: theoretical and substantive issues

The development and implementation of governmental policies for black families provides a special case of the problems of family social policy discussed above. A myriad of social-historical factors combine to stamp black families in the United States indelibly with unique circumstances which distinguish them, and any governmental attempt to deal with their problems, from white families. An effective way of illustrating this point is by turning to the literature on black families. The rationale for this strategy is obvious: fundamental research informs and directs policy research that serves as the general basis for policy decisions. This is to say that in the United States, as elsewhere, both social policy programmes and strategies for their implementation are normally justified on the basis of academic research. The theoretical frameworks, data and interpretations drawn from such research all eventually feed into the policy-making machinery to provide a foundation for informed decision-making. While the percolation effect, whereby academic research models and findings are translated over time into concrete social programmes, may be direct and immediate, more often than not this translation is indirect and delayed. The end result of this process is the implementation of social programmes whose intellectual traditions are unclear. We see the utility of social programmes debated and decided largely in terms of secondary features (that is, cost, publicity value, political expediency). On the other hand, little or no attention is paid to the basic issues of how valid the underlying premises of the programmes are, and the level of empirical support that exists for such positions. Thus it becomes imperative for us to understand the way in which black families are treated in terms of United States scholarship, for this very treatment predicts their treatment in United States social policy.

Theory and method in the study of black families

While the majority of theoretical weaknesses characterizing black family studies are symptomatic of deficits in the area of family studies as a whole (see Allen and James, 1998 and Hill *et al.*, 1993 for discussion of these deficits), there are theoretical problems unique to the study of black families. In part, these problems arise from fundamental ideological differences among researchers. The competing ideologies in black family studies may be represented as three distinct theoretical perspectives: 'cultural equivalent', 'cultural deviant', and 'cultural variant' (Allen, 1978b; 1995).

The *cultural equivalent* perspective on black family life is exemplified by researchers who fail to acknowledge that black families constitute distinct cultural forms, fundamentally different from white families. In their attempts to de-emphasize or negate the unique characteristics of black families and to highlight characteristics shared with white families, these researchers merely succeed in creating caricatures – black families depicted as darkly-tinted facsimiles of white families. Thus Bernard (1966, pp. 41–50) speaks of 'culturally White' black families; Frazier (1964, p. 190) refers to one group of black families as 'Black Puritans'; and Scanzoni (1971, pp. 323–5) suggests that black and white family differences are reducible to social class differences. By failing to recognize the uniqueness of the black family experience, the 'cultural equivalent' perspective does black families a grave injustice. The perspective makes the implicit value judgement that black families constitute legitimate forms only insofar as their structures and processes replicate those of white, middle-class families.

The *cultural deviant* perspective does not ignore the distinctive qualities possessed by black families. Instead, researchers who employ this perspective acknowledge the unique traits of the black family but then penalize them for being different. Such research attributes differences between black and white families to various alleged weaknesses in the black family. To this extent, the 'cultural deviant' perspective makes explicit the normative judgements left implicit by the 'cultural equivalent' perspective. Adopting white, middle-class families as the 'healthy' norm, researchers label those black families that deviate from this norm as 'pathological'. Qualities that distinguish black from white families are taken as indices of dysfunction. Therefore, the more at odds a black family is with the white, middle-class family model, the more pathological in orientation that family is judged to be. Moynihan (1965, p. 5) exemplifies this perspective in his widely quoted conclusion that 'at the heart of the deterioration of the fabric of Negro society is the deterioration of the Negro family', while Frazier (1964, pp. 404–5) speaks of 'widespread disorganization' in black family patterns. Similarly, Rainwater (1970, pp. 155–87) characterizes black males as ineffectual, irresponsible mates and parents, and Schulz (1969, pp. 67–9) concludes that black families are matriarchies. The combined writings of 'deviance' perspectivists are injurious to the image of black families since they lend questionable support to common myths portraying black families (and, by inference, black people) as basically pathological in nature.

The *cultural variant* perspective views the black family as a form, distinct from the white family. Unlike the 'cultural deviant' perspective, however, the 'cultural variant' perspective does not automatically interpret distinctive qualities in black family life as signs of pathology. Rather, this perspective acknowledges that black and white families operate under different situational constraints and in response to different cultural imperatives. As a consequence, the former's structures, processes and functions differ in many respects. This perspective recognizes and makes culture-relative evaluations of differences between black and white families. Billingsley (1968), for example, views the black family as an 'ethnic subsystem' of the larger society. Developing the notion of adaptive functioning, he views the black family as amazingly adept at fulfilling the 'bio-psycho-social' needs of its members in spite of extreme hardship. He argues that black families strategically adopt forms that facilitate the efficient performance of assigned functions (Billingsley, 1968, pp. 22–33). The idea of adaptive functioning is also reflected in Stack's (1974, pp. 124–6) reference to the culturally adaptive functions of economic 'exchange' relationships among urban black families; Rodman's (1971, p. 197) interpretation of what are normally referred to as 'problems' in lower-class black families (e.g. illegitimacy, female-headed households) as adaptive 'solutions'; and Ladner's (1971, pp. 44–66) description of changing female adolescent socialization patterns in black families as responses to shifting environmental conditions. The 'cultural variant' perspective of black family life recognizes that while family functions are universal, cultural values and situational constraints vary; thus, different structural adaptations are often required. Since 'theory' is intricately linked with 'method' and the two are mutually determinative, we now must turn to the consideration of salient methodological issues in the study of black families.

Experience suggests that one's research methodology can only be as good as one's theory, for theory provides the procedural guidelines for research. In this sense, good theory construction (in the sense of problem formulation) represents the first step in the methodological sequence. Inadequate problem conceptualization and poor theory construction have historically plagued the area of black family studies. For the most part, researchers have been bound in their approaches by models that are largely ethnocentric and inflexible (Hill *et al.*, 1993; Billingsley, 1992; Staples, 1971; Allen, 1978a). For this reason, it is not sufficient to deal solely with issues of data collection and analysis; attention must also be directed to the founding assumptions from which the central research hypotheses of a study are derived. The question, therefore, transcends issues of survey research versus experimental research, descriptive versus causal analyses, or nonparametric versus parametric statistics, and *becomes one largely of perspective*. Is the researcher's perspective sufficiently flexible to allow for the application of new, more appropriate research models and analytical techniques?

Within the last two decades, researchers have begun to make substantial advances in the development of alternative research models for the study of black families (Allen and James, 1998). Perhaps the most dramatic gains are attributable to research employing ethnographic or participant-observation approaches. Working from the premise that subjects are best understood when the researcher shares their day-to-day experiences, these researchers study black families in natural settings. Their findings have generated a rich volume of 'fresh' hypotheses concerning family support systems (Stack, 1974), Black female roles (Ladner, 1971) and extended-family ties (Aschenbrenner, 1975). Progress towards the development of alternative research models for the study of black families has been made on other methodological fronts as well. Hill (1971) and Herzog (1966) used census data to propose alternative interpretations of black family behaviour at the aggregate level, while Heiss (1975) and Hyman and Reed (1969) relied on secondary analysis of survey data to refute long-standing assumptions about the instability of black family structure. Alternative interpretations of early black family patterns have also been proposed by a group of quantitative social-historians (Lammermeier, 1972; Gutman, 1975). Perhaps the most important development is the theoretical/methodological approach to African-American families which emphasizes a holistic perspective. Scholars such as Billingsley (1992) and Hill *et al.* (1993) insist on the need to locate families in broader context and the need to study Black members as parts of a larger organic whole – the family.

Omissions in black family studies and their consequences for social policy

Billingsley (1970) identifies four areas of social science scholarship that have been presented with both the opportunity and the necessity to describe, analyse and explain the character of black family life in the US. Of these four areas, 'studies of social welfare problems and programs' are most important to us here, for studies of this genre inform social policy in our society. In this area of concern, Billingsley notes little systematic attention to the roles, structures or cultural foundations of black families. Instead, they tend either to be overlooked or (where they are addressed) are portrayed in a distorted light. It becomes readily apparent that many of the 'informed' social policy decisions that affect black families were not well informed at all. Guided by research that labelled black families as pathological, employed inapplicable models of family life, and applied inappropriate methodological/statistical techniques, policymakers formulated policies that were inimical to the welfare of the very black families which they were supposedly intended to help (Hill *et al.*, 1993). Ultimately, we must indict American scholarship and its treatment of black families, for it has provided more of a hindrance than an aid to the process of formulating enlightened social policy.

The consequences of the academic community's shortcomings in the treatment of black families have been detrimental on two levels. At one level, the general population, who ultimately passes judgement on government policy decisions, continues to be ignorant about black family life. Consequently, misguided views of black people and black families persist and fuel national resistance to the implementation of necessary social programmes. On another level, policymakers themselves are impaired by faulty research conclusions about black families – conclusions that contribute to the enactment of inadequate, ill-conceived social programmes. Concerned, sincere legislators and government officials are left without the knowledge essential to any successful attempt to address the needs of black families systematically and programmatically. In sum, the record of United States academics has been at best patchy and at worst destructive.

Black families: protectors of the realm

Of all the functions performed by family systems in contemporary society, perhaps the most important is that of protectorate. Families serve as buffer mechanisms, intervening between their members and the larger society (Spencer *et al.*, 1985). In their roles as advocate, stabilizer and defender of individuals who are confronted with at times overwhelming societal forces, families certainly make real and tangible contributions to the maintenance of personal mental health. Some family sociologists even go so far as to suggest that institutional division of labour in the society has evolved to a point where families now exist primarily for purposes of emotional gratification. They argue that the majority of other traditional family functions have long since been assumed by other institutions in the society. While I shy away from such a drastic conclusion, I am thoroughly convinced of the primary role played by families (or their less formal, though no less real, substitutes) in the maintenance of stable personalities. For this reason, I believe that understanding of family variations in 'coping' styles, skills and patterns is essential if we are to grasp fully the range of alternative models for preventative and corrective action in the arena of mental health.

In my opinion, black families present prototypes of effective family systems in their performance of these mental health maintenance functions. In spite of historic deprivation, discrimination and the many other problems they face, black families have continually produced creative, productive, stable individuals. They have successfully nurtured and maintained their members through centuries of societal indifference, if not outright hostility, toward their welfare. Paradoxically, black families have received very little credit for their admirable work in this sphere. Negativism and oversights in research approaches continue to retard recognition of the skill and dedication with which black families marshal limited resources to maintain positive mental health in the black community.

Limited research experience contributes to our lack of information about black family coping styles and skills (Toliver, 1998). However, Hill (1971; 1997) and Hill *et al.* (1993) identify important types of black family coping behaviour relevant to the maintenance of physical well-being and positive mental health.

Role flexibility: due to historic necessity, black families have displayed amazing flexibility in family member role definitions, responsibilities and performances. Children commonly assist with the care and socialization of younger siblings; children and wives are expected to share economic responsibilities with the husband-father; sex role expectations are less stereotypic; and alternative family arrangements or configurations are more prevalent than is true among families in the wider society. Such flexibility in individual roles is an obvious asset in dealing with and adjusting to the pressures or strains of modern living.

Close-knit kinship systems: as a rule, black families tend to be well integrated into larger kin-friend networks. Researchers have shown such relationships to represent invaluable ways of supplementing material, emotional and social resources. Coping is enhanced because the family finds itself with a larger pool of resources upon which to draw.

Culture-specific norms: black communities are characterized in a majority of cases by bicultural norms. Individuals draw upon 'mainstream' and 'subcultural' values – as the situation dictates – for prescriptions of what constitutes appropriate behaviours. Thus, African-Americans are better able to cope, since alternative cultural values allow them to 'stretch' conventional norms to fit the imperatives of the situation.

Parallel institutions: institutions in the black community that parallel those in the white community also contribute substantially to personal adjustment. Individuals denied access to organizations and institutions in the wider society often find satisfying alternatives in their black community-based counterparts (for example, black businesses, fraternal orders, leadership roles in black institutions). In addition, certain black institutions, most notably the Church, have traditionally represented invaluable sources of individual support and comfort in the struggle for adjustment to the rigours of life.

Race and personal identity/pride: membership in and identification with the race have also been shown to yield positive benefits for black Americans. A stronger sense of purpose, greater security in self, better management of frustration and more strongly developed self-identities are a few of the commonly cited outgrowths of such racial pride and identification.

These have obvious relevance to public mental health. I suspect that future research will reveal many others. Certainly, attention should be paid to identifying the inherent strengths of black families; subsequently, mental health delivery systems could be organized to complement those mental health maintenance functions already in existence. I am proposing here that government mental health delivery systems be integrated with indigenous mental health maintenance networks in order to achieve maximal coverage of black community mental health needs. As English (1983, p. 14) notes, 'Theory suggests that when used in some combination or sequential pattern, the effectiveness of family, extended kin resources, indigenous community-based care-givers and bureaucratic mental health services is maximized'. A key issue involves the need to first secure adequate input from the intended target population. The subjects must be consulted about their mental health needs and traditional service avenues with an eye toward achieving an effective interface between indigenous mental health maintenance activities and government-sponsored mental health delivery systems.

While it is important to accentuate the strengths of black families in the maintenance of positive mental heath, we should not lose sight of reality. Large numbers of black people and black families find themselves in precarious and deteriorating positions. The increasingly severe economic situation of the country finds black families losing many of the gains achieved during the 1960s. In fact, the economic stability of sizeable numbers of black families is worse now – relative to whites –

than at any other time during the past 25 years. Census statistics on black–white occupational classifications and annual incomes attest to this fact (Farley and Allen, 1989; Oliver and Shapiro, 1995). Since black families, along with all families in post-industrial societies, rely heavily on societal institutions for the creation and maintenance of environments conducive to their positive development, we must recognize the limits of mere coping. A sincere commitment by the public and private sectors to the improvement of black community economic status is a necessary condition for fostering physical well-being and positive mental health in black families. Black individuals receive significant emotional support in the loving, caring environments of their families. What they, and those families, lack and need most are additional structural supports from the society in the form of jobs, effective schools, adequate incomes, quality housing and equality of opportunity (Billingsley, 1992; Hill *et al.*, 1993; Conley, 1999). Until such structural supports are widely available, the maintenance of positive well-being and mental health in black communities will continue to be problematic. As common sense tells us, emotional support – no matter how plentiful – only goes so far in a society that values economics above all else.

Summary, conclusions and implications

Government policies were shown often to work at cross-purposes with the welfare of black families. However, some value did come from this examination of national family policy and its consequences for black families. We found social policies directed at black families to be characterized by many of the same deficiencies that exist in the area of family social policy generally. Among those deficiencies was a host of historical traditions and practices in this country which, when taken as a whole, prevented the development of well-articulated, national family policy. In addition, social policy relating to the black family was characterized by a unique set of problems that collectively hampered the creation and implementation of well-conceived, effective programmes. These problems were attributable in large part to outmoded research traditions that continued to yield faulty interpretations of the character of black family life in this country. Predictably, the social policies and programmes based on such shaky conceptual and empirical foundations fell short of stated goals. As our discussion indicates, such social programmes tend only to substitute one set of problems for another. In a manner analogous to social programmes that shift drug addict dependencies from heroin to methadone, black families have often been shifted from one category of social problems to another by well-intentioned legislation (Edin and Lein, 1997). Unfortunately, rarely do resultant government policies or programmes provide for a complete 'kicking of the habit'. How are we to move beyond temporary, ineffective and contradictory responses to the needs of black families in governmental social policies and programmes?

Proposals to redirect government social policy with respect to black families are best stated in terms of two areas of concern: academic/policy research and legislative processes. The former is perhaps the more appropriate concern here, given its influence over the latter. As noted before, policymakers rely on input from academic and policy research to guide their decision-making.

Academic research on black families remains in dire need of substantial refinements in theory and methods (Allen and James, 1998). It is only through such refinements that social and behavioural scientists will begin to generate a store of dependable knowledge about the nature of black family life, which can then serve as a basis for informed decision-making by policymakers.

Policy-related research in the area of black family studies also needs to be drastically upgraded (Hill, 1993). Researchers interested in having an impact on governmental decision-making must begin to design their research and write-up results in such a way so as to ensure that findings will come to the attention of the government policy-making machinery. In addition, social policy researchers must develop alternative methods for the evaluation of government legislation and programme implementation in order to better assess how these affect black families.

The goals outlined for improvement of policy and academic research on black families can only be accomplished by commitments on the parts of private and public agents to fund the training of specialists in this area of concern. Through a combination of postdoctoral training programmes, establishment of family policy research programmes and the founding of family institutes, a larger pool of professionals who understand the complex links between government family policy and black family life can be created. While this educational effort could very well occur in conjunction with other ongoing training projects aimed at developing strategies/techniques for family policy impact analysis, it would be wise to consider other alternatives. Foremost among these would be the establishment and funding of predominantly black-controlled and staffed academic research centres. As numerous authors point out, many of the deficits observed in research on black families are directly attributable to the absence of a black perspective.

On the matter of legislative processes, the most helpful action which policymakers could undertake would be to begin a review of extant legislation, programmes and procedures in order to assess the intended and unintended consequences for black families. Where those consequences are negative, these policymakers should be prepared to take corrective action against punitive regulations, legislation and practices. Legislators have been shown to rely heaviest on general data in decision-making, the very type of data most susceptible to distortion. It would behoove policymakers, therefore, to develop systematic procedures that allow input into the decision-making process from scholars as well as from the affected families.

For emphasis, I must pause on the point of black family input into the family social policy decision-making process. All too often, these families' 'voices' go unheeded (Hill *et al.*, 1993, pp. 147–249). The process of controlling, redefining and judging their lives moves forward relentlessly, without their input. They are treated as objects, disembodied, disempowered, dismissed. The notion is that the 'experts', usually white, know best. The fact is that they do not. Black families must be made full partners in the formulation and implementation of social policy that affect their existence.

If the higher goals sought by national family policy advocates are to be achieved, if government is ever to begin formulating sensible family policy, then the US as a nation must become more self-conscious of social policies and programmes in the area of family. It is particularly important that the nation re-examine the consequences of social policy based on the assumption of a white, middle-class, conjugal nuclear family model. The overwhelming majority of American families do not fit this pattern (for example, black, Chicano, single-parent, lower-class families). In conclusion, our need as a nation for formalized, comprehensive family policy is dire. Resources are available to develop an encompassing national family policy that is sensitive to the needs of all families. What we lack at this point is a commitment to this goal.

This country is currently at a crossroads, brought on by the insistent pressures of economic stagnation, spiralling inflation, shrinking resources and an increasingly conservative political climate (Omi and Winant, 1994). The dilemmas facing the country require detailed examination of our established way of life. The historic assumptions of unbridled growth, infinite possibilities and the absence of limits – fundamental elements of our cultural ethos – have now run head-on into the realities of limits imposed by contemporary global and national circumstances. These circumstances require that we question the future viability of a system imbued in the belief that developed nations, a minority of the world's population, are entitled to control and consume the overwhelming majority of the world's resources (Chomsky, 1999). Challenges to the persistence of such inequities on the world scene will undoubtedly become more frequent and strident as the voices of the Third World achieve a higher pitch, wider impact and more unified economic/political clout. We shall see more agitation for changes in the world order such as the struggle between 'North' and 'South' nations within the United States, the oil embargo, the North–South Conference in Mexico, the United Nations Conference on the International Control of Information Flow and the conflicts between UNESCO and the United States. At root, these examples represent challenges to the presumed rights of 10 per cent of the world's population to control 90 per cent of the world's natural, economic, political and information resources.

The task confronting the US in the twenty-first century will be to develop new standards of the appropriate, to generate new values (Collins, 1998; Glazer, 1997). Where will such redirection of values come from if not from the educated elite, those who teach the next generation and head its key institutions? In all fairness, it must be recognized that many of the justifications for the *status quo* are generated by the society's intelligentsia – its universities, major corporations, lawyers, doctors and professors. The relevance of this point to the shifting world order derives from the critical role played by the US in the maintenance of the current world order and the striking parallels between how black Americans (an exploited, internal 'Other') are treated, as compared with the treatment accorded exploited 'Others' on the world scene (Takaki, 1990). Therefore, until this society redirects its relationships with and definitions of black Americans – that is, until this society learns and institutes new values – it will be unable to redefine its posture towards other people of colour in the US and towards a largely non-white, Third World.

> The problem of the twentieth century is the problem of the colour line, the question as to how far differences of race, which show themselves chiefly in the colour of the skin and texture of the hair, are going to be made hereafter, the basis for denying to over half the world the right of sharing to their utmost ability the opportunities and privileges of modern civilisation.
>
> W. E. B. Du Bois, Report of the Pan African Conference,
> July 23–25, 1990, Westminster Town Hall,
> London (Lewis, 1995, p. 639)

References

Allen, W. R. (1978a) Black Family Research in the United States: a Review, Assessment and Extension, *Journal of Comparative Family Studies*, 9, 167–89.

Allen W. R. (1978b) Towards Applicable Theories of Black Family Life, *Journal of Marriage and the Family*, 40, 117–29.

Allen, W. R. (1995) African American Family Life in Societal Context: Crisis and Hope, *Sociological Forum* 10(4), 569–92.

Allen, W. R. and James, A. (1998) Comparative Perspectives on Black Family Life, Special Issue of the *Journal of Comparative Family Studies*, Vols I and II, 29, 1–2.

Aschenbrenner, J. (1975) *Lifelines: Black Families in Chicago*, Holt, Rinehart and Winston, Chicago, IL.

Ball, D. W. (1972) The 'Family' as a Sociological Problem: Conceptualization of the Taken-for-Granted as Prologue to Social Problems Analysis, *Social Problems*, 19 (3), 295–307.

Bernard, J. (1966) *Marriage and Family Among Negroes*, Prentice-Hall, Englewood Cliffs, NJ.

Billingsley, A. (1968) *Black Families in White America*, Prentice-Hall, Englewood Cliffs, NJ.

Billingsley, A. (1970) Black Families and White Social Science, *Journal of Social Issues* 26 (3), 127–42.

Billingsley, A. (1992) *Climbing Jacob's Ladder: the Enduring Legacy of African–American Families*, Simon and Schuster, New York.

Chilman, C. S. (1973) Public Social Policy and Families in the 1970s, *Social Casework*, 575–585.

Chomsky, N. (1999) *Profit Over People: Neoliberalism and Global Order*, Seven Stories Press, New York.

Collins, P. H. (1998) *Fighting Words: Black Women and the Search for Justice*, University of Minnesota Press, Minneapolis, MN.

Conley, D. (1999) *Being Black, Living in the Red: Race, Wealth and Social Policy in America*. University of California Press, Los Angeles, CA.

Edin, K. and Lein, L. (1997) *Making Ends Meet: How Single Mothers Survive Welfare and Low-Wage Work*, Russell Sage Foundation, New York.

English, R. (1983) *The Challenge of Mental Health: Minorities and Their World Views*, School of Social Work, University of Texas, Austin, TX.

Farley, R. and Allen, W. R. (1989) *The Color Line and the Quality of Life in America*, Oxford University Press, New York.

Frazier, E. F. (1939, reprinted in 1964) *The Negro Family in the United States*, University of Chicago Press, Chicago, IL.

Glazer, N. (1997) *We Are All Multiculturalists Now*, Harvard University Press, Cambridge, MA.

Gutman, H. (1975) *The Black Family in Slavery and Freedom, 1750–1925*, Pantheon, New York.

Heiss, J. (1975) *The Case of the Black Family*, Columbia, New York.

Herzog, E. (1966) Is There a Breakdown in the Negro Family?, *Social Work*, 11, 3–10.

Hill, R. (1971) *The Strengths of Black Families*. Emerson Hall, New York.

Hill, R. (1997) *The Strengths of African American Families: Twenty-Five Years Later*, R&B Publishers, Washington, DC.

Hill, R., *et al.* (1993) *Research on the African American Family: a Holistic Perspective,* Auburn House, Westport, CT.

Hyman, H. and Reed J. (1969) Black Matriarchy Reconsidered: Evidence from Secondary Analysis of Sample Surveys, *Public Opinion Quarterly,* 33, 346–54.

Ladner, J. (1971) *Tomorrow's Tomorrow,* Doubleday, Garden City, NY.

Laing, R. D. (1971) *The Politics of the Family,* Random House, New York.

Lammermeier, P. (1972) The Urban Black Family of the Nineteenth Century, *Journal of Marriage and the Family.*

Lewis, D. L. (ed.) (1995) *W. E. B. Du Bois: a Reader,* Henry Holt, New York.

Moynihan, D. P. (1965) *The Negro Family: the Case for National Action,* US Department of Labor, Washington, DC.

Oliver, M. and Shapiro, T. (1995) *Black Wealth/White Wealth: a New Perspective on Racial Inequality.* Routledge, New York.

Omi, M. and Winant, H. (1994) *Racial Formation in the United States,* Routledge, New York.

Rainwater, L. (1970) *Behind Ghetto Walls: Black Families in a Federal Slum,* Aldine, Chicago, IL.

Rodman, H. (1971) *Lower Class Families,* Oxford, New York.

Scanzoni, J. (1971) *The Black Family in Modern Society,* Allyn and Bacon, Boston, MA.

Schorr, A. L. (1962) Family Policy in the United States, *International Sociological Science Journal,* 452–67.

Schulz, D. (1969) *Coming Up Black,* Prentice-Hall, Englewood Cliffs, NJ.

Spencer, M. B., Brookins, G. K. and Allen, W. R. (1985) *Beginnings: the Social and Affective Development of Black Children,* Lawrence Erlbaum Associates, Hillside, NJ.

Stack, C. (1974) *All Our Kin,* Harper and Row, New York.

Staples, R. (1971) Towards a Sociology of the Black Family, *Journal of Marriage and the Family,* 33, 19–38.

Sussman, M. (1971) Family Systems in the 1970s: Analysis, Policies and Programs, *The Annals of the American Academy of Political and Social Science,* 396.

Takaki, R. (1990) *Iron Cages: Race and Culture in 19th Century America,* Oxford University Press, New York.

Toliver, S. D. (1998) *Black Families in Corporate America,* Sage Publications, Thousand Oaks, CA.

4

The Racialization of Social Scientific Research on South Africa

Rupert Taylor and Mark Orkin

Within the domain of social scientific knowledge production in South Africa, there has been a socio-politically influential group of methodologically 'mainstream' sociologists and political scientists. Reflecting common-sense appearances and following the dictates of empirical-analytical social science – including the application of statistical methods and the canon of objectivity (Fay, 1975) – the study of South African society has been framed within the imagery and logic of 'race' and 'ethnicity'; such that, for many years, efforts to engineer social change away from apartheid were predicated on the 'factual' existence of these two concepts.

In line with such understanding there was a general concern to develop and promote a particular consociational and federal vision of South African political life. And this vision was taken forward politically during the 1970s and 1980s – with the active involvement of many of its academic proponents – by Chief Buthelezi and his Inkatha party. Then, as Inkatha's position became marginalized, the vision was adapted and extended as a negotiating platform by *verligte* ('enlightened') Afrikaner Nationalists led by F. W. de Klerk, who in 1989 succeeded P. W. Botha as leader of the National Party and opened negotiations with the liberation movements (MacDonald, 1992; O'Meara, 1996).

A brief historical account of the context in which mainstream work and its 'vision' arose will be helpful. H. F. Verwoerd who, as Prime Minister (1958–66), transformed the piecemeal implementation of pre-WWII segregation into the post-war design of grand apartheid, was himself a sociologist. Before the war, Verwoerd held a Chair in sociology at the University of Stellenbosch, one of the first universities after the University of Chicago to have such a department. The intellectual justifications of the apartheid design were bolstered in the two decades after the war by the South African Bureau of Racial Affairs (Gordon, 1991). Most of SABRA's social scientific subscribers were Afrikaans-speaking members of the *Broederbond* (League of Brothers), a secret politico-cultural organization comprised of most male members of the ruling Afrikaner elite (Wilkins and Strydom, 1978). In turn, SABRA members dominated SASOV, the 'Whites-only' *Suid-Afrikaanse Sociolo-gievereniging* (South African Sociological Association), and were also to be found in its counterpart organization in political science, in which some English-speaking social scientists uneasily participated.

'Racial' segregation was legislatively imposed upon universities in 1959. The African National Congress (ANC) and Pan-Africanist Congress (PAC) were banned a year later; their leaders went into exile or under-ground, and most of the latter group were captured in 1964. Until the end of the decade, above-ground opposition to apartheid was sustained in liberal terms by the non-racial National Union of South African Students (NUSAS), by Helen Suzman in Parliament, and by the *Rand Daily Mail* newspaper. At the beginning of the 1970s, English-speaking social scientists (mainly of this liberal persuasion), broke away from SASOV and, together with a couple of renegade anti-*Broederbond* Afri-kaans academics, established the non-racial and regional Association for Sociology in Southern Africa.[1] Social anthropologists and political scien-tists of like mind also became active in ASSA. Ironically, this occurred just as the influence was spreading, both in 'racially' segregated schools and in the specially-established 'ethnic' universities of the radical and separatist Black Consciousness Movement led by Steve Biko – which soon developed a research strand of its own (Pityana, 1981).

Among English-speaking social scientists within South Africa, who were concerned with what was termed 'race relations', the dominant outlook during the 1960s and 1970s thus had a liberal political intent, in opposition to the prevailing legislatively enacted racism of apartheid (Horrell, 1971). This pressing concern with 'race' readily found a social scientific locus in 'plural society theory', then in its heyday. From this perspective, analyses of South Africa centred on 'ethnicity' for its under-standing of the genesis and process of 'racial' categorization prevalent in everyday as well as political and legal discourse and practice (van den Berghe, 1967; Kuper, 1974); and the chosen methodologies were those of empirical social science.[2]

This developing mix of liberal politics and pluralist thinking soon faced radical challenges. In the early 1970s, NUSAS students, inspired by the renaissance of Marxism in Europe, helped revive African trade unionism through taking part in previously dormant industrial councils and setting up industrial aid societies. And young Marxist social scientists who had undertaken postgraduate degrees in England or France, and were participating in nascent worker organizations, began to establish or re-cast industrial sociology courses in sociology departments (Webster, 1991). At the same time, a Marxist-inspired revision of South African social and labour history was beginning to unfold, primarily in England, initiated by South African social scientists and historians in exile (Wright, 1977; Johnstone, 1982). By the mid-1980s it was being argued that neo-Marxist sociology was dominant in some sociology departments at English-language South African universities (Jubber, 1983).

The revival of Marxist thought was, however, marked by a number of failings (Posel, 1983). Most notably, there has been an inability to rise above crude materialism to specify theoretically how class intersects with non-economic forces, and there has been a 'misconceptualisation of the sources of power and privilege in South Africa' (MacDonald and James, 1993, p. 388). Moreover, as Marxist writings have been predominantly historical and anti-empirical in approach, there has been – with rare exception (Fisher, 1978) – little use made of surveys or serious attention to attitudinal data, especially of a quantitative nature. As a result, in the 1980s, emphasis on 'race' and 'ethnicity' was not significantly displaced but remained the taken-for-granted starting-point in much social scientific research. 'Race' and 'ethnicity' continued to be seen as independent sociological factors, having their own effects and determinate relationships with a bearing on the future trajectory of South Africa.

The mainstream network

In the apartheid years, most society-centred analyses concerned with promoting visions of a future South Africa took 'race' and 'ethnicity' as descriptive and analytical categories, and proceeded to see the key players as 'racial' and 'ethnic' groups. In this regard, since the 1970s and especially over the 1980s, a closely-knit network of scholars, together with the associated intellectual framework, can be explicitly identified by linkages in the literature. Taking the major mainstream social scientific books on South Africa published between 1971 and 1993, and charting interlocks through social network analysis (Scott, 1991) – in terms of co-authorship, contributors (in the case of edited books), preface acknowledgements and dust-cover endorsements – the central connections can be presented as a sociogram (Diagram 4.1). This network of individuals forms the hegemonic core of the mainstream, in which the standards for other works were set in terms of the types of questions posed and data used. The sociogram clearly reveals a marked pattern of mutual validation, with individual writers using each other's work and advice to legitimate their own writing.

The key books include Hanf *et al.* (1978/1981) *South Africa: the Prospects of Peaceful Change*, Adam and Giliomee (1979) *Ethnic Power Mobilized*, van Zyl Slabbert and Welsh (1979) *South Africa's Options*, Lijphart (1985) *Power-Sharing in South Africa*, Adam and Moodley (1986) *South Africa Without Apartheid*, Giliomee and Schlemmer (1989) *From Apartheid to Nation-Building* and Horowitz (1991) *A Democratic South Africa?*.[3] Focus falls on books because they are more widely read and cited than journal articles (Blau, 1973), and offer more detailed and sustained overviews of South African society. Attention is given to acknowledgements in the prefaces rather than cross-citations because the former are stronger indications of shared values. It is evident that this is not a parochial network. It has been linked into, and consolidated by, global dimensions of social science. The network includes the internationally-known academics, Adam, Lijphart and Hanf. It is, however, a network within which – in terms of apartheid 'racial' designations – 'black' social scientists have been present only at the margins.

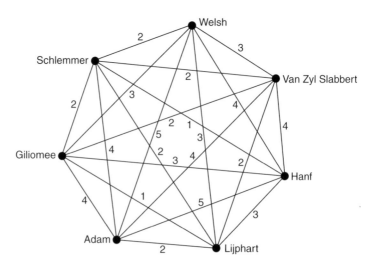

Diagram 4.1   Individuals interlocked through 15 leading social scientific books on South Africa, 1971–93.

There are various other ways in which the network has been pervasive and interlocked. Many of the individuals identified in Diagram 4.1 have formed part of an international academic community. There have been dozens of international conferences on South Africa; most notably, the conference on 'Change in Contemporary South Africa' at Mount Kisco (United States) in 1975, the 'International Conference on Intergroup Accommodation in Plural Societies' at Cape Town (South Africa) in 1977, and 'The Prospects for Peaceful Change in South Africa' confer-ence at Titisee (Germany) in 1978. The first two of these conferences resulted in key books (Thompson and Butler, 1975; Rhoodie, 1978). The network has also been interlocked through membership of professional associations and the editorial boards of South Africa's leading social scientific journals such as *Politikon, Social Dynamics* and the *Journal of Contemporary African Studies.*

This has not been an 'invisible' college (Crane, 1972) but a clearly visible social circle in which there has been a considerable degree of face-to-face contact. Most of the 'stars' identified in Diagram 4.1 (those individuals with the highest number of interlocks) have been opinion leaders in as much as they have frequently contributed to the press, radio and television. They have frequently written articles for *The Star* (Johannesburg) and *Cape Times*, for business-oriented magazines such as *Leadership, South Africa International* and South Africa's version of the *New Statesman, Die Suid-Afrikaan*. These are the individuals who have most been sought after to give keynote speeches to high-profile confer-ences, workshops and briefings.

Although not totally unified, and with some individuals having shifted ground over the years, this network has been marked by a particular approach (the empirical-analytical) which guides research to a set of problems – the reform of a 'racially' and 'ethnically' divided society – and as such constitutes a 'paradigm' (Kuhn, 1970). But just how has seeing South Africa in terms of 'race' and 'ethnicity' helped to explain South African society? And how has mainstream work sought to establish a position critically distinct from apartheid thinking? Indeed, has it been able to move substantively beyond the 'official', 'racial' and 'ethnic' classifications of apartheid ideology, especially given the ruling National Party's shift, in the 1950–60s, from 'racial' to cultural rhetoric, from 'race' to 'ethnicity'?

Basically, the mainstream has subjected 'race' and 'ethnicity' to a more sophisticated understanding than that offered by apartheid ideo-logues. 'Race' and 'ethnicity' have been seen as more fluid and context-ual, and it was argued that they should not have been unjustly used to allocate distinct rights and set legislative boundaries between people. The National Party's classifications were seen as false, for, as Lijphart puts it, 'the constituent segments of this plural society can be finally determined only by a process of free and voluntary affiliation and free competition' (Lijphart, 1985, p. 50). It was argued that once we move away from imposed 'invidious distinctions' based on 'race' and the 'artificial' aspects of 'ethnicity' created by apartheid, the political saliency of 'race' (but not its reality) will submerge and 'ethnicity' will emerge as something of value to be defended. Here, as Adam and Moodley stated in *South Africa Without Apartheid*, 'Good racial relations would be ethnic relations' (1986, p. 16, repeating Banton 1983, p. 397).

In the context of such understanding, it was consistently urged that South Africa ought to move towards an open pluralism by creating institutions that accommodate 'racial' and 'ethnic' differences, and that would allow for voluntary 'racial' and 'ethnic' group attachments and freedom of association. This is a central theme that runs from the early days of the Spro-Cas [Study Project on Christianity in Apartheid Society] (1973) *Political Alternatives* report through to the demise of apartheid (Rich, 1989). The theme evolved, from attempts in the 1970s to chart an evolutionary course away from separate development, by linking 'homeland' and non-'homeland' areas in a consociational federalist system, through national debates on consociational power-sharing in the 1980s, to proposals for constitutional structures and mechanisms during the transition years (1990–94). On this basis, the mainstream network first countered the 'ethno-national' racially-based grand apartheid design of Verwoerd but then moved to moderate the non-racial unitary state design of the ANC. Now, with the advent of South Africa's new democracy, the future is viewed in pessimistic light; given the country's 'racial' and 'ethnic' divisions, it is argued, 'consolidation may take a long time' (Schlemmer, 1994, p. 22) or even that 'the evolution of a liberal democracy is most unlikely' (Giliomee, 1995, p. 104).

Unanswered questions

There are, however, serious failings in the mainstream approach to 'race' and 'ethnicity' – at both a theoretical and empirical level. These are now considered in turn. At the theoretical level, there has been a failure to provide a coherent position on 'race' and 'ethnicity'. Instead, what has been offered are definitions of 'race' and 'ethnicity' which are sometimes overlapping, sometimes synonymous and sometimes dovetailing with definitions of 'nationalism', 'culture' or 'social group'. The main-stream paradigm has presented an eclectic and changing mix of 'pri-mordial', instrumental and social constructivist approaches to 'race' and 'ethnicity' in order to try and give specific meaning to presumed inner attributes and account for their independent causal significance.

'Race' and 'ethnicity' are considered of primary import in the South African context – why? What are the essential differences for which 'race' and 'ethnicity' account? Thoughtful answers have not been con-spicuous. In *Ethnic Power Mobilized* (1979), for example, Adam and Giliomee saw 'race' and 'ethnicity' as explaining something which 'class' could not; but just what this was, was not clearly explained. They failed to specify theoretically just how 'race' and 'ethnicity' are constituted as separate orders in society, and dialectically interact (Wolpe, 1986). To move analysis forward there was an increasing rejec-tion of the kind of simple 'primordialism' which infused Lijphart's (1985) *Power-Sharing in South Africa* in favour of an effort to forge a convergence of 'primordialism' with a careful measure of social con-structivism. In this view, while it is assumed that there is a prior 'prim-ordial' infrastructure, 'racial' and 'ethnic' consciousness are treated as latent universal potentialities which only come to the fore under certain social contexts to meet or serve people's socio-political interests. But just how do we explain where 'racial' and 'ethnic' consciousness comes from in the first place?

In the search for an answer, in the case of 'ethnicity' in particular, focus has centred on social psychological processes of group formation and the 'need' for group identity. Giliomee (1990), for example, has seen the potency of 'ethnicity' in terms of 'the psychological demands for the affirmation of group worth'; Schlemmer (1991) has written that 'ethni-city' 'offers the immediate rewards of ego-expansion and psychological gratification'; and Horowitz has maintained that 'the sources of ethnic conflict reside, above all, in the struggle for relative group worth' (1985, p. 143). There is, however, a serious problem with this. While such social psychological approaches may help explain the intensity of social cleav-ages it is not made clear how they explain their specific nature. Just how do social psychological mechanisms link to 'ethnicity' as opposed to other factors, such as 'class'? What is the specificity of 'ethnicity' in and of itself? How do 'group differences' relate to 'ethnic differences'?

These questions remain unanswered. From Lijphart's recourse to 'primordialism', to Horowitz's 'careful measure' of social constructivism, there remains the common belief that there is 'something there'. But we are never told what specifically *is* 'there'; in the final analysis there has been, and remains, a failure to establish a coherent position that offers valid answers as to the thinghood of 'race' and 'ethnicity'. In consequence, we encounter a theoretical dead-end. The search for a convincing theory of 'race' and 'ethnicity', in the key works, has been unsuccessful. In light of this it is hard, at a *socio-theoretical* level, to see why we should use such terms as 'black' and 'white', 'Zulu' and 'Xhosa' except as the *end-product* of an explanation of why they continue to occur in everyday life. Nonetheless, mainstream social scientists proceeded 'to tell the story', granting 'race' and 'ethnicity' independent causal significance.

The reason why mainstream work has remained under-theorized is that considerable reliance has been placed on the strength of 'race' and 'ethnicity' at the level of empirical evidence, especially as revealed in quantitative data. As Horowitz has written, empirical survey data proves the 'continuing importance of racial, ethnic and subethnic identities in South Africa' (1991, p. 85). This reflects the ontological and epistemological primacy which empirical-analytical social science ascribes to what can allegedly be observed directly; such that truth-claims must be consistent with the empirical 'facts' collected and revealed in an 'objective' manner (Fay, 1975).

This, however, is to be led from one set of criticisms to another. For, there has been a reluctance to recognize that to view society in terms of 'racial' and 'ethnic' categories is to work with totalizing concepts of group identity which tend to deny 'internal' differences and cross-cutting commonalties, mask diversity and multiple identifications, and conceal the contingency and ambiguity of every identity. In particular, a central focus on the categories of 'race' and 'ethnicity' has resulted in the neglect of the complexity of social differentiation with regard to age, gender, religion, education, occupation, wealth, status, region and urbanization. There has been little attempt in mainstream texts to disentangle 'race' and 'ethnicity' analytically from other factors. None of the key books give any real concern to dealing with complex causal relations where an attempt is made to control and handle many variables: no sophisticated multivariate analyses have been designed to tease out the independent effects, if any, of 'race' and 'ethnicity' (and in this sense the mainstream's professed commitment to empirical-analytical social science falls short).

Typical of this is Giliomee and Schlemmer's use, in *From Apartheid to Nation-Building*, of a survey of 'black' industrial workers to show that differences in 'ethnic' attitudes in 'endorsing the answer category of "angry and impatient" with regard to feelings about the political situation in South Africa' varied between 'Zulu' [62 per cent] 'Xhosa' [44 per cent] and 'Sotho' [45 per cent] (1989, p. 168). Is it the case that 'ethnic' category is related to political choices without the mediation of other factors? Such recourse to 'ethnicity' is not self-explanatory. More recently, this shortcoming has been reflected in the view that the April 1994 election was little more than a straight 'racial census', with 'whites' voting for the National Party, and 'blacks' voting for the ANC; 'one can use the term "racial census" for the outcome of the 1994 election: the choice of political party correlated with the position in the racial or ethnic hierarchy of a particular group' (Giliomee, 1996, p. 97; also see Schlemmer, 1994; Johnson and Schlemmer, 1996). But why should 'race' be taken as the most important determinant of voting behaviour? Simply to show correlations between 'race' and people's voting behaviour can actually say nothing about causation. It cannot be assumed automatically that 'race' determined the way people voted. What of other social background characteristics such as age, gender, religion, level of education and class location (consider Mattes, 1995)? In any event, it cannot simply be said that the political parties in South Africa represent exclusive 'racial' interests; particularly with regard to the ANC, but also in terms of the new National Party.

What has transpired in mainstream work is that the determining salience of 'race' and 'ethnicity' has simply been inferred, never shown. There has been no attempt to spin out a *fully-specified* theory of the connections between 'race'/'ethnicity' and other variables (such as political attitudes and voting), so as to yield empirically testable predictions or propositions. 'Race' and 'ethnicity' should not be left to speak for themselves, they stand in need of further explanation. People may indeed place value on considering themselves as 'black' or 'white', 'Zulu' or 'Xhosa', but the question is: how and why do these conceptions of identity have meaning?

Moreover, while there is indeed much evidence to show that most South Africans subscribe (in one form or another) to 'racial' and 'ethnic' terms of identity, there is also counter-evidence which shows that some South Africans refuse to accord 'race' any significance, and that some African people have not internalized 'ethnic' labels but have seen them as partial and imposed, with no subjective significance in day-to-day interaction.[4] People have contested the 'collective selves' promoted by apartheid society; notably through non-racialism, which is based on the principled rejection of a racialized understanding of South African society. There are many examples of the presence of non-racialism as subjective lived experience, especially for people located within organizations and institutions that have professed a non-racial standpoint: these include the ANC, South African Communist Party, Congress of South African Trade Unions, the South African Council of Churches and Southern African Catholic Bishops Conference, the English-language universities, and many smaller professional, labour and civic organizations (Foster, 1991; Norval, 1996). Mainstream scholars have not given a *voice* to the non-racial alternatives projected by many anti-apartheid organizations.

Just as seriously, there is scant recognition in mainstream work of the need for more contextual and interpretative research methods which would probe the subjective experiences, perceptions and feelings that shape people's responses. To stress the empirical 'facts' of 'race' and 'ethnicity' is not to offer 'insight into the genesis of the present patterns of response and their relationship to the intrinsic meaning of what is experienced' (Adorno, 1972, p. 245; also see Keat, 1979). In particular, by their recourse to socio-psychological notions of 'ethnic' identification, mainstream writings have tended to neglect the diachronic dimension, that is, change over time. For instance, they have thus underplayed – or misrepresented – what has been conspicuous about the pattern of support for African political parties since the mid-1970s: the relatively steady growth in support, across all language-groupings, for the ANC.[5]

Through such omissions, empirical social research promotes the objectification of 'the Other' such that the presumed 'facts' of 'race' and 'ethnicity' come to actually frame survey questions and the collation of findings. The two major social scientific surveys – Hanf *et al.* (1978) and the Buthelezi Commission (1982) – both conducted separate standardized surveys for 'black' and 'white' opinion and offered restricted, selective and even manipulative choices in questions and answers.[6]

More than this, the use of externally imposed 'racial' and 'ethnic' categorizations can lead to debilitating circular reasoning in which the meaning of non-racial and non-ethnic awareness is never fairly confronted. In Horowitz's *A Democratic South Africa?*, for example, we find that the belief in 'ethnicity' remains unchallenged regardless of empirical findings. In one case, it is concluded that 'When Xhosa provide a nonethnic response to an identity question on a sample survey, they are reflecting their view of South African society' (1991, pp. 69–70). But how can non-ethnic responses be attributed to 'ethnicity'? Similarly, Adam and Moodley, in *The Opening of the Apartheid Mind*, argued against the non-racialism of the ANC by pointing to estimated voting preferences according to 'race' in opinion polls conducted over 1991 and 1992 which indicate that the ANC holds less attraction to 'Indians', 'Coloureds' and 'Whites' than the National Party (Adam and Moodley, 1993, p. 76). But what, at this level, is the value of analysing non-racialism in terms of 'race'? After all, a 'racially' mixed organization is not necessarily non-racial (Taylor, 1994).

In sum, there are clearly a range of unresolved and largely unrecognized tensions and obstacles in mainstream research. It has not been shown exactly why and how 'race' and 'ethnicity' are sociologically useful categories for analysis. It has not actually been made clear how 'race' and 'ethnicity' help 'explain' South African society. Seekings has aptly summarized our argument: mainstream scholars 'have generally assumed rather than demonstrated that [*race and ethnicity*] provide the basis of South African society, have not probed the meaning of the categories around which their analysis revolves, and have failed to explore the relationship between race, ethnicity and other forms of social differentiation' (Seekings, 1995, pp. 60–1). Not surprisingly, mainstream scholars have now found themselves at a loss to account for the advent of a non-racial democracy which has rejected specific forms of protection for 'racial' or 'ethnic' group politics.

Constraints on understanding

To begin to explain why mainstream social science has not understood 'race' and 'ethnicity' we must recognize how the root causes of these problems can be traced to the emphasis placed on an empiricist conception of data and 'the interest in controlling an objectified environmental world' (Apel, 1979, p. 6; also see Habermas, 1988). Centrally, the objectification of the 'facts' and commitment to objectivity in the process of enquiry which are characteristic of empirical-analytical social science, renders social enquiry highly susceptible to the sway of South Africa's racialized social order. This is because the question of 'objectivity' with regard to 'race' and 'ethnicity' is not as innocent as presumed. To use these terms, as mainstream scholars do, is to take a position. It is to state that one believes such 'things' exist and should count as preformed data. To be objective on 'race' and 'ethnicity' is not a non-ideological, value-free standpoint; objectivity is implicated in the failings of mainstream work and should not be regarded as being beyond question.

The problem is that empirical social science fails to see society as an active subject. It 'confuses the epiphenomenon – what the world has made of us – with the thing itself' (Adorno, 1972, p. 244; also see

Bernstein, 1979). The racialization of social scientific research, whereby 'racial' and 'ethnic' identity are taken for granted, occurs through the silence of empiricism; through the 'forgetting' of a history in which racism in South Africa is seen as grounded in nineteenth-century Western thought (and earlier colonial frameworks), and is a product of European modernity (Crais, 1992); a history in which 'racial' and 'ethnic' conceptualization has been socially constructed to serve as ways for ordering, controlling and ruling society.

Once 'race' and 'ethnicity' are seen as categories invented in a social process to pursue social differentiation and perpetuate inequality, it is clear that 'race' and 'ethnicity' do not exist outside meanings imputed by people. And it follows that to use them *uncritically* is to engage in inscription, not description; it is to use words that uphold investments of power and privilege. Looked at from this perspective, mainstream social science has not only reflected South Africa's racialized social order but has actually been implicated in its very constitution.

Part of the problem is that there has been a failure to see how 'race' and 'ethnicity' themselves have entered social science in terms of specific theories and methods, especially through discredited nineteenth-century anthropological theories (Barkan, 1992; Harding, 1993). There has been a failure to see the concepts as residues of pre-Enlightenment thought rooted in Europe.

The racialization of mainstream work, the assumption that there are to one extent or another such givens as 'racial' and 'ethnic' groups, also has roots in the weight of the earlier social scientific orthodoxy which conceptualized South African society in terms of the 'sociology of race relations' and 'plural society theory', both of which are marked by an inability to take 'race' as problematic in itself. For instance, the work of Kuper (1974) and van den Berghe (1967) – both of whom are cited, or personally acknowledged, in many of the key texts – treats 'race' as an irreducible constituent of human identity, having independent causal significance.[7]

To understand more thoroughly the racialization of mainstream research, and to account for its wide acceptance, we have to turn to consider the social relations between knowledge and power in South Africa under National Party rule. We have to understand how the production and use of social scientific knowledge was determined and reinforced by its location in, and connections with, the power structure of apartheid South Africa. The extent to which the mainstream has been tied to various institutional agendas and political interventions is shown in Diagram 4.2. The diagram locates all those individuals identified in our analysis of the 15 key books in a wide research field which intersects with the apartheid state, big business, regionally-focused reformist projects, independent policy research institutes and political parties.[8]

The diagram points towards the fact that, for some, there has been a considerable degree of status, prestige and influence; an influence which also stretches to the exercise of significant authority over academia and the politics of publishing.[9] Of the 37 individuals identified in the socio-gram only one – in terms of apartheid designations – is 'black'.

When one considers this research field in more detail, it becomes apparent that the direct ties to state programmes became more prominent in the 1980s as the National Party turned to the reform of apartheid. Many in the mainstream played a part in debates around the 1983

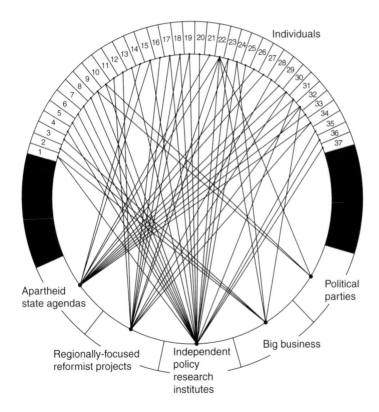

Diagram 4.2 The mainstream social scientific research field, 1971–93.

Constitution, such as in submissions to the Constitutional Committee where the work of Lijphart was of central import (Worrall, 1981; Taylor, 1990). There has also been much association with the para-statal Human Sciences Research Council (HSRC), which is the major source of funding for social science research within South Africa, and has been responsible for channelling funds that run into many millions of rand into techno-cratic research or programmes linked to National Party goals. Here, mainstream involvement included participation in HSRC committees, projects and publications, most notably the large-scale interdisciplinary 1985 Investigation into Intergroup Relations.[10]

Ties with the key regionally-focused reform projects – which did not directly involve the National Party (or the ANC) – have included the Quail (1980), Lombard (1980) and Buthelezi (1982) Commissions, and the Natal/KwaZulu Indaba (1986). All of these projects advocated forms of regional consociational federalism. The Quail Commission spoke of a 'multiracial condominium'. The Lombard Commission proposed regional government for KwaZulu/Natal. The Buthelezi Commission and Indaba saw KwaZulu/Natal as a model for state government in a consociational-federal South Africa – a position which was central to Inkatha's platform throughout the 1980s (Maré, 1987).

Apart from these projects, mainstream work has been carried forward through a wide range of influential 'think-tanks' that include the South African Institute of Race Relations, the Centre for Policy Studies and the Urban Foundation. Under apartheid, the programmes of these institutes generally fused dominant political interests with mainstream goals through focusing on specific policy issues.

The mainstream's reformist orientation has been closely aligned to the political interests of the Progressive Federal Party/Democratic Party and Inkatha (van Zyl Slabbert was once PFP Leader of the Opposition, Schlem-mer was once Director of the Inkatha Institute), and has dovetailed with big business concern over capitalist stability. In fact, the links with capital are more important than Figure 4.2 indicates, as several major policy research institutes and projects have been funded by big business. The giant Anglo-American Corporation provided major funding for the 'South Africa Beyond Apartheid' project and was a prominent participant in the Buthelezi Commission – in which Adam, Giliomee, Lijphart and Schlemmer were all involved.[11] The South African Sugar Association and Durban Chamber of Commerce initiated the Lombard Commission. Likewise, the Indaba was heavily sponsored by local capital. In addition, various forms of corporate sponsorship and funding have come from Mobil, Shell, First National Bank, Barlow Rand and Anton Rupert.

By locating the mainstream paradigm in this wider research field it is apparent that it has had considerable institutional backing. And this, it should be recognized, is because of its concern with social engineering and the connections of empirical-analytical social science with the idea of control (Habermas, 1971; Fay, 1975). A concern to reform the political agenda incrementally through co-operation rather than transform it radically, has had real material advantages for social scientific research and contributed to significant National Party policy changes, but it has entailed an intellectual price: the neglect of critical thinking. It has helped ensure that certain kinds of questions do not get asked. It has helped prevent many from seeing South Africa in an illuminating way.

It is time, however, to oblige those who adhere to the mainstream paradigm to confront, through critical self-reflection, the deeper assumptions and structure of interests underlying such work. Mainstream social scientific research must begin to face the fact that its strongly empiricist beliefs have prevented serious theorizing on 'race' and 'ethnicity'. Such beliefs limit our powers of explanation in that we are led towards seeing 'race' and 'ethnicity' as objectively given, and away from investigating deeper questions around how they have been socially constructed, through state-making imperatives, as conceptual systems for constituting reality and establishing relations of power and forms of inequality. Moreover, there is a need to recognize how the racialization of social research is compounded by the way in which apartheid state policies closed the space for critical intellectual work and impacted on academia such that most work has been, and is, undertaken by those whom apartheid designated 'white'; today, the HSRC continues to struggle with low credibility and over 80 per cent of permanent university staff are 'white', with the majority of 'black' academics employed at the bottom of the employment ladder.[12]

The way forward

Insofar as the network of mainstream scholars 'retains intellectual influence, it is in part precisely because nobody else has put forward major interpretations of contemporary South Africa that tackle head-on "common sense" views on race and ethnicity' (Seekings, 1995, p. 62). Thus, the way forward must rest on presenting new principles of sociological method – a new paradigm – for understanding the meaning of 'race' and 'ethnicity'.

To begin with, 'race' and 'ethnicity' must be understood as *ideologies* of 'race' and 'ethnicity' (Guillaumin, 1995). Instead of seeing the terms as free-standing, and enduring, independent phenomena to be examined and understood on their own terms, there is a need to totally reject notions of 'racial' and 'ethnic' determinism and to shift focus to the material conditions and social relations which work to generate and reproduce 'race' and 'ethnicity', to show how they have been socially constructed. This compels scholars to deconstruct *preconceived* notions and assumptions so that these do not uncritically appear in data collection, empirical analysis and theoretical discussion. To the extent that social science analyses take 'race' and 'ethnicity' as given, and uncritically infers correlation to social and political behaviour, it is poor social science: the significance of 'race' and 'ethnicity' must be demonstrated within a broader analysis.

That people may believe in 'race' and 'ethnicity' at the everyday level, and explain their actions in such terms, must be acknowledged. But this does not mean accepting their 'thinghood'; it simply means they have been given value because 'race' and 'ethnicity' are notionally normative, and the extent to which this is the case is precisely what has to be *explained* from a non-racial, non-ethnic standpoint. Indeed, what is required is a social science capable of helping to move people beyond such self-perceptions through promoting the emergence of non-racialism.

The way for social research to proceed is, first, to accept the need to move away from the value placed on ascriptive social categories to focus on the categories of self-identification, to give people their own *voice*, and understand the *process* and *structure* of ideological thinking. As 'racial' and 'ethnic' identities are not simply given, but are shifting political constructs, present conditions must be researched, through qualitative methods and more sophisticated statistical techniques, to find the extent to which 'racial' and 'ethnic' thinking really does form part of people's social consciousness. To what extent, and why, have people internalized apartheid ideology and work within 'racial' and 'ethnic' logic? Is there, in everyday life, a formal consistency to 'racial' and 'ethnic' thinking or is it marked by contradictions and dilemmas? And, in terms of a belief in 'race' and 'ethnicity', where is this at its strongest in present-day South Africa?

Simultaneously, social research must begin to chart fully, and analyse the evidence for, the presence and impact of a non-racial outlook, with its alternative interpretation of self-identity which rejects and resists racial politics. A number of empirical studies conducted in South Africa since 1994 reveal that people do actively use 'racial' and 'ethnic' categories in thinking about their identity. It is also evident that there are 'a wide diversity of identities in South Africa...and most importantly... either when people are able to offer it on their own, or where they have chance to select the option, clear minorities of South Africans take the opportunity to call themselves a South African' (Mattes, 1997, p. 21). Surveys undertaken by the Institute for Democracy in South Africa have found that those people identifying themselves as 'South African' has increased from 13 per cent in 1994 to 22 per cent in 1995, whereas those giving a 'racial' or 'ethnic' answer declined from 51 per cent to 45 per cent (ibid., p. 12).

Overall, the way forward requires the development of a critical methodology tied to more sensitive and sophisticated forms of empirical analysis. In this, as social science is a social activity, it is not a question of whether quantitative methods are more 'scientific' than qualitative methods but a question of how such techniques are used (Aronowitz, 1988, p. 135). Centrally, we must refine methods that do not bypass the question of 'meaning' but break-down the immediacy of 'race' and 'ethnicity' by placing diachronic focus on the process and politics of subject formation. In addition, the limitations of conventional survey research can be transcended by exploring the relation of respondents to non-racial, non-ethnic understanding. This can be advanced through building reciprocity into the research design and questioning respondents on issues of feasible concern to them which they might not otherwise have raised for themselves.[13]

Although there is, as yet, not much of a critical tradition in quantitative social science (Irvine *et al.*, 1979), we should move to advancing more sophisticated statistical techniques of data analysis that recognize the importance of diachronic data and are not tied to the hypothetico-deductive orthodoxy; as, for example, through the use of modelling tools such as log-linear analysis. Such techniques would allow us to identify the evolving orientations of human subjects and thus inform emancipatory practice around 'race' and 'ethnicity'. By measuring the extent to which people have internalized dominant 'racial' and 'ethnic' ideologies and are engaged in processes of social self-transformation towards non-racial, non-ethnic understanding, we can arrive at quasi-causal generalizations, and try to identify workable points of progressive social intervention.[14] Quantitative techniques can uncover evidence on which emancipatory transformation can rely as long as it is recognized that quasi-causal explanation is 'only a heuristic means of deepening human self-understanding' (Apel, 1979, p. 43; also see Fay, 1975).

In sum, what is required, to escape racialization, is a deeper level of theoretical analysis in which empirical social research must be placed in a broader meta-factual context where we seek 'a unity of knowledge combining moral and political with empirical understanding' (Harding, 1986, p. 241; also see Horkheimer, 1972). Empirical social research must come to serve as 'a type of *historical analysis* of contemporary social forces' (Agger, 1977, p. 19) that uncovers the potential for non-racial, non-ethnic understanding. In approaching 'race' and 'ethnicity', we must move to embrace a critical social science, where, as Apel asserts, 'the leading knowledge-interest is...directed to...deepening of self-understanding by critical-emancipatory self-reflection' (1979, p. 43). By taking non-racialism as the standpoint for constituting the subject and subjects of critical activity, critical social science can be reclaimed and rejuvenated as being politically relevant.[15] Today, in South Africa, with the 'end of apartheid' and changing relations of power, there are real spaces for the development of such work.

Notes

The authors are grateful for the comments of: Sebouh Aslanian, Charles Crothers, Don Foster, Robert Gordon, Adam Habib, Thomas G. Karis, Tom Lodge, Stanford M. Lyman, Michael MacDonald, Robert B. Mattes, Graeme Moodie, Ephraim Nimni, S. Ortega Habib, Marie Poinsot, Adamantia Pollis, Peter Ratcliffe, Paul Robeson Jr., Jeremy Seekings, A. W. Stadler, Per Strand, Charles Tilly, Arthur J. Vidich and Elke Zuern.

1   See 'Editor's Preface' in Helm (1977). For an account of ASSA's role, see Webster (1991). SASOV amalgamated with ASSA in 1992, to form the non-racial South African Sociological Association, SASA.

2   Many of these empirical, usually attitudinal, studies are outlined in Lever (1978). See also Morse and Orpen (1975).

3   The rest of the 15 key books are: Adam (1971) *Modernizing Racial Domination*; Study Project on Christianity in Apartheid Society [Spro-Cas] (1973) *South Africa's Political Alternatives*; Thompson and Butler (1975) *Change in Contemporary South Africa*; Rhoodie (1978) *Intergroup Accommodation in Plural Societies*; van der Merwe and Schrire (1980) *Race and Ethnicity: South African and International Perspectives*; Berger and Godsell (1988) *A Future South Africa: Visions, Strategies and Realities*; Giliomee and Gagiano (1991) *The Elusive Search for Peace: South Africa, Israel and Northern Ireland*; Adam and Moodley (1993) *The Opening of the Apartheid Mind*. The selection of key books is supported by citation analysis. The *Social Sciences Citation Index*, January 1986 to December 1996, gives 180 citations to the work of Adam, 112 to Giliomee and 71 to Schlemmer. Lijphart is one of the world's most cited political scientists. Diagram 4.1 represents the core of the network charted from the key books in that it shows all those individuals who are fully interlocked with each other (although the entire network is too complicated to show completely). The numbers on Diagram 4.1 indicate the particular number of interlocks connecting any two individuals.

4   On the rejection of 'race', see Frederikse (1990). On the rejection of 'ethnicity', see the surveys of: Brandel-Syrier (1971), Edelstein (1974), Mayer (1975), Dreyer (1989).

5 In this regard, contrast Horowitz (1991, pp. 48–61) with Orkin (1989a, p. 84).
6 The Hanf *et al.* questionnaire first asked respondents if they had heard of Inkatha and what they thought the organization could do for them. Immediately afterwards it asked respondents for their leadership choice. See Orkin (1989a, p. 296).
7 See, in particular, Wolpe (1986, pp. 111–12). On the reductionism of 'race relations theory' also see Miles (1989). For a critique of 'plural society theory', see Johnstone (1976).
8 Diagram 4.2 refers to the following institutions and projects: apartheid state agendas (constitutional designs, Human Sciences Research Council, South African Bureau of Racial Affairs); big business (Anglo-American Corporation, South Africa Foundation, Urban Foundation); reformist projects (Quail, Lombard and Buthelezi Commissions); policy research institutes (South African Institute of Race Relations, Africa Institute, Centre for Intergroup Studies, Centre for Policy Studies, Institute for a Democratic Alternative in South Africa, South African Institute of International Affairs, Institute for Multi-Party Democracy); political parties (Progressive Federal Party/ Democratic Party, Inkatha). The sources used included a wide range of circulars, reports and publications of the above mentioned bodies; it also included confidential discussions with key informants. The 37 individuals charted on Diagram 4.2 are: (1) M. Spicer; (2) P. Berger; (3) A. Bernstein; (4) N. Charton; (5) T. R. H. Davenport; (6) R. M. de Villiers; (7) A. du Toit; (8) B. Naudé; (9) D. Welsh; (10) F. van Zyl Slabbert; (11) A. Lijphart; (12) R. I. Rotberg; (13) M. Savage; (14) D. A. Kotzé; (15) H. W. van der Merwe; (16) W. B. Vosloo; (17) H. Adam; (18) O. Dhlomo; (19) H. Giliomee; (20) A. Boraine; (21) P. Le Roux; (22) L. Schlemmer; (23) G. C. Olivier; (24) G. G. Maasdorp; (25) A. S. Matthews; (26) N. J. Rhoodie; (27) N. M. Stultz; (28) J. L. Sadie; (29) B. C. Lategan; (30) M. Wiechers; (31) W. J. Breytenbach; (32) R. M. Godsell; (33) B. G. Ranchod; (34) J. A. Lombard; (35) J. Dugard; (36) D. Schreiner; (37) W. de Klerk. These individuals represent the sum of those people uncovered in the network analysis of the 15 key books who have at least one direct interlock with the institutions and projects cited above.
9 Both the Human Sciences Research Council and the South African Institute of Race Relations publish reports and books under their own imprint.
10 On the HSRC see: Marais *et al.* (1988), Cloete and Muller (1991). The HSRC (1985) Investigation into Intergroup Relations accepted 93 research tenders and 12 special projects. For a critique of HSRC (1985), see Goldberg (1993, pp. 177–84).
11 The 'South Africa Beyond Apartheid' project resulted in the publication of Berger and Godsell (1988). Anglo-American's Chairperson, H. F. Oppenheimer, was appointed to the Buthelezi Commission. Constituted by Buthelezi in 1980, the Commission was a 44 member body, appointed by the KwaZulu legislature.
12 See National Commission on Higher Education (1996). On how the racialization of academia influences the question of 'who studies what?', see Jansen (1991).
13 In this regard, see: Laslett and Rapoport (1975), Carr-Hill (1984), Lather (1991).

14   For the possibilities of such work, see Orkin (1989b). Orkin shows, through
     use of log-linear analysis, how Buthelezi's 'ethnic' boundary was breached
     outwards between 1978–80 in the direction of the non-racial inclusivism of
     the ANC, as an actor's subjective political efficacy was enhanced by a deter-
     mination to transcend 'ethnicity' rather than invert or manipulate it. Also
     see Orkin (1992).
15   On the promise of a critical social science, see Fay (1987).

References

Adam, H. (1971) *Modernizing Racial Domination: the Dynamics of South African
    Politics*, Berkeley, University of California Press.
Adam, H. and Giliomee, H. (1979) *Ethnic Power Mobilized: Can South Africa
    Change?*, New Haven, Yale University Press.
Adam, H. and Moodley, K. (1986) *South Africa Without Apartheid: Dismantling
    Racial Domination*, Cape Town, Maskew Miller Longman.
Adam, H. and Moodley, K. (1993) *The Opening of the Apartheid Mind*, Berkeley,
    University of California Press.
Adorno, T. W. (1972) Sociology and Empirical Research, in P. Connerton (ed.)
    Critical Sociology: Selected Readings, Harmondsworth, Penguin, pp. 237–57.
Agger, B. (1977) Dialectical Sensibility I: Critical Theory, Scientism and Empiri-
    cism, *Canadian Journal of Political and Social Theory*, (1)1, 3–34.
Apel, K. O. (1979) Types of Social Science in Light of Human Cognitive Interests,
    in S. C. Brown (ed.), *Philosophical Disputes in the Social Science*, Brighton, Har-
    vester, pp. 3–50.
Aronowitz, S. (1988) *Science as Power: Discourse and Ideology in Modern Society*,
    Minneapolis, University of Minnesota Press.
Banton, M. (1983) *Racial and Ethnic Competition*, Cambridge, Cambridge Univer-
    sity Press.
Barkan, E. (1992) *The Retreat of Scientific Racism*, Cambridge, Cambridge Univer-
    sity Press.
Berger, P. and Godsell, B. (eds) (1988) *A Future South Africa: Visions, Strategies and
    Realities*, Boulder, Westview Press.
Bernstein, R. J. (1979) *The Restructuring of Social and Political Theory*, London,
    Methuen.
Blau, P. M. (1973) *The Organization of Academic Work*, New York, Wiley.
Brandel-Syrier, M. (1971) *Reeftown Elite*, London, Routledge and Kegan Paul.
Buthelezi Commission (1982) *The Requirements for Stability and Development in
    KwaZulu and Natal*, 2 Volumes, Durban, H+H Publications.
Carr-Hill, R. (1984) Radicalizing Survey Methodology, *Quality & Quantity* 18(3),
    275–92.
Cloete, N. and Muller, J. (1991) Human Sciences Research Council Incorporated
    (Pty) Ltd: Social Science Research, Markets and Accountability in South Africa,
    in J. D. Jansen (ed.), *Knowledge and Power in South Africa*, Johannesburg, Skota-
    ville, pp. 141–57.
Crais, C. C. (1992) Race, the State, and the Silence of History in the Making of
    Modern South Africa, paper presented to African Studies Association, Seattle.
Crane, D. (1972) *Invisible Colleges*, Chicago, University of Chicago Press.

Dreyer, L. (1989) *The Modern African Elite of South Africa*, London, Macmillan – now Palgrave.

Edelstein, M. (1974) *What Do Young Africans Think?*, Johannesburg, South African Institute of Race Relations.

Fay, B. (1975) *Social Theory and Political Practice*, London, Allen and Unwin.

Fay, B. (1987) *Critical Social Science: Liberation and Its Limits*, Ithaca, Cornell University Press.

Fisher, F. (1978) Class Consciousness among Colonized Workers in South Africa, in L. Schlemmer and E. Webster (eds), *Change, Reform and Economic Growth in South Africa*, Johannesburg, Ravan, pp. 197–223.

Foster, D. (1991) On Racism: Virulent Mythologies and Fragile Threads, Inaugural Lecture, University of Cape Town, New Series 161.

Frederikse, J. (1990) *The Unbreakable Thread: Non-Racialism in South Africa*, Johannesburg, Ravan.

Giliomee, H. (1990) Rocks Litter 'Building a Nation' Road, *The Sunday Star*, Johannesburg, 18 November.

Giliomee, H. (1995) Democratization in South Africa, *Political Science Quarterly*, 110(1), pp. 83–104.

Giliomee, H. (1996) A Politically Incorrect View of Non-Racialism and Majority Rule, in W. James, D. Caliguire and K. Cullinan (eds), *Now That We Are Free: Coloured Communities in a Democratic South Africa*, Cape Town, Idasa, pp. 94–9.

Giliomee, H. and Gagiano, J. (eds) (1991) *The Elusive Search for Peace: South Africa, Israel and Northern Ireland*, Cape Town, Oxford University Press.

Giliomee, H. and Schlemmer, L. (1989) *From Apartheid to Nation-Building*, Cape Town: Oxford University Press.

Goldberg, D. T. (1993) *Racist Culture*, Oxford, Blackwell.

Gordon, R. (1991) Serving the Volk with Volkekunde: On the Rise of South African Anthropology, in J. D. Jansen (ed.), *Knowledge and Power in South Africa*, Johannesburg, Skotaville, pp. 79–97.

Guillaumin, C. (1995) *Racism, Sexism, Power and Ideology*, London/New York, Routledge.

Habermas, J. (1971) Technology and Science as Ideology, in J. Habermas, *Toward a Rational Society*, Boston, Beacon Press, pp. 81–122.

Habermas, J. (1988) *On The Logic of the Social Sciences*, Cambridge, Mass., MIT Press.

Hanf, T., Weiland, H. and Vierdag, G. (1978) *Südafrika: Friedlicher Wandel?*, München/Mainz, Kaiser-Grünewald. English translation published in 1981 as *South Africa: the Prospects for Peaceful Change*, London, Rex Collings.

Harding, S. (1986) *The Science Question in Feminism*, Ithaca, Cornell University Press.

Harding, S. (ed.) (1993) *The 'Racial' Economy of Science: Toward a Democratic Future*, Bloomington, Indiana, Indiana University Press.

Helm, B. (ed.) (1977) *Society in Southern Africa*, Johannesburg, Association for Sociology in Southern Africa.

Horkheimer, M. (1972) Traditional and Critical Theory, in P. Connerton (ed.), *Critical Sociology: Selected Readings*, Harmondsworth, Penguin, pp. 206–24.

Horowitz, D. (1985) *Ethnic Groups in Conflict*, Berkeley, University of California Press.

Horowitz, D. (1991) *A Democratic South Africa? Constitutional Engineering in a Divided Society*, Berkeley, University of California Press.

Horrell, M. (1971) *Legislation and Race Relations*, Johannesburg, South African Institute of Race Relations.

Human Sciences Research Council (1985) *The South African Society: Realities and Future Prospects*, Pretoria, HSRC.

Irvine, J., Miles, I. and Evans, J. (eds) (1979) *Demystifying Social Statistics*, London, Pluto.

Jansen, J. D. (1991) Knowledge and Power in the World System: the South African Case, in J. D. Jansen (ed.), *Knowledge and Power in South Africa*, Johannesburg, Skotaville, pp. 17–52.

Johnson, R. W. and Schlemmer, L. (eds) (1996) *Launching Democracy in South Africa: the First Open Election, April 1994*, New Haven/London, Yale University Press.

Johnstone, F. (1976) *Race, Class and Gold*, London, Routledge & Kegan Paul.

Johnstone, F. (1982) 'Most Painful to Our Hearts': South Africa Through the Eyes of the New School, *Canadian Journal of African Studies* 16(1), pp. 5–26.

Jubber, K. (1983) Sociology and its Social Context: the Case of the Rise of Marxist Sociology in South Africa, *Social Dynamics*, 9(2), pp. 50–63.

Keat, R. (1979) Positivism and Statistics in Social Science, in J. Irvine, I. Miles and J. Evans (eds), *Demystifying Social Statistics*, London, Pluto, pp. 75–86.

Kuhn, T. S. (1970) *The Structure of Scientific Revolutions*, Chicago, Chicago University Press.

Kuper, L. (1974) *Race, Class and Power*, London, Duckworth.

Laslett, B. and Rapoport, R. (1975) Collaborative Interviewing and Interactive Research, *Journal of Marriage and the Family*, 37(4), pp. 968–77.

Lather, P. (1991) *Getting Smart: Feminist Research and Pedagogy With/in the Postmodern*, London, Routledge.

Lever, H. (1978) *South African Society*, Johannesburg, Jonathan Ball.

Lijphart, A. (1985) *Power-Sharing in South Africa*, Policy Papers in International Affairs Number 24, Institute of International Studies, University of California, Berkeley.

Lombard Report (1980) *Alternatives to the Consolidation of KwaZulu: Progress Report*, Bureau for Economic Policy and Analysis (BEPA), University of Pretoria, Special Focus Number 2, Pretoria, BEPA.

MacDonald, M. (1992) The Siren's Song: the Political Logic of Power-Sharing in South Africa, *Journal of Southern African Studies*, 18(4), pp. 709–25.

MacDonald, M. and James, W. (1993) The Hand on the Tiller: the Politics of State and Class in South Africa, *Journal of Modern African Studies*, 31(3), pp. 387–405.

Marais, H. C. *et al.* (1988) Human Sciences Research in South Africa: Focal Points, Resources and Achievements, in H. C. Marais (ed.), *South Africa: Perspectives on the Future*, Pinetown, Owen Burgess, pp. 17–38.

Maré, G. (1987) 'Mixed, Capitalist and Free': the Aims of the Natal Option, in G. Moss and I. Obery (eds), *South African Review 4*, Johannesburg, Ravan, pp. 508–23.

Mattes, R. (1995) The (Limited) Impact of Race and Ethnicity on Partisan Identification in South Africa's First Open Election, paper presented to Colloquium of International Political Science Association's Research Committee on Politics and Ethnicity, Johannesburg.

Mattes, R. (1997) The Role of Identity in Building a Common Democratic Culture in South Africa, paper presented at National Identity and Democracy Conference, University of the Western Cape.

Mayer, P. (1975) Class, Status and Ethnicity as Perceived by Johannesburg Africans, in L. Thompson and J. Butler (eds), *Change in Contemporary South Africa*, Berkeley, University of California Press, pp. 138–67.

Miles, R. (1989) *Racism*, London, Routledge.

Morse, J. and Orpen, C. (eds) (1975) *Contemporary South Africa: Social Psychological Perspectives*, Johannesburg, Juta.

National Commission on Higher Education (1996) *A Framework for Transition*, Report, Pretoria.

Norval, A. (1996) *Deconstructing Apartheid Discourse*, London, Verso.

O'Meara, D. (1996) *Forty Lost Years: the Apartheid State and the Politics of the National Party, 1948–1994*, Johannesburg, Ravan.

Orkin, M. (1989a) Politics, Social Change, and Black Attitudes to Sanctions, in M. Orkin (ed.), *Sanctions Against Apartheid*, Cape Town, David Philip, pp. 81–102.

Orkin, M. (1989b) 'Of Sacrifice and Struggle': Ideology and Identity among Black High-School Students, PhD thesis, University of the Witwatersrand, Johannesburg.

Orkin, M. (1992) Beyond Alienation and Anomie: the Emancipatory Efficacy of Liberation Ideologies in South Africa, in F. Geyer and W. R. Heinz (eds), *Alienation, Society, and the Individual*, New Brunswick, Transaction, pp. 195–211.

Pityana, N. (1981) The Black Consciousness Movement and Social Research, in J. Rex (ed.), *Apartheid and Social Research*, Paris, UNESCO, pp. 161–84.

Posel, D. (1983) The Race-Class Debate in South African Historiography, *Social Dynamics*, 9(1), pp. 50–66.

Quail Commission (1980) *Ciskei Commission Report*, Pretoria, Conference Associates.

Rhoodie, N. (ed.) (1978) *Intergroup Accommodation in Plural Societies*, London, Macmillan Press (now Palgrave) for the Institute for Plural Societies, University of Pretoria.

Rich, P. B. (1989) Doctrines of 'Change' in South Africa, in J. D. Brewer (ed.), *Can South Africa Survive? Five Minutes to Midnight*, London, Macmillan – now Palgrave, pp. 281–311.

Schlemmer, L. (1991) Ethnicity Nettle must be Recognised and Grasped, *The Saturday Star*, Johannesburg, 20 July.

Schlemmer, L. (1994) Birth of Democracy, *Indicator SA*, 11(3), pp. 17–22.

Scott, J. (1991) *Social Network Analysis: a Handbook*, London, Sage.

Seekings, J. (1995) Some Comments on 'The Racialisation of Social Scientific Research on South Africa', *South African Sociological Review*, 7(2), pp. 60–9.

Study Project on Christianity in Apartheid Society [Spro-Cas] (1973) *South Africa's Political Alternatives*, Johannesburg, Ravan Press.

Taylor, R. (1990) The State of Political Science in South Africa: a Survey of the Profession, *Politikon*, 17(2), pp. 115–29.

Taylor, R. (1994) South Africa: From 'Race' to Non-Racialism?', in P. Ratcliffe (ed.), *'Race', Ethnicity and Nation: International Perspectives on Social Conflict*, London: UCL Press, pp. 91–107.

Thompson, L. and Butler, J. (eds) (1975) *Change in Contemporary South African*, Berkeley, University of California Press.

van den Berghe, P. (1967) *South Africa: a Study in Conflict*, Berkeley, University of California Press.

van der Merwe, H. W. and Schrire, R. (eds) (1980) *Race and Ethnicity: South African and International Perspectives*, Cape Town, David Philip.

van Zyl Slabbert, F. and Welsh, D. (1979) *South Africa's Options: Strategies for Sharing Power*, Cape Town, David Philip.

Webster, E. (1991) The Search for a Critical Sociology in South Africa, in J. D. Jansen (ed.), *Knowledge and Power in South Africa*, Johannesburg, Skotaville, pp. 69–78.

Wilkins, I. and Strydom, H. (1978) *The Super-Afrikaners*, Johannesburg, Jonathan Ball.

Wolpe, H. (1986) Class Concepts, Class Struggle and Racism, in J. Rex and D. Mason (eds), *Theories of Race and Ethnic Relations*, Cambridge, Cambridge University Press, pp. 110–30.

Worrall, D. (1981) The Constitutional Committee of the President's Council, *Politikon*, 8(2), pp. 27–34.

Wright, H. M. (1977) *The Burden of the Present: Liberal-Radical Controversy over South African History*, Cape Town, David Philip.

5

Independence, Incorporation and Policy Research: an Australian Case Study[1]

Christine Inglis

At the end of the twentieth century the model of sociology as an objective, value-free social science, which had been so successfully institutionalized in the academy over the last century, is increasingly under challenge. One of these challenges consists of pressures for greater 'relevance' by governments and the public who are major financial sponsors of the universities and academic enterprises. For some, 'relevance' signifies that sociological research serves the interests of the state and dominant social groups by providing legitimation and support for their actions and policies. For others, 'relevance' means that sociology addresses issues of major social importance and identifiable social 'problems'. Pressures for relevance also come from those outside the mainstream. For those disillusioned with society, and outside the dominant majority, 'relevance' becomes a call to redress the injustices they face. In the contemporary world, ethnic and racial minorities are increasingly gaining a voice and pressing their claims for a critique of society by academics, including sociologists. Sociological research on migration and ethnic and racial diversity hence faces numerous conflicting pressures influencing both the research and its status.

Another challenge to the model of sociology as an objective, value-free, endeavour comes from the increasing difficulties in obtaining 'independent' sources of funding which allow sociologists to undertake research without the appearance of being 'committed' or 'indebted' to a specific individual, organization or political/philosophical position. In many countries, the absence – or decline in the availability – of funds from higher education funding agencies (operating at arms length from the government which provides their finance), has been aggravated by the increasing costs associated with modern large-scale survey techniques and a growth in the numbers of researchers seeking assistance.

Such challenges are forcing sociologists to confront anew their relationship as social researchers to their sources of funds and their social, academic and intellectual responsibilities. In doing so it involves a reconceptualization of their relationship to the state as a major source of funds and, through its diverse policies, a major stakeholder in social change. The dilemma concerns how sociologists can reconcile a commitment to the more traditional models of independent and basic (or pure) research with financial and social pressures to become more involved in applied and policy-oriented research. Much of the debate about the role of the sociologist and the relationship between sociology, the state and social change has been characterized by simplistic depictions of the relationship in which 'incorporation' in applied or non-university funded research is viewed as negating objectivity and 'independence'.

Often ignored in such debates is a body of literature developed in the wake of such classical studies as Robert Lynd's *Knowledge for What? The Place of Social Science in American Culture* (1939) and Lerner and Lasswell's *The Policy Sciences* (1951). The themes of this literature on policy research are diverse. They range from methodological textbooks (Nagel and Neef, 1979) to more analytical accounts of issues such as the motivations underlying involvement in applied, policy-oriented research (Bulmer, 1986; Weiss, 1991), models of how social research influences policy (Weiss, 1991), or how research may be made more accessible and useful to policy-makers (Auriat, 1998). Case studies have illustrated the importance of the socio-historical context in determining the research participation by sociologists and other social scientists in government-funded policy research institutions (Shotland and Mark, 1985; Bulmer, 1987; Wagner *et al.*, 1991). Through an examination of the Australian Bureau of Immigration Research, a state-supported, quasi-autonomous research organization working in a highly contentious area of public policy, this chapter explores the relationship between incorporation and independence. The focus is not on how sociologists and other social scientists can influence government policies and social change but, rather, the potential for working with policy-oriented research organizations in a manner which resolves some of the dilemmas of reconciling opportunities for 'basic' and 'applied' research.

Central to such an analysis is an understanding of the social and institutional context in which the Bureau operates (Inglis, 1994). A brief account of these issues is given below. This is followed by a consideration of the structure and operation of the Bureau and an assessment of its significance for Australian research on migration and ethnic issues. The chapter concludes with reflections on the implications of this case study for the relationship between researchers and government-funded research agencies.

The institutional and social context to research on migration and ethnic relations

The 1980s and 1990s were a period of major economic and social change in Australia. Fundamental economic restructuring initiated by a government that aimed to reposition Australia to respond positively to the impact of globalization and changes in the world economy, inevitably impacted on the lives of ordinary citizens. Large numbers of native-born Australians are experiencing its negative effects. The decline of rural communities and widespread unemployment have contributed to a sense of alienation. The replacement of policies of assimilation by those of multiculturalism have created a climate where migrants, especially the large numbers of recently arrived (and visible) Asian migrants, can readily become scapegoats for the venting of frustrations.

Compounding these developments is a class dimension in which the cosmopolitan, elite groups concentrated in the cities are seen as abandoning the Australian working and rural population. Epitomizing this approach are references to the 'little Aussie battler' and the need to step back from a 'black armband' view of history in which Aboriginal–White relations are reassessed via increasing calls for apologies for past treatment of the Aboriginal population as a pre-requisite for formal reconciliation[2]. These concerns have coalesced with earlier anxieties about the impact of immigration.

By the late-1960s, the potential social impact of large numbers of newly arrived European migrants was being linked by some conservationists to anxieties about the effects of large-scale migration on the physical environment. Given this coalescence of anti-immigrant sentiment, a distinctive focus among some highly vocal opponents of immigration emerged. This is the belief that the project of nation-building (with which immigration has been associated historically) is now, under multiculturalism, leading to a destruction of an Australian identity which had developed over a century and a half of predominantly British settlement (Fincher, in press). Giving particular power to this anti-immigration stance is its combination of instrumental and affective concerns. Its supporters, which included some academics, became active opponents of the work of the Bureau, which was seen as symbolizing and supporting policies which were changing irrevocably both the physical and social environment of the nation. One effect is that immigration no longer attracts the bipartisan political support which it once did.

As part of its larger project to restructure the Australian economy, the Australian government in 1990 created a new system of higher education through a series of amalgamations and redesignations which obliterated the former distinction between universities and the teaching-oriented colleges of advanced education. All were now universities and expected to undertake research (although at the same time they were advised that government funds for their operation would be reduced). Student fees and paid contract work were to be the main alternative sources of income. The impact of these changes was particularly severe on the social sciences and humanities. As a review of the social sciences in Australian universities has pointed out, the effect was to reduce drastically the resources available for social science research at a time when more researchers were competing for funds from the traditional source of independent funding, the Australian Research Council (ARC). Between 1992 and 1995 there was virtually no increase in real expenditure on research in the social sciences (and expenditure on the humanities actually declined) at a time when the increase in real expenditure in the natural sciences grew by 23 per cent (Academy of the Social Sciences in Australia, 1998, pp. 26–70). In contrast to the natural sciences, which received less than 20 per cent of their funding from the higher education sector, 80 per cent of the research expenditure in the social sciences in the mid-1990s came from the higher education sector via the ARC. The remainder of the funding for social science research involving, in the main, contract work, came from general government funding (16.5 per cent), private non-profit sources (2.3 per cent) and business enterprises (1.4 per cent) (ibid., p. 26). The report also noted that the level of research support for social science researchers by government departments through consultancies for contract research and in-house funding had declined to a two-decade low (ibid., p. 31).

Within sociology, the effect of the changes on the research infrastructure was considerable. Noting the success rate of less than 20 per cent in the ARC large grant applications (which are the major source of sociological research funding), Western (1998, p. 230) forecast increasing difficulty in obtaining funding. This especially applied to 'curiosity-driven', or basic, research because it was not seen as providing immediate economic benefits; hence the shift towards what he described as mission-oriented, or applied, research. In this way, the short-term political interests of government were viewed as increasingly likely to affect research priorities (ibid., p. 231).

Although the situation in the social sciences and sociology deteriorated in the 1990s, the opportunities for research funding had already been limited. By the 1970s, researchers working in areas such as immigration and ethnic relations were experiencing difficulties in accessing funds (Inglis, 1994, p. 72; 1999; Jupp, 1998, p. 115). This was despite the fact that immigration and ethnic diversity were major features of Australian society, with a quarter of the population overseas-born and some 40 per cent either immigrants or the children of immigrants. One response by researchers was to move increasingly towards more qualitative studies relying on small sample sizes and towards research which utilized secondary data sources such as official statistics and policy documents. Another response was for researchers to undertake consultancy and applied research.

Funding for such research had increased from the 1970s in conjunction with the government's shift towards a policy of multiculturalism, something which inevitably required it to play a more interventionist role in the process of immigrant incorporation. Since this policy required the government to address issues of concern to the various ethnic communities, it needed mechanisms whereby it could establish their needs as part of the process of policy formulation. Also needed was information on strategies for implementation of policy as well as evaluations of the outcomes of policy initiatives. One means of obtaining this body of information was through consultations with (ethnic) community groups and leaders, but governments also sought additional sources of input. Limitations in the research capacity of the bureaucracy meant that government turned to outside research consultants.

While some consultancy work was undertaken by commercial market research agencies, academic researchers also became increasingly involved as the more traditional avenues for research funding declined. As the focus of research shifted towards areas of policy concern, the resulting emphasis was on grounded research, which focused on specific social problems in institutional areas such as education, health, welfare, the labour market and the media. Inevitably, the pressures were towards description and policy analysis rather than addressing broader theoretical issues.

The 'independence' of the funding agencies and their research soon became a political issue. This involved the Australian Institute of Multicultural Affairs (AIMA), which the federal government set up in 1979 under the direction of a close adviser of the Liberal Prime Minister, Malcolm Fraser. From the beginning there was scepticism about the independence of AIMA because of these close connections with the ruling political party (Stosser, 1989; Jupp, 1998, p. 115). This scepticism was not dispelled by claims of alterations being made to the evaluation reports submitted by academic consultants. Subsequently, when a Labor Government replaced the Fraser Government in 1983, a major review of AIMA was undertaken, and it was closed down in 1986.

   This closure coincided with the setting up of the Office of Multicultural Affairs (OMA), which was located within the department of the prime minister and cabinet with the task of promoting and advising on the development of appropriate policies by federal government departments. Initially, it actively funded a variety of research projects addressing specific areas of policy need (similar to AIMA) such as multiculturalism and ethnic relations (Nieuwenhuysen, 1990, p. 41). It is against this background of increasing academic involvement in contract research on matters of immigration and ethnic relations that the Bureau of Immigration Research was created.

The structure and operation of the Bureau of Immigration Research

The Bureau of Immigration Research was established in May 1989 following a recommendation by the 1988 Committee to Advise on Australia's Immigration Policies (1988, pp. 103–4). In recommending the creation of the Bureau, the committee was seeking to address what it viewed as widespread ignorance and misunderstanding of the immigration programme in the community. The objectives of the Bureau, as identified by the committee, were to provide the government with access to professional and independent research, to assist in the formulation of its immigration policies and to encourage informed public debate on immigration matters (ibid., pp. 103–4). From its foundation, the Bureau was attached to the department responsible for immigration[3] although it was a separate division of that department with autonomy for independent choice of research topics, authors and publication decisions. From its inception the Bureau's director was at pains to highlights its dissimilarities to AIMA (Nieuwenhuysen, 1990).

   In an effort to underline the independence and separate identity of the Bureau, its headquarters were shifted to Melbourne. Only the Bureau's major library and the statistical and research unit, which had formerly been part of the department's headquarters, remained in Canberra (with the department). Other steps to ensure the independence of the Bureau included the appointment of a director, John Nieuwenhuysen, a respected academic economist who had been research director for the privately-funded Committee for the Economic Development of Australia, which had undertaken a major study on the economics of immigration (Norman and Meikle, 1985). Apart from the deputy director and those staff who were transferred to the Bureau from the department's Statistical and Research Unit, other staff were recruited from outside the department, including academics and some staff who had worked with the former AIMA.

The Bureau had an appointed advisory committee whose chairs were all prominent academics. The first (Glenn Withers) was an economist with a long-standing involvement in immigration issues. Other members of the initial committee drawn from the National Population Council included academics, trade union representatives and individuals with links to ethnic communities and government. Subsequent chairs were a social work professor (David Cox) with a background in refugee issues, and a sociologist (Stephen Castles) with a major record of research on immigration in Europe and Australia. Regional reference groups located in each State and Territory of Australia provided additional advice for the advisory committee and Bureau. Membership of these reference groups again included academics, community members, government representatives and a representative of the Department of Immigration. Their tasks included the monitoring of research projects, considering applications for research grants and identifying areas for future research (BIPR Review Committee, 1994, p. 7).

In Australian terms, the size of the Bureau's research budget was considerable. While averaging $1.5 million annually for external researchers, in its first year nearly $2.2 million was allocated to external research consultancies with somewhat lower levels in later years as a result of general reductions in the department's budget in 1991–92. In 1993–94, $2.3 million alone was allocated to the Bureau's Longitudinal Survey of Immigrants to Australia contracted out to a market research agency (ibid., pp. 8–9). When closed in 1996, the Bureau's total budget was in excess of $6 million, much of it still supporting external consultants – 19 external contract projects being commissioned that year (Department of Immigration and Multicultural Affairs, 1997, p. 24).

The Bureau funded in-house research by its own staff as well as commissioning research undertaken by external consultants. Topics were identified by the Bureau and its advisory committee, and also by the governmental joint Commonwealth, State and Territories Steering

Committee's Australian Population and Immigration Research Programme. Applicants were required to respond to specific tender documents, which often prescribed the scope and methodology of the research project. In addition, the Bureau operated a research grants programme in which applicants proposed their own research topics, although this was within the framework of the priority areas the Bureau outlined in its call for applications.

In the first three years of the Bureau's existence, commissioned research accounted for two-thirds of the external research funds, but in the next two years the division of funds between commissioned research and research grants was approximately equal (BIPR Review Committee 1994, p. 9). Many of the external consultants who undertook contract or general research projects were academics. Others came from major business consultancy firms and, latterly, from community organizations. Selection ultimately rested with the reference and advisory groups, although the Bureau's research managers undertook preliminary vetting of applications and proposals. The actual application and selection process operated along lines which resembled those with which academics were familiar from their applications for funding to the major body supporting 'basic' or 'pure' academic research, the Australian Research Council.

Throughout its existence, the research activities of the Bureau were divided between the economic and social research sections each headed by an assistant director, with the Canberra unit being the responsibility of the deputy director. As the Bureau's research responsibilities expanded, these were incorporated within one or other of these sections. The first major extension to the Bureau's responsibilities came in 1993 as a result of a recommendation in the National Population Council's (1991) report that the Bureau's brief should be extended to include population policy and research.

Accompanying the extension of responsibilities was a change in name to the Bureau of Immigration and Population Research (BIPR). These changes were a response to an extensive debate (noted earlier) about the desirability of immigration – given high levels of unemployment and claims that Australia's fragile eco-systems could not support higher levels of population. Criticisms had begun to be expressed forcefully by groups and individuals (including some members of the Bureau's advisory committee) that the Bureau was 'pro-migration' (Nieuwenhuysen, 1995, p. 3). Through a broadening of the Bureau's research agenda to locate migration within the wider framework of population issues, it was hoped to deflect criticisms of the Bureau's focus.

A year later, the scope of the Bureau's research was again extended to include issues of long-term settlement and community relations. The Bureau's name now changed for a third time to become the Bureau of Immigration, Multicultural and Population Research (BIMPR). Different pressures led to this change. When the Bureau was established in 1989, an arrangement had been reached with the Office of Multicultural Affairs (OMA), which was strategically located in the office of prime minister and cabinet (where it had responsibility for monitoring the implementation of the official policy of multiculturalism). As part of this role, OMA also sponsored research into matters of settlement and inter-ethnic relations. The two agencies had agreed that 'migration', BIR's brief, would be limited to the first two years of settlement while, after this period, the issues would come within the brief of OMA (Nieuwenhuysen, 1995).

By 1995, OMA had effectively withdrawn from sponsoring or supporting research on multicultural issues. At the same time, ethnic community groups[4] were expressing concerns about the Bureau's failure to address issues of community concern adequately. These views had been put to the Review of the Bureau (in 1993–94) as part of a regular 3–5 year cycle of reviews within the Commonwealth public service. One of the review's recommendations was that the Bureau should become more involved in projects related to, and involving participation by, ethnic community groups (BIPR Review Committee, 1994, p. 17).

During 1995, tensions between the director of the Bureau and the then minister for immigration (Senator Nick Bolkus) became public when the senator required the director to withdraw invitations to speak at the biennial National Outlook Conference from six individuals who might be critical of aspects of the government's immigration policy (Healy, 1994). The tension was associated with the far more 'hands on' role towards the immigration portfolio by Bolkus than either of his two predecessors, Senator Robert Ray, under whom the Bureau had been set up, and Gerry Hand. By 1996, the director had resigned to take up the position of Executive Director of the Committee for the Economic Development of Australia. Before a new director could be appointed a federal election was called.

The election was won resoundingly by the Opposition Liberal National Country Party coalition, which formed a government under the leadership of John Howard. Apart from favouring neo-liberal social policies, Howard was known to be hostile to immigration and multicultural policies which he felt were leading to the downplaying of an Australian identity based on the British heritage. He had also made clear his opposition to OMA, so it came as no surprise when it was summarily closed. Its director, who had only recently been appointed under Bolkus' patronage, was then reassigned to take charge of the Bureau. To the surprise of some observers, in July 1996, four months after the elections, the announcement was made that the Bureau was to be 'restructured' in the name of budgetary savings. What this effectively meant was its closure. The only parts which survived were the statistics section (which was reabsorbed into the Department of Immigration) and the Longitudinal Survey of Immigrants to Australia.

The Bureau's closure was widely seen as resulting from the continuing, strong lobbying by interest groups opposed to immigration (Healy, 1994, p. 39). Strengthening the opponents' claims of pro-immigration bias had been the active involvement of the former minister, which ranged from interventions in the speaker panels at the National Outlook Conference, to other areas of his portfolio, including nominations of Labor Party supporters and activists to positions on statutory bodies such as the Immigration Review Tribunal (ibid.). Significantly, the anti-immigration lobby's targeting of the Bureau accorded both with sections of the bureaucracy opposed to the Bureau's independence and the new prime minister, who displayed his own strongly held views on immigration in 1988 by departing from the traditional bipartisan approach to immigration policy.

The research role of the Bureau

In view of the central concerns of the current volume we need to ask two related questions at this point: what influence did the Bureau, which was only in existence from 1989 to 1996, have on research on migration and settlement, and what was the impact of this research? One criterion is obviously the quantity of research which it sponsored, and the publications which resulted from it. Apart from funding research, the Bureau played a very active role in disseminating the results of its research, both through publications and through national conferences and seminars. At the time of the review in 1994, five years after the Bureau's foundation, it had already published 248 statistical reports, bulletins and monographs. From its inception in 1989 until shortly after its closure, the Bureau published over 240 research reports apart from various statistical publications, bulletins and other materials.[5] This represents a substantial achievement, given that the Bureau only began commissioning research late in 1989. Indeed, in 1994, one author commented that:

recent years have seen a veritable explosion of publications on immigration and settlement issues. Foremost here has been the active publication program of the BIPR itself, which alone now constitutes the most comprehensive collection of immigration and settlement research of any nation in the world.

(Wooden, *et al.*, 1994, p. 1)

By 1996, a prominent international expert was commenting how 'in a matter of only a few years, Australia leapfrogged over virtually all other countries in the quantity and quality of its research on immigration and associated issues' (Papademetriou, 1996, p. 8).

When the Bureau was set up in 1989, it was widely believed that economic issues would dominate its research agenda. This expectation was derived from the CAAIP review's emphasis on the value of immigration as a means of contributing to economic development in a context where the government, responding to the pressures of globalization, was undertaking a major restructuring of the Australian economy. The Committee's position was consistent with the broader economic rationalist focus of the government in all areas of policy development (Pusey, 1991). Apart from creating a policy culture in which the only 'meaningful' information was economic, there was also a marked preference for 'hard' data, by which was meant quantitative data. These were to be obtained, in the absence of standard economic indicators, from large-scale social surveys.

Although noted as a more general preference among policy-makers, such criteria assumed a special significance (Auriat, 1998, p. 281). The appointment of an economist to head the Bureau confirmed the expectation that economic research would be given priority. In the first years of the Bureau's operation, such research was dominant, although there was a gradual shift from macro-economic studies to those at a micro-level which sought to disaggregate the economic effects of migration (BIPR Review Committee, 1994, p. 9). In a report prepared for the second National Immigration Outlook conference in 1992, the director emphasized the salience of the economic recession of the period, coupled with the impact of immigration on the environment and urban infrastructure, for the Bureau's research agenda (Nieuwenhuysen, 1992, p. 2). However, mirroring its name changes, other, and in particular, social research aspects, gained greater prominence. The shifts were well documented in the Director's Report to the Third National Immigration and Population Outlook conference in 1995 (Nieuwenhuysen, 1995). Complementing research on the economic impact of migration and its effects on the labour market and industrial relations, was a wide range of social research on settlement, education, health, housing, ageing and policy formulation.

Despite the director's assertion that the Bureau was free to 'ultimately determine the terms of reference of its research projects' (ibid., p. 25), the selection of topics was directed by external local and international developments affecting immigration. Other influences on the agenda included the expectations of what the 1994 review referred to as 'clients' and 'stakeholders' within the bureaucracy, and public debates in which a variety of lobby groups were actively involved. Absent from this lobbying were academic and disciplinary associations because, although they welcomed increased research opportunities, there was no unity as to research priorities.[6]

That a variety of influences operated in the selection of the Bureau's research agenda does not, in itself, indicate that the actual quality of the research undertaken was diminished. There are, of course, many 'quality' criteria. One measure derives from the perceptions of the Bureau's 'clients', nearly 30 per cent of whom described themselves as 'academics' in the Review Committee's postal survey. Of the 600–plus individuals who knew about the Bureau's research, a high proportion gave it a positive ranking on issues such as quality (94.1 per cent), usefulness (91.2 per cent), credibility (89.8 per cent) and independence (82.4 per cent). When the responses were restricted to those who gave a ranking of either 'excellent' or 'very good', the results still showed two-thirds expressing these views for quality (69.9 per cent), usefulness (65.8 per cent) and credibility (65.1 per cent). Little more than half (53.5 per cent), however, rated the 'independence' of the research so highly (BIPR Review Committee, 1994, p. 53). The juxtaposition of strong support for the quality, usefulness and credibility of the research against weaker assessments of its independence suggests a disjuncture between methodological and social criteria of evaluation.

Underlying these perceptions are various, more specific, criteria which influence such assessments. These include questions about the adequacy of the methodology, the data collection process and the analysis of the results. As a way of ensuring the credibility of its research, the Bureau did adopt an explicit (and transparent) set of processes for selecting external researchers. This involved specifying the criteria to be considered (Bureau of Immigration, Multicultural and Population Research, n.d.):

- skills and expertise in research (both general and specific to the topic);

- mastery of the project brief and understanding of the key issues;
- the availability of research support facilities and infrastructure needed to support the project;
- expected quantity and quality of the data, analysis, documentation and reporting; and,
- management, cost and administrative efficiency and, in some cases, timing of the project.

Application of these criteria led to few objections. Similarly, the Bureau's procedures for refereeing completed research reports prior to publication attracted little attention. All reports were submitted to officers in the Department of Immigration who checked, in particular, the accuracy of statements about the programme. Then external referees with expertise in the area were used to assess the quality and adequacy of the research. In contrast to the earlier experience of AIMA, these procedures did not lead to claims that the Bureau and department had attempted to suppress research findings.

In adopting these procedures for selecting researchers, and then evaluating the outcomes of the research, the Bureau was striving to ensure that its research was credible within the canons of academic social science. Where it might be seen to have departed from the 'openness' of these canons was in the way its tenders for contracted research were often quite specific about the questions to be answered and methodology to be used. Such specification can, with considerable reason, be seen as influencing the type of results which can be obtained. Suspicions about such procedures were not sustained by the Review Committee but continued to underlie accusations of lack of independence and even 'bias' from the anti-immigration lobby (Healy, 1994, p. 40; Betts, 1996, pp. 221–2).

These concerns about the orientation, or scope, of the research questions supported by the Bureau had their origins in its role as a policy-oriented organization. An ongoing tension for such an organization is how to balance its status as an 'independent, professional research body' while disseminating knowledge about the implications of, and links between, government policies on immigration and population, facilitating the government's development of relevant policies, increasing community knowledge, and understanding and encouraging informed public debate (Bureau of Immigration Multicultural and Population Research, n.d.). Paradoxically (given the claims of the anti-immigration lobby), the review of the Bureau made it clear that there were substantial concerns by many bureaucrats about the Bureau's *limitations* in delivering sufficiently specific policy options based on its research agenda (BIPR Review Committee, 1994, pp. 25–7). Social, rather than economic, research was specifically identified as having less policy relevance (ibid., p. 26), a result not entirely surprising given the established policy culture favouring economic and other 'hard' data.

In his Report for the 1995 National Outlook Conference, the director of the Bureau took issue with the narrow view of policy relevance contained in the review's critique (Nieuwenhuysen, 1995, pp. 16–17):

> There is a danger that, in considering the Bureau's policy contribution, it might be supposed that this means only or mainly establishing direct links between research output and specific policy initiatives and changes. Instead, I believe that in assessing the Bureau's contribution to providing 'a basis for Government policy formulations' a broader criterion of judgment should be used.
>
> This criterion should be the extent to which Bureau research output is employed in key policy debate, as well as how frequently it is used in support of advice to relevant central decision-making processes, such as in DIEA [Department of Immigration and Ethnic Affairs] submissions to Cabinet and in major relevant reports, inquiries, or academic publications, as well as in media discussions such as editorials.

In terms of the broader criteria identified by the director, the Bureau was extremely active in bringing research to public attention in a manner completely unfamiliar to most academic research. The Bureau held numerous high profile conferences, attracting considerable coverage by both the print and electronic media. It also prepared materials which specifically targeted the school-age population, these publications containing information drawn from its research activities. It therefore undoubtedly made a contribution to more informed public debate. As the annual reports of the Bureau show, its research material was also widely incorporated into a variety of governmental decision-making processes (Nieuwenhuysen, 1992; 1995, p. 18).

A further set of criteria by which to judge the bureau's contribution derives from sociological concerns about the role of its research in contributing both to the development of sociological expertise and to conceptual and theoretical advances. Although social research remained subordinate to economic research, the availability of funding for commissioned research (and the research grants programme) provided a major impetus to research in the whole area of immigration and settlement issues among sociologists and other social scientists. As a result of funding opportunities, conferences and the easier access to statistical data, many researchers were attracted to work in the area, thereby generating increased expertise. At the level of conceptual and theoretical development, direct outcomes of the Bureau's research are less clear.

The emphasis on publishing research reports promptly was an important contribution to the accumulation of knowledge and the establishment of baseline data. But, the policy-oriented focus of the research, including in some cases a range of constraints on the scope and methodologies to be employed, made it less directly appropriate for use in developing alternative conceptual or theoretical frameworks. Apart from the limitations in the formulation of the research, researchers operated under severe time constraints, especially when they were also engaged in full-time teaching. This made it extremely difficult to indulge in the reflection necessary to draw out the conceptual and theoretical implications of their research findings after they had prepared the more 'descriptive' report for the Bureau.

Despite these limitations, the research funding did provide opportunities for researchers to explore new forms of migration patterns and migrant groupings. This demonstrated the necessity of developing new ways of conceptualizing immigration and its links to globalization. Without Bureau funding and easy access to migration data and policy information, much research pertinent to these reconceptualizations could not have been undertaken. For many researchers, an exposure to policy-oriented research was itself an invaluable opportunity to gain a more extensive understanding of the policy-making process.

Research after the Bureau

The closure of the Bureau in 1996 was only one of many steps undertaken by the new Howard Coalition Federal Government so as to be seen to be 'tough' on immigration and multiculturalism. At the same time, it was also seeking to restructure Australian society towards a free market model based on principles of 'user-pays' and 'small government'. As a consequence, consultancy-based research opportunities in the area of migration and ethnic relations declined at a time of increased competition for research funding from the traditional academic source, the Australian Research Council. As noted earlier, the success rate for funding from ARC large grants (which in the social sciences means $20,000 or over), is less than 20 per cent. In the 1999 round, only seven successful large-grant applications were concerned with migration or ethnic relations: and even this represented a slight increase from the two previous years. No research fellowships were awarded in the area; nor were there any successful applications in the category of SPIRT grants, which involve collaborative projects between academe and industry. The latter is particularly noteworthy in that it clearly demonstrates how allowing market forces to determine research agendas may not ensure that important areas of social research are addressed.

In the absence of funding from ARC large grants or consultancies, researchers in the area of migration and ethnic relations have again been forced to tailor their research activities to the limited resources available. With increasing teaching and administrative pressures on university staff, postgraduate students' research has become the major ongoing work in the area. Much of this research is concerned with identity and 'cultural studies', which were beyond the research agenda of the Bureau. Aside from the current popularity of the cultural studies paradigm, such topics are often related to students' own personal search for identity, especially when, as is increasingly the case, they come from ethnic minority backgrounds. Such topics, with their reliance on more quali- tative methodologies, also have the advantage of being 'low cost' and requiring limited material resources.

The negative consequences of having only limited research informa- tion on migration and ethnic relations were all too graphically demon- strated in the so-called 'Hanson Debate', named after the member of federal parliament who came to prominence in the 1996 elections on a populist anti-immigration, anti-Aboriginal platform. In 1998, her One Nation Party won 11 seats in the Queensland State elections (although only one senator was elected to the federal parliament in the elections later in the year). In 1999, the political strength of the Party declined considerably. Six of the Queensland Parliamentarians defected from the Party (soon to be followed by the remaining five), and only one Party representative was elected in the 1999 New South Wales state elections. During 1996 and 1997, Hanson's swingeing critiques of Asian migration and ethnic groups (and a raft of other policies and developments in Australia) went largely uncontested. Compounding government inaction was the absence of ready public access to data and research findings, something which could have refuted her many highly err- oneous claims. In the absence of the Bureau, with its brief to ensure 'informed public debate', no other institution had the capacity and will to fill the void. While Hanson demonstrated, in her disregard for census data, an unwillingness to be swayed by sound 'empirical evidence', the real significance of the lack of data was that the general public were also unable to evaluate her claims (Fincher, in press).

While several recent specialist conferences indicate renewed academic interest in migration, multiculturalism and ethnic relations, research funds remain elusive. Although the Department of Immigration and Multicultural Affairs is now beginning once again to employ external research consultants, the model followed in contracting the research is not that of the former Bureau, with its emphasis on open and transparent processes. Inevitably, this raises concerns about (limited) opportunities to evaluate and challenge government policies. The Bureau's director claimed that an important element of its freedom lay in its ability to:

- formulate terms of reference after consultation;
- choose authors and launch and function conference speakers, as well as to invite attendees of its choice to all functions without restriction;
- publish results, whatever the conclusions (that is, whether or not they are embarrassing to, or critical of, government) and subject only to quality control; and
- publicize the projects as it chooses (Nieuwenhuysen, 1995, p. 26).

Given the government's disinterest in multiculturalism and its clear preference for small government and the privatization of social services, research-derived knowledge has little relevance for the formulation of government policies. But this is only a partial explanation which ignores the broader political agenda associated with the presentation and control of knowledge on sensitive political issues. Commenting on the post-Bureau construction of knowledge about immigration and multiculturalism (as evidenced by the limited Department of Immigration involvement in research, and dissemination of information, about these matters), a prominent academic and former Bureau staffer notes a reduction in the sophistication with which these issues are discussed and 'a dumbing down' of immigration-related discussion sponsored by the government (Fincher, in press). She sees this as a government response to a political constituency (whose significance was highlighted by the success of 'One Nation') which is not sophisticated in its inter-pretation and perception of immigration and which actively resents the intellectualization of public discourse.

Conclusion

For many Australian sociologists, researching in what had become, dur-ing the 1980s, the politically highly contentious area of migration and ethnic relations, the Bureau provided instructive insights into how 'incorporation' via acceptance of government grants could exist alongside a reasonably high level of 'independence' in the research process. The greatest control exercised by the Bureau was in its commissioned research, where parameters in terms of questions to be addressed and methodologies to be used were more tightly specified than in the research grant programme. Other 'controls' concerning performance criteria, refereeing and publication can be seen as providing a framework of accountability which scarcely contravenes academic 'independence'. The Bureau's commitment to publicise and publish its funded research was extremely positive for academic researchers since it disseminated their research, thereby contributing to their scholarly publications and their university's research performance (which in turn directly affected the university's level of government funding).

The Bureau's emphasis on economic, rather than social, research reflected the strength of policy-makers' perception of the greater relevance of economic research both because of the government focus on economic restructuring and the belief in the greater value of economic research findings. The latter view is not unique to Australian policy-makers and highlights the challenge for sociologists to persuade policy-makers of the worth of their research by actively demonstrating the reliability and validity of their results. Not all those who undertook social research for the Bureau may have been as effective in this area, especially when one appreciates that the Bureau commissioned research not only from academics but from a range of outside consultants with diverse backgrounds and expertise. Claims that social research lacks policy relevance reflects as much on the ability of policy-makers to clarify their precise policy concerns as it does on sociologists to translate these concerns into viable research questions and to communicate their results in a clear fashion. That said, it also needs to be acknowledged that any policy recommendation or decision relies on a range of assumptions, preferences and desired outcomes which contextualize the research findings.

The political dimension of the Bureau's work was certainly a factor in its relationship with the academic community. Not all sociologists became involved with the Bureau. For some, this was because the Bureau's research agenda was not relevant to their specific research interests. For others it was because of a desire to avoid potential problems associated with 'incorporation'; an understandable response in the light of the less than happy relationships between independent researchers and the earlier Australian Institute of Multicultural Affairs.

There was also a third group of researchers who were highly critical of the whole national project of immigration and multiculturalism. Some had actually been incorporated into Bureau activities, having received external grants and been on its committee and conference programmes. [This was, in fact, an important element of the Bureau's strategy of seeking to develop a balanced debate on these issues (Betts, 1996, p. 213).] Yet, this did not prevent them claiming that the Bureau was biased, and lacked independence. They contended that the Bureau had never really questioned the role of immigration as an integral element in nation-building, although the type of additional research which might have been undertaken to answer such a question, was never made clear. Two issues were of particular concern to these academics: the impact of immigration on population growth and consequent destruction of the physical environment; and, migration's impact on social cohesion and national identity. While the Bureau sponsored research on both areas, the absence of strongly negative findings on the impact failed to satisfy these critics.

As this example demonstrates, it is all too easy for activists who fail to change the research programme of an agency from within, to undermine its credibility with accusations of 'bias' and 'lack of independence'. It is, of course, somewhat paradoxical that the Bureau's 'neutrality' and openness to a range of views failed to insulate it from such damaging allegations. Perhaps somewhat naively, the Bureau actually contributed to its own demise by providing a platform for the expression of these hostile views. This contrasts sharply with the more traditional peer review process which operates in the context of 'academic' research funding: here, assertions of bias tend to surface in the context of personal and/or professional rivalries.

During the 1980s, a range of Australian government-funded research agencies were closed in areas such as education (Education Research and Development Committee), the economy (Bureau of Labour Market Research, Economic Planning Advisory Council) and migration and ethnic relations (the Bureau and AIMA). Their cases illustrate how claims of loss of 'independence' and 'bias' are critical to survival, although loss of ministerial and governmental support (often rationalized in terms of budgetary constraints) provides the final *coup-de-grâce*. The agencies adopted different structural models but, as the Director of the Bureau indicated in 1995, formal arrangements to ensure independence cannot substitute for:

> observances in practice by the several players-the Minister, the Secretary, the advisory groups and the Director-of certain conventions or customs related to the Bureau's freedom.
>
> (Nieuwenhuysen, 1995, p. 26)

The needs for Australian research on migration and ethnic relations continue but in a climate of declining levels of funding for basic research. Should the government again fund a policy-oriented research agency, the former Bureau provides a model which goes a considerable way to reconciling the dilemma of 'incorporation' and 'independence' for sociologists and other social scientists. Nevertheless, the history of the Bureau is a reminder that such agencies operate in a political environment where research excellence alone cannot ensure survival.

Notes

1   A complete study of the Bureau of Immigration Research remains to be undertaken. In preparing this paper I have benefited from the comments of a number of individuals, including James Jupp, Siew Ean Khoo and Glenn Withers, all of whom I thank for their assistance.
2   Both of these phrases, together with an emphasis on the distinctively Australian nature of 'mateship', which he wished included in a pre-amble to the Constitution, have been extensively used by the current Prime Minister, John Howard, who closed down the Bureau soon after coming into office in 1996.
3   In 1989, the department was called the Department of Immigration, Local Government and Ethnic Affairs but it then changed its name to the Department of Immigration and Ethnic Affairs before, in 1996, being renamed the Department of Immigration and Multicultural Affairs, following a further restructuring of the Australian Public Service.
4   In Australia, the term 'ethnic community group' refers to groups which are organised on the basis of shared ethnicity. These range from small, informally-organized single-interest bodies involving leisure/cultural pursuits, to more formal, large-scale organizations concerned with welfare, educational and lobbying activities. These latter groups are major participants in the regular government consultations with 'ethnic communities', are an integral element of multicultural policy formulation, and were particularly active in identifying community welfare issues which they felt the Bureau was ignoring.
5   Given the somewhat precipitate nature of the Bureau's closure, there is no accurate list of precisely what it did publish. Much of the work of staff at this time consisted of trying to close down existing research projects and many of these later appeared in in-house publications and a variety of journals and other outlets. The present figure is based on material contained in the Annual Reports of the Department.
6   While academics *were* involved in lobbying, it was as individuals with particular views on immigration rather than as part of a considered 'academic lobby'.

References

Academy of the Social Sciences in Australia (1998) *Challenges for the Social Sciences in Australia*, Canberra, AGPS.

Auriat, N. (1998) Social Policy and Social Enquiry: Reopening Debate, *International Social Science Journal*, (156), 275–87.

Betts, K. (1996) Explaining Australian Immigration, *Journal of the Australian Population Association*, 13(2), 195–229.

BIPR Review Committee (1994) *Evaluation of the Bureau of Immigration and Population Research*, Canberra, AGPS.

Bulmer, M. (1986) *Social Science and Social Policy*, London, Allen & Unwin.

Bulmer, M. (ed.) (1987) *Social Science Research and Government: Comparative Essays on Britain and the United States*, Cambridge, Cambridge University Press.

Bureau of Immigration, Multicultural and Population Research (n.d.). *BIMPR Commissioned Research: Information and Guidelines for Tenders*.

Committee to Advise On Australia's Immigration Policies (1988). *Immigration: a Commitment to Australia*, Canberra, AGPS.

Department of Immigration and Multicultural Affairs (1997) *Annual Report 1996–97*, Canberra, Department of Immigration and Multicultural Affairs.

Fincher, R. (in press) Immigration Research in the Politics of an Anxious Nation, *Environment and Planning D: Society and Space*, 19.

Healy, E. (1994). The Management of the Immigration Portfolio Under Senator Bolkus, *People and Place*, 2(4), 37–45.

Inglis, C. (1994) Linkages Between Methodology, Research and Theory in Race and Ethnic Relations: the Case of Australia, in P. Ratcliffe (ed.) '*Race', Ethnicity and Nation: International Perspectives on Social Conflict*, London, UCL Press, pp. 68–90.

Inglis, C. (1999) Changements dans les formes de l'immigration, les politiques d'intégration et les programmes de recherche en Australie, in I. Simon-Barouh and V. de Rudder (eds), *Migrations internationales et relations interethnique: recherche, politique et société*, L'Harmattan, Paris, pp. 129–62.

Jupp, J. (1998) *Ethnic, Multicultural and Immigration Studies: Challenges for the Social Sciences and Australia*, Academy of the Social Sciences in Australia. Canberra, AGPS, 113–18.

Lerner, D. and Lasswell, H. (eds) (1951) *The Policy Sciences*, Stanford, Stanford University Press.

Lynd, R. (1939) *Knowledge for What? The Place of Social Science in American Culture*, Princeton, Princeton University Press.

Nagel, S. S. and Neef, M. (1979) *Policy Analysis in Social Science Research*, Beverley Hills/London, Sage Publications.

National Population Council (1991). *Population Issues and Australia's Future: Environment, Economy and Society*, Canberra, AGPS.

Nieuwenhuysen, J. (1990) The Bureau of Immigration Research: a Vital Opportunity, *Canberra Bulletin of Public Administration*, 60, 41–3.

Nieuwenhuysen, J. (1992) *An Overview of Recent Research On Australian Immigration*, Canberra, AGPS.

Nieuwenhuysen, J. (1995) *The Recent Work of the Bureau of Immigration, Multicultural and Population Research: Background for the Third National Immigration and Population Outlook Conference, Adelaide 22–24 February 1995*, Canberra, AGPS.

Norman, N. R. and Meikle, K. (1985) *The Economic Effects of Immigration on Australia*, Melbourne, CEDA/DIEA.

Papademetriou, D. (1996) Vale John Nieuwenhuysen, *BIMPR Bulletin*, No. 16.

Pusey, M. (1991). *Economic Rationalism in Canberra: a Nation-Building State Changes its Mind*, New York, Cambridge University Press.

Shotland, R. L. and Mark, M. M. (eds) (1985) *Social Science and Social Policy*, Beverley Hills/London, Sage Publications.

Stosser, S. (1989) The Bureau of Immigration Research-Government Reinventing the Wheel, *Canberra Bulletin of Public Administration*, 59, 39–40.

Wagner, P., *et al.* (eds) (1991) *Social Sciences and Modern States: National Experiences and Theoretical Crossroads*, Cambridge, Cambridge University Press.

Weiss, C. (1991) Policy Research: Data, Ideas or Arguments, in P. Wagner *et al.*, op.cit., 307–32.

Western, J. (1998) 'Sociology' *Challenges for the Social Sciences in Australia*, Academy of the Social Sciences in Australia, Canberra, AGPS, 223–32.

Wooden, M., *et al.* (1994) *Australian Immigration: a Survey of the Issues*, Canberra, AGPS.

Part III

Western European Societies: Ex-Colonial Powers

6

'Race' and Ethnicity Research in Britain: Key Ethical and Political Considerations

Peter Ratcliffe

Introduction

We are principally concerned with the vexed question of the role of sociology in effecting meaningful social change, in a context where research is clearly mediated by, and contingent on, various elements of the 'state', not least academe itself (as intimated in Chapter 1). It will be argued that our role is, or at least can/(should?) be, much broader than that conceptualized/anticipated in mainstream 'social policy' debates in the UK (Bulmer, 1978; 1982; 1986).

This entails firstly a look at the historical context of research in Britain and in particular its links with social policy formation and the generation of change processes. We then relate this specifically to the extant literature on 'race' and 'ethnicity'. This entails an appraisal of both the intended and unintended consequences of such work, and the ethical and political concerns (and obligations) of the professional sociologist. It also entails situating research in its social and institutional context. This involves questions such as: Why do the research at all? What are the implications of certain forms of funding? What are the limitations inherent in research conducted in certain institutional settings and employing certain methodological strategies? Does the identity of the researcher(s) matter (in the sense of their 'race'/ethnicity/gender/class)?

Finally, there is an appraisal of shifts in the research agenda. It will be seen, for example, that there have been major changes since the present author's rather cursory analysis of the research scene a little over a decade ago (Ratcliffe, 1988); not least because of structural constraints on the conduct of academic life emanating from central government policy. The imposition on the university sector of the four-yearly Research Assessment Exercise (RAE) has had much wider implications than the generation of league tables based on 'productivity levels': it has actually influenced the very nature of the research agenda itself.

Social research in Britain: an historical perspective

There is, in Britain, a long tradition of research on matters social. Witness the celebrated poverty studies of the nineteenth century by Mayhew (1862), and Booth (1894; 1897) not to mention Engels' study of the British working class in 1844 (Engels, 1968). This tradition was continued into the present century by major figures such as Rowntree (1902; 1941). Concern by government to produce quantifiable social indicators could be argued to go back even further, to the beginning of the nineteenth century and the first Population Census of 1801. On the other hand, government-sponsored social research is a relatively recent phenomenon, perhaps dating back only a half century or so, to the setting up of the Government Social Survey in 1941 and the Government Statistical Service in 1946. Previously, this research was generally the province of a few wealthy philanthropists.

The only institutional support came from the London School of Economics, founded in 1896, 'by a group led by Sidney and Beatrice Webb and devoted exclusively to the study of the social sciences' (Bulmer, 1978, p. 4). There is no space here to devote to a detailed account of this 'policy' research (for that was how it was generally conceptualized), nor is it within our remit to do so. What is of concern is whether there is a tradition not only of *doing* research but also of channelling findings into the policy domain, and acting thereon. The obvious answer to this somewhat simplistic question is, of course, that there is not. But, Bulmer (1986) quite rightly argues that even a more complex 'rational model' does not accord with empirical reality. Rather, a process of 'permeation' takes place. In an earlier work, for example, Bulmer (1986, p. 12) quotes Keynes 'famous claim . . . for economics' that:

> The ideas of economists and political philosophers, both when they are right and when they are wrong, are more powerful than is usually understood. Indeed, the world is ruled by little else. Practical men (*sic*), who believe themselves to be quite exempt from any intellectual influences, are usually the slaves of some defunct economist. Madmen in authority, who hear voices in the air, are distilling their frenzy from some academic scribbler of a few years back. I am sure that the

power of vested interests is vastly exaggerated compared with the gradual encroachment of ideas.

Where I would take issue with Bulmer is that he lets this quote ride without further comment. It seems inconceivable that ideas permeate governmental decision-making on an apparently haphazard basis and independent of 'vested interests'. We would argue that the latter concerns and the 'political project' of the party in power not only influence the selection of the appropriate 'defunct economist' or 'academic scribbler' but also guide it to the parts of her/his work (suitably interpreted) which accord with its ideas. Selective permeation is much more likely to be the end result, therefore.

Before assessing the role of sociologists (of 'race'/ethnicity) in influencing the policy/research agendas of government departments and quangos (QUAsi, Non-Governmental OrganizationS), however, we must take stock of some fundamental changes in the political climate for research over the last two decades. As intimated above, the filtering or selective permeation of findings has been the norm in contemporary Britain. But this is not the whole story, or course. There is often direct political control over the nature of research undertaken, which may take the form of closing (or winding down) units which do work of which the government disapproves, and the setting up of alternative 'friendly' organizations. There is also careful monitoring of who receives research funds and the threat of the ultimate sanction: the refusal to publish (in the absence of 'significant' amendment) in the case of government-sponsored research. There is considerable evidence of all of these. Moreover, there has been a policy of selective cutbacks in general research funding combined with the purposive channelling of such funds as are made available. The story, then, is one of a much higher government profile in the control of research output.

There are two major objections to this line of argument: first, that it simply misrepresents the case and exaggerates the importance of the government's role in the research enterprise. The second follows on from this. One might argue that it presents an overly simplistic, or even functionalist, account of the state's role in research. But this would be to misrepresent the argument.

The government in power does not, and cannot, have the capability to exercise complete control over the vast panoply of research outlets, and nor would it necessarily wish to. Any government, as we shall see, can to a point 'live with' uncomfortable research findings, and might indeed at times act on these results in order to retain a veneer of liberalism and of a participatory democracy. In some ways more important, however, is the level of autonomy still exercised by individual sociologists and their ability to effect change beyond the aegis of 'the state' (in all its guises).

What is being suggested is that government control over research has vastly increased over the last two decades, and continues to do so despite the election of a 'New Labour' government in May 1997. Indeed, following the Robbins expansion of Higher Education in the 1960s, the 'purse strings' had already begun to be tightened by the early 1970s. The days of heady expansionism of the university system were over, and this affected the social sciences and humanities perhaps more than any other areas of research.

There had been a certain openness to outside ideas within goverment circles, reflected in some sense by the birth in 1971 of the Central Policy Review Staff (CPRS). This was a clear acknowledgement that there was a need for a body independent of departments of state to collate material and to advise the government of the day. True, appointments to positions at the CPRS tended to be 'political'; this was to be expected, as was the purge of personnel following a change in government. But the staff were often respected academics who could not be counted upon to simply 'toe the party line'. And this was something which increasingly upset Margaret Thatcher as Prime Minister. As Bulmer (1986) argues, the CPRS came to be seen as an 'interest group' within government. It came as a great surprise, therefore, that it was summarily closed down in 1983.

It came as no surprise either that the university system came under the microscope in the early 1980s. Some sections of the government (back-benchers as well as front) were deeply suspicious of the 'newer' academic disciplines such as sociology; others were openly hostile, suggesting that (as evidenced by the 1968 unrest) they were the hotbeds of revolution, an idea more than faintly absurd. One of the main targets at the time was the Social Sciences Research Council (SSRC), the major source of support for postgraduate and academic research in the social sciences. It was generally believed that hostility from major front-bench speakers such as Sir Keith (later Lord) Joseph, the then Minister for Education, was indicative of a general wish of the government to close this body down.

Much to their dismay, the report by Lord Rothschild (interestingly, the first head of CPRS, and a respected natural scientist) was broadly supportive, a result (which, incidentally, underlines the earlier point about the dangers of an overly functionalist model of power relations). To save face, however, and to give a clear warning to the council that its agenda was a matter of concern to the government, its name was changed to the Economic and Social Research Council (ESRC). Joseph, for example, had made clear his feeling that there was not, and could not be, something called 'social science'. 'Science' was a term only to be applied to the 'hard' natural science disciplines. The inclusion of the word 'economic' in the council's title was a clear hint that research in this area was to be prioritized. In some ways an even more fundamental attack on the discipline of sociology, though, was the removal of 'specialist subject' status in teacher training programmes in colleges and departments of education at around the same time; the aim clearly being to undermine its teaching in schools and to precipitate its marginalization even prior to the introduction of the core curriculum enshrined in the 1988 Education Reform Act.

To argue that economics was to be prioritized is true, but without explanation conceals a more fundamental truth. The aim was effectively to attempt a takeover of the discipline's agenda by raising the profile of Friedmanite (or neo-Friedmanite) monetarist economics. This new 'agenda' was clearly stated in publications such as the *Salisbury Review* and in a highly controversial Channel 4 television series entitled '*The New Enlightenment*' narrated by Professor Kenneth Minogue, a prominent (Conservative) political scientist. The latter clearly expressed the perceived 'need' to provide 'respectable', authoritative research/public relations organizations from which to argue the new economic orthodoxy. One such body was the Centre for Policy Studies (CPS), not to be confused with the Policy Studies Institute (PSI) a well respected 'independent' research unit, whose work will be discussed later.

Importantly, the atmosphere in British universities was also changing significantly. The often savage cutbacks during the earlier part of the decade, following the University Grants Committee (UGC) review, threw the system open to the play of 'market forces'. The keywords were now 'competition' and the 'maximization of research income'. But it appeared to a large number of those working in the universities that whereas for example, competition in one sense could be a good thing leading to an improvement in the quality and volume of research, the notion of competition here was linked to what I described in an earlier work as 'the pervading ethos of "radical individualism"' (Ratcliffe, 1988, p. 1). There appeared to be a move towards an atomization of the research enterprise, an emphasis on the individual's output rather than her/his contribution to a collective intellectual effort.

Universities were forced to rely on the generation of external funds, through research grants and (crucially) overseas students' income (which had become a significant issue, given the major increase in their fees in relation to those of 'home' students). To put it perhaps a little crudely, fund-raising became the name of the game, thus deflecting effort away from what arguably most saw as the real purpose of universities. The implications for the development of a subject such as sociology were clear. If research income was the key to success for the individual and their department then the subject's future agenda is likely to be affected in significant ways.

In the 1990s, a new monster of the Thatcher government reared its head, the RAE. To its eternal discredit, academe ('even' the sociological profession) accepted it with barely a whimper. The end result was an even more dangerous subversion of the intellectual enterprise, not least because of the prioritization of research council funding and publication in international peer-reviewed journals. Just how serious this was for work in the area of 'race and ethnic relations' will be explored in later sections of this chapter.

The sociologist and social change: some initial thoughts

(a) Whatever the academic argument in favour of doing a specific piece of research it is politically naive and potentially dangerous to see research as autonomous from its contextual political environment, and (b) governments and other interested groups necessarily take a strong role and have a stake in academic research about so-called deviants in society.

(Solomos, 1989a, p. 5)

Although written in the context of debates surrounding the Moynihan report on the black family in the US (Rainwater and Yancy, 1967), this statement expresses succinctly one of the major problems facing the researcher. The 'contextual political environment' we take to encompass not only interested *groups* such as the government, media, police and rightist political organizations, but also what could be described as the pervading normative cultural values at an individualized level (ideological forms seen as historically entrenched within hegemonic power relations). Thus academic research, however well intentioned, can be co-opted and subverted.

But this presupposes answers to the key questions 'why do research?' and 'who is it for?' The contention of this paper is that much, perhaps most, research in the area of 'race' (at least until the 'postmodern turn' of the 1990s) has been undertaken with a view to exposing sources of inequality, and ultimately working towards their eradication. This may, or may not, imply an appeal to policy change. It may, or may not, involve action research geared to the empowerment of subordinate groups. One thing is clear. Beyond the obvious, rather trite, point that 'all research is political' one could argue that 'some of it is more political than others'. Given the ideological legacy of slavery and colonialism, no research on 'race' in Britain can lay claim to being 'purely academic', in the sense of its content being divorced from contemporary material conditions and discourse. Hence, even research which explicitly eschews concerns about 'racial' inequality nevertheless contributes (unintentionally) to such debates.

The chapter argues, therefore, that one cannot absent oneself from the fray. This has to be the case when an issue as 'basic' as nomenclature remains hotly contested terrain (Modood, 1988; Ratcliffe, 1994). Conceptual precision, a *sine qua non* on the part of the academic sociologist, acquires a political dimension; not to mention a theoretically reflexive quality. The terminology clearly involves a social construction of the world which is, or should be, 'negotiable'. This is particularly of concern when our imposed labels are seen as unacceptable, or worse repressive, by the 'subjects' of our research. A constant reassessment of terms would appear to be the minimal requirement of an ethically sound research strategy.

There is no space, nor really the need, to rehearse the detailed arguments once again here: they have after all been extensively dealt with elsewhere (see, for example, Ratcliffe, 1994; 1996: esp. Chapter 1). But, importantly, they draw attention to the politics of the research process, specifically the differential power relationship between the researcher and the researched (Jenkins, 1987; Wenger, 1987). A further point should not be forgotten, that although (normally) 'powerful' in the context of the research act, the sociologist is powerless in one important respect. They are not in a position *directly* to influence the cultural reproduction of racist (or sexist) discourse. The sociologist's rejection of the concept of 'race' as an ideological construct (Miles, 1982; 1989; 1993) has not, and will not, result in its abandonment at street level nor for that matter in the 'corridors of power' nor, importantly, by the media.

All of these matters have implications for social change processes. As we saw earlier, the latter embodies ideological as well as material ontological relations. As to the former, sociologists can, irrespective of research context, ensure that they avoid the reproduction of repressive forms of discourse. At the level of action, the power to change depends to a large extent on context, funding, the will to envisage and effect change, and so on. Four major research sites are considered here: central government, local government, quangos (especially the Commission for Racial Equality-CRE) and, finally, 'independent' research organizations and academic departments. Because of its statutory duty to effect 'social change', we begin with the CRE.

The Commission for Racial Equality as a potential vehicle for change

The CRE came into being as a direct result of the 1976 Race Relations Act, and fused the legal and research functions of the Race Relations Board (RRB) and the Community Relations Commission (CRC) respectively. This was some 11 years since the first piece of legislation to outlaw discrimination based on 'race, colour or creed', years during which most would agree that little was achieved either in terms of reducing levels of racial hostility or in changing the way in which minorities were routinely treated in the street, at work, at school and so on. The weakness of the 1965 and 1968 Acts suggested to all a lack of political will to attack the root causes of the problem (Sivanandan, 1976). Two factors confirmed these views.

First, despite clear inequalities in substantive material conditions, it had taken 13 years since the first attempted Private Members Bill for any legislation to enter the Statute book. Second, and more importantly, accompanying this legislation were a host of measures to curb immigration to Britain. Most of the literature regards each Immigration Act from 1962 onwards as overtly racist in being geared essentially to curbing the influx of black people to Britain (Sivanandan, 1976; Moore and Wallace, 1975; Gilroy, 1987; Solomos, 1993). Others see many aspects of this legislation as simultaneously sexist (WING, 1985). The unwillingness of governments (of whatever political hue) to enact effective anti-discrimination legislation, combined with the introduction of ever-more restrictive immigration control, explains why minority communities had little faith in the 'race industry' (Gilroy, 1987).

Despite the strengthening of the legislation with the advent of the 1976 Race Relations Act, the CRE faced an uphill struggle. It now had the power to *subpoena* documents and witnesses and had a strategic role in the sense of being able to initiate investigations where a *prima facie* case of discrimination appeared to exist. No longer was it limited to dealing with *individual* cases of discrimination. It had the statutory duty to ensure compliance with the Act, directly via its London-based and regional staff, and indirectly through a panoply of local Community

Relations Councils (CRCs). Compliance was, and is, approached by a combination of conciliation, advice, arbitration and, as a last resort, investigation (or the threat of it).

It would be churlish to argue that there have been no positive achievements. 'Ethnic monitoring', which the CRE still sees as the central plank of its policy, is now fairly widespread. By the end of the 1980s it was estimated, for example, that over 30 per cent of major employers had some form of monitoring scheme in place (Bunting, 1990). In local government, required to conform to section 71 of the Act (which outlaws discrimination in both employment and service delivery), monitoring is also increasingly common, especially in housing and social services (CRE, 1994). And after much debate, the government finally accepted the case for an 'ethnic question' to be included in the 1991 Population Census. All of this came about not solely as a result of lobbying from the CRE: many academics had been adding their voices (though not always in unison) over the years, amongst them Martin Bulmer whose work we have already referred to and Michael Banton the title of whose book *Promoting Racial Harmony* (1985) encapsulates the consistent ethos of the CRE.

CRE investigations uncovered blatant cases of discriminatory behaviour, underpinned often with the most virulent forms of racism. As demonstrated by the late Professor Valerie Karn (1997), who dedicated her life to undermining the 'ethnic penalty', the CRE's work spanned all the major social institutions: education, housing, health and welfare as well as employment. Sociologists became increasingly involved in the CRE's work as researchers and consultants.

There were a number of 'showpiece' investigations in the late-1980s. The study of St. George's Hospital Medical School in London (CRE, 1988) employed the current author as consultant. Here, an apparent lack of success on the part of minority applicants (and women) led to an evaluation of the admissions process. When the focus of attention turned to the computer programme used to pre-select likely candidates for interview, a disturbing factor emerged. It was seen to attach negative weightings on the basis of 'race and gender'. The interview process then acted as an additional filter, reducing yet further the numbers of minorities and women who had survived the computer pre-selection phase despite its inbuilt biases.

As with an earlier investigation into the housing policies of Hackney Council (CRE, 1984), the impact, at least in terms of public debate, was immediate. A BBC TV programme in the current affairs series 'Panorama' was devoted to the CRE report. Shockwaves permeated much of the Higher Education sector as internal management meetings were called to consider student recruitment policies and a number of seminars and conferences pulled together admissions tutors and other interested parties from universities throughout the country.

Once again in a consultancy role, I was involved in the CRE's formal investigation into recruitment practices in the accountancy profession. And once again, despite some variations between firms, discrimination on the basis of 'race' appeared disturbingly common. So the evidence is there, as was the case in the investigations outlined above. But could the CRE, with its existing powers, effect real change where it proved the existence of discrimination? And, if it could, was the effect inevitably localized (that is, impacting only on the firms/organizations investigated)?

The answer to the first question has to be a qualified 'yes'. But, as to the wider impact of 'showpiece' investigations, it has to be said that, but for the immediate flurry of activity following a report's publication, few changes in broader organizational culture have been discernable. A sense of frustration was clearly reflected in the comments of Michael Day (then CRE Chair) reported in the *Guardian* newspaper of 13 June 1990. In a speech commemorating 25 years of race relations legislation he said:

> It would be wrong to say that some government departments have not been solidly behind us. But there are other departments, and the collective voice which one would want to come down from the top, which don't seem to recognise our efforts or what we're about. *There is an element of tokenism in the legislation*, and I'm getting impatient at the slow pace of change.
>
> (my emphasis)

Further,

> We haven't been clear enough in our message in the past that we're about social justice of a fundamental kind. But we need investment; in buildings, in technology. If you're really in business, an organisation has to reflect this to attract the best people and achieve results. It's got to be impressive or the cause looks apologetic and rundown. If you're going to give minority groups space and justice, *the political will has to be there*; there has to be a sense of outrage, there has to be a passion as well as professionalism behind it. If we as an organisation aren't tuned into the anger that black people feel, we cannot com-

municate it back to *the people who all too often don't want to hear.*
(my emphasis)

Others would be less charitable. Anil Sivanandan, Director of the Institute of Race Relations and long-time critic of the 'race industry' was quoted (in the same article) as saying, in characteristically dismissive style: 'It is not good enough to say the CRE has no teeth. It has no bloody gums'. He argued further that the major effect of its work was the creation of a black 'managerial class, whose job, through the buffer institutions of the CRE and CRCs, was to manage racism for the State'.

Although these remarks were made a decade ago, they remain in large part pertinent today. True, the CRE at the turn of the century is a very different organization from what it was in 1990, and the political mood has shifted with the election of a New Labour government in May 1997. The appointment of Herman (now Sir Herman) Ouseley as Chair marked a radical change in ethos. Here was a prominent black activist with a highly successful local government career in London behind him. Local CRCs were renamed (re-badged?) Racial Equality Councils (RECs) so as to downplay old-style conciliation and suggest a more proactive role, the CRE marketed itself aggressively (employing, ironically, Saatchi and Saatchi, the agency which had previously worked on Margaret Thatcher's image makeover), and the investigative approach was gradually replaced by the concept of partnership. Monitoring was still a key theme, but the CRE would work with organizations to achieve the goal of equality.

Old problems remain, however. Annual budgets have been reduced inexorably through the 1990s, inevitably limiting its effectiveness given the size of the task at hand. The political will Michael Day sought is still not in evidence, despite more positive noises from the current government. Those committed to true equality agree that the current legislation is woefully weak (Sanders, 1998): the CRE (and much of academe) has been arguing the case since the mid-1980s. The current government has committed itself to strengthening it during the 2000 session, but early signs are that changes are likely to be minor: Labour strategists/ 'spin doctors' appearing to fear the political consequences of more radical action. Some have used the retreat from affirmative action in the US as a justification for relative inaction, implying that more positive measures privilege black people at the expense of the indigenous (white) population! 'Contract compliance', whereby companies are disqualified from public sector business unless they employ an appropriate number of minority staff, remains on the agenda. [The government prefers to see its concept of 'Best Value' solely in economic terms.] Finally, the level of existing penalties and the threat of 'non-discrimination notices' hardly serve as adequate deterrents.

So, the dilemma for sociologists is whether they should, given these problems, support the CRE's work. The author's personal view is confirmed by his actions. Some action is better than none, as long as this is only part of a wider strategy to be outlined below. Further, to oppose or belittle the CRE and its work, would be to play into the hands of those who oppose its mission. There is little evidence that its demise would lead to the development of grassroots black political movements (which in any case can, and do, flourish irrespective of the CRE's existence).

The sociologist and government departments

The problems faced by sociologists working within departments of state is in many ways self-evident. For one thing, with the exception of 'Government Statisticians', who are equivalent in rank to Administrative Staff (and therefore promotable through grades leading, for example, to the post of Permanent Secretary or its equivalent), researchers (defined as those directly involved in the collation of data to aid policy formulation), are generally badly paid and of relatively low status. As a consequence, their agendas will be set by others and they are, in isolation, powerless to influence the course of policy development.

The Office for National Statistics is, at least, part of the Cabinet Office, and senior statisticians advise ministers on matters relevant to their skills. Theoretically, they have a window (however opaque) on policy (Bulmer 1982; 1986). Some windows are even half open in that external (academic) advice is now usually sought even in the case of 'in-house' projects. Having said this, 'permeation' rather than paradigm shift is likely to characterize the process of change, leading to frustration on the part of researchers who see their reports lie fallow on the desks of their seniors, or blocked by their political masters. They are forbidden by the Official Secrets Act from divulging the content of (unpublished) reports to third parties.

All of this underlines the disjuncture between research and action, and differential relations of power within 'the powerful'. And, of course, there is action in theory and action in practice. In-house researchers inevitably have one eye firmly set on their career goals. External academic consultants undertake this work for a variety of motives, and it would be naive to suggest these were all noble (in the sense of a serious intent to redress social inequalities): money, kudos and prestige all come to mind. The ultimate effect is likely to be carefully worded documents which fail to challenge the *status quo* fundamentally. Even then, radical statements can be co-opted by ministers to display sensitivity to the problems of 'minorities' without actually *doing* anything. To illustrate limits to the efficacy of agency, two examples are considered here: first, the introduction (in 1991) of an 'ethnic group' question in the decennial census and, secondly, the role of public inquiries and commissions in respect of policy formulation.

As noted earlier, social scientists and the CRE had been lobbying government since the late-1970s on the census issue. The argument, accepted by the then Labour government, was that this would provide the only way of monitoring nationally the effectiveness of the 1976 Race Relations Act. It was argued that existing methods of population estimation based on birthplace would become increasingly flawed as ever-larger proportions of minority communities would be British-born. The idea was rejected by the incoming Conservative administration of Margaret Thatcher on the grounds that ethnic (and class) inequalities were part of an outmoded (socialist) ideology. They could also point to the fact that many inner-urban black residents objected to the question (Sillitoe, 1978). As a consequence, it was dropped from the 1981 schedule.

Black residents who objected to the question were generally concerned about the uses to which the data might be put, a concern shared by some social scientists. Others were unhappy with, or suspicious about, the proposed categories. It was pretty clear, for example, that putative 'skin colour' provided the organizational logic behind the categories: leading people to the obvious conclusion that it was not *ethnicity* which interested the state but '*race*', seen in terms of phenotype. There is an important sense in which this *is* the key issue, in that it usually constitutes the basis on which discrimination takes place: in other words, the latter is a function of ascribed identity and not self-defined identity (Ratcliffe, 1996: Ch.1).

Given that the principal reason for including the topic in the census was to assess levels of inequality, it is reasonable to ask what use have been made of the data. Not surprisingly, the academic literature is replete with analyses not only of the published tabulations but also of data from the Samples of Anonymized Records (SARs) which were produced for the first time (following pressure once again from academe, and lengthy debates about the ethical implications – Dale and Marsh, 1993) Importantly for the current argument, the Office of Population Censuses and Surveys, the forerunner of ONS, also invited a number of senior academics to produce a 4-volume series entitled *Ethnicity in the 1991 Census*. These appeared between 1996 and 1997.

One particular chain of events provides a fascinating insight into the then government's sensitivity as to the data's use. The current author was commissioned to edit Volume 3, dealing with the changing spatial patterns of Britain's minorities (Ratcliffe, 1996). OPCS/ONS were essentially looking for a description of the data (letting 'the facts speak for themselves'), whereas I and most of my academic contributors felt the need to go beyond this, giving an appraisal of the reasons behind the observed residential patterns. This inevitably involved a reflection on the 'racial' dynamics of labour and housing markets and the successes, and failures, of urban policy to redress the sharp material inequalities which inevitably emerged.

The crunch came with a chapter written by two highly respected academics, one a very senior urban analyst with a long history of large-scale funded research, much of it from government departments such as the Department of the Environment (DoE). Their chapter linked the analysis of 1991 census data to patterns of urban inequality, and used a wide swathe of research evidence to reflect on policy matters. ONS, and importantly their colleagues from the Home Office, objected to the chapter on the grounds that it 'didn't use enough census data' and that it contained 'too much of the authors' own views'. I, as editor, strongly defended the chapter on the basis that the 'views' were not 'their own' but stemmed from published research findings, and insisted that it be included in the volume subject to relatively minor amendments (largely unrelated to the ONS's concerns). Disagreement then led to arbitration, with the chapter being sent to two professors nominated by ONS. Given their highly conservative views, their responses were predictable. One said repeatedly that the paper 'wasn't scientific enough', the other defended the ONS's line on the policy issues. The chapter was dropped from the published volume, but much of the spirit of the 'offending material' was included in my concluding chapter since I felt it was essential in a volume such as this to reflect on the evidence which the census data provided of failures of government policy. After all, the whole point of including the 'ethnic group' question in the census was to able to reflect on the success of policy such as the 1976 Race Relations Act!

On publication, the book caused a furore. The Home Office were reportedly angry with the direct references to government policy, and the right-wing media led by the *Daily Mail* embarked on a scurrilous campaign to embarrass the ONS (for failing to censor the volume) and to discredit me, my work, and even the university which employed me (Heffer, 1996). This explains why the final volume (Karn, 1997) was subject to a high level of scrutiny by the ONS (and the Home Office). There was an attempt to force the editor to make radical changes to the concluding chapter, which again contained reflections on policy (in the fields of education, housing and employment) based on a copious quantity of published findings from the academic literature and CRE formal investigations. A stand-off ensued and, to her eternal credit, the editor refused to back down. The volume was published retaining the critical final chapter.

The problems in retaining intellectual autonomy in research emanating from external stimuli, for example, successful grant applications to government departments from universities and research institutes, will be dealt with below. Here, we are concerned with the involvement of social scientists in Government Commissions and Public Inquiries (including their aftermath). Unlike routine in-house research, or research put out to tender, this is usually geared explicitly to finding policy solutions to pressing social problems (as perceived by government). In the area of 'race', this usually involves an inquest into outbreaks of violence as was the case with Lord Scarman's investigation of the Brixton (and Toxteth) disorders of 1981, the enquiry led by Lord Gifford into the 1985 disturbances on the Broadwater Farm Estate in North London, and the Bradford Commission undertaken in the wake of the Bradford 'riots' of 1995.

The case of Scarman illustrates clearly the ways in which critical reports can be marginalized, and hence neutralized. While one might have wished the report (Scarman, 1981) to have gone rather further than it did (or to have been conducted by other people) it was critical of the police and saw the material conditions of life in Brixton as an important element of the problem. It made specific recommendations in terms of policing strategy, to remove 'racial' confrontationism and suggested that efforts should be made to recruit officers from minority communities. Now, one might have qualms with this or other aspects of his work, but he did unequivocally call 'for a radical national programme of action to tackle the roots of racial inequality' (Solomos, 1989b, p. 18). Tellingly, though, Solomos describes the 'lukewarm response' to the report as '(a) good example of the dominant political response to racial inequality during the 1980s' (ibid., p. 18). Few (if any) of his recommendations have been carried out systematically, and one is left with the feeling that the report was essentially a *substitute* for substantive action rather than a facilitator of such action.

True, there was a flurry of policy activity in Brixton itself for a while with, for example, US visitors suggesting ways in which 'black business' could contribute to the area's regeneration. Thus, colour-blind adaptations of Thatcher's economic policy were seen as a panacea for inner-city problems. Elsewhere, showpiece projects and relatively minor injections of funds have been used to project the image of a progressive, caring and responsive 'state' to the wider community, while hoping also to assuage local discontent. Hence, in Liverpool, scene of the Toxteth 'riots' of 1981, an International Garden Centre was opened on derelict land and encouragement was given to the development of the Docks area.

In Birmingham, where the area of Handsworth erupted during September 1985, a formal police-led inquiry was followed by a report published by West Midlands County Council (1986). This pooled the expertise of politicians such as Keith Vaz and the prominent black sociologists Stuart Hall and Paul Gilroy. It pointed to years of official neglect, of top-down policy-making from a 'white' bureaucracy, and misguided urban renewal strategies which failed to provide work for local people (thereby failing to generate sustainable communities). The actual response was less ambitious. The Broughton Road venture was opened with a flurry of publicity by the then leader of Birmingham City Council, Dick Knowles, and Kenneth Clarke MP, Secretary of State for Industry. But this was an extremely small scheme involving the improvement of 38 houses and ultimately providing 100 units accommodating some 180 people. Although 24 training places were made available for local young people (18–24 years of age) it was very much a one-off venture. The Heartlands project in East Birmingham represented an attempt to solve the 'inner city problem' by removing the 'inner city' and its residents (the 'problem'?).

Both the Gifford report (1986) and the Bradford Commission (1996) saw poverty, social conditions and policing as key issues in their locality. The latter document owed much to the efforts of Sheila Allen (Professor of Sociology at the University of Bradford) and one of the appointed commissioners. As befits the work of one who has committed the whole of her life to exposing and redressing 'race' and gender inequality, the report paints a complex picture of multiple failure in respect of social and urban policy; thereby rejecting simplistic accounts which pointed to policing *or* prostitution *or* poverty *or* inter-generational conflict.

In reflecting on the history of these studies over the past two decades, one obvious conclusion emerges. Although much has been learnt, little has been acted upon. This was brought home by the brutal murder of a black teenager in South London in 1993, Stephen Lawrence. Pressure from his parents finally persuaded the new government to institute a public inquiry with Sir William Macpherson as Chair. The conclusions, published as a mammoth report in 1999, tell an all-too-familiar story: a catalogue of failure by the police, in this case the Metropolitan Police under Commissioner Sir Paul Condon. It argued that, as a result of multiple incompetence grounded in 'institutional racism', Stephen's killers had been allowed to remain free. It also argued, importantly, that institutional racism was not confined to the police and criminal justice system.

Jack Straw, as Home Secretary, immediately promised action to redress the problems highlighted by the report, but as yet little has been offered apart from promising to include the police within the remit of the race relations legislation. Yet all of the problems have been known about for decades, not least from the Scarman inquiry and decades of research by sociologists across the gamut of social institutions. The current government appears more willing than previous administrations to *listen* to what we as a profession have to say, but *action* is less assured. This is particularly so, as there is also evidence of an almost pathological fear of the 'race' issue, where its spin-doctors see a potential loss of votes. Its focus on 'social exclusion' remains strangely colour-blind.

Local authorities and the 'race issue'

> Once again . . . the experience of local authorities seems to mirror that of central government initiatives, since there has been a gap between the promise embodied in policy statements and the actual achievements of policies.
>
> (Solomos, 1989b, p. 15)

Such was one gloomy conclusion to an evaluation of the attempts by local authorities in the 1980s to achieve the *stated* goals of racial equality. This was in spite of a myriad of 'race advisors', 'race units', in-house policy research teams and 'ethnic monitoring' sections. We need to ask why this should be the case and, more pertinently perhaps, what can be done about it. Clearly, the political will needs to be there, but some sociologists have argued that *our* role should be more overtly 'political'.

Ben-Tovim *et al.* (1986) argued that theirs was an explicitly Marxian approach fusing 'theory and practice' and rejecting positivistic, quantitative methods and also the ethnographic case-study model. Explicitly rejecting the notion of value-free research, they adopted an explicitly anti-racist stance, identifying with and working alongside local political groups. Largely because of this, one suspects, they were refused access to the two local authorities whose 'race equality' policies they intended to study – Wolverhampton and Liverpool.

They would defend their rejection of a basic canon of sociological research, that of not influencing that which is to be observed, on the grounds that their aim was to *change* not simply to *expose*. This would be totally unexceptionable were real change to be promotable from the outside, that is, through political action and external pressure on a local authority. In practice, one suspects that the possibilities of this happening are slight. Ball (1990, p. 17) argues that fusing the roles of researcher and political activist is difficult to reconcile with the expectations of the academic world, with its emphasis on individual achievement, objectivity and academic publication. On the other hand, this is at least a matter of individual choice, that is, whether to 'play the academic game' or not. Also, there is always the option for us (*qua* individual citizens) to engage with real world issues; in so doing engaging in *action* and not necessarily *action research*.

There are three principal types of local authority-based study. One is 'in-house' research. The second is commissioned research, where the authority defines the agenda. The other is where a third party defines the research focus and the team are not employees of the authority. Here, we focus on the first two; the third being deferred to the next section of the chapter.

As in the case of in-house research in government departments, local authority researchers are usually in the unenviable position of having the major parameters of their work defined, and financially delimited, by others. They also suffer from the same constraints in terms of the limits on autonomy, that is, reports can contain criticism of authorities' policies but an overstepping of the mark can lead to seriously curtailed promotion chances! On the other hand they can be, and often are, highly critical of *central* government policy. But, as with central government researchers, they rarely hold management positions with a clear, unequivocal link to the decision-making process.

In the case of research on 'race', one often finds a situation which accords with Sivanandan's view, quoted earlier, of bodies tending to 'manage racism', and fulfil a 'buffer function'. Local politicians, council committees and area/line managers, can effectively channel problems to in-house research essentially to neutralize them (given the researchers' low status). If awkward questions are raised thereafter managers can then claim to be 'taking action'.

The researchers are also used at times to settle internal squabbles, or 'keep councillors happy'. If there is one defining characteristic of their work, then, it is a lack of antonomy compounded by the lack of power to promote, let alone effect, policy change. Discussions with many researchers over the past two decades reveal that, all too often, authorities are not at all clear in their own minds as to the job description of the person concerned. This is particularly serious in the current context if the 'research' relates to an issue such as 'ethnic monitoring'. During a workshop held in 1988 at Salford University on the theme of 'Monitoring for Racial Bias in Housing Allocations', and attended by monitoring staff from a variety of local authorities and housing associations, a number of significant concerns emerged:

- rather than developing their skills, many had come to the workshop to find out what monitoring was all about!
- where data are being assembled, the mere *collection* of the data was usually equated with *action*;
- where monitoring reports contained specific proposals for redressing inequalities, managers often failed to push for their implementation.

Once again, in the final analysis, it came down to a question of political will, or rather the lack of it. Local authorities like to argue that they respond to legislation, and of course, were keen to bid for Section 11 funding (under the 1966 Local Government Act) to support posts ostensibly dealing with service delivery in a multi-ethnic context. They have not been so keen, however, to examine their own institutional ethos. Issues of racism and sexism, insofar as they are recognized to exist, are perceived as individual problems, soluble by discussion and conciliation. Institutional racism is deemed not to exist outside the textbooks of 'race relations' analysts (despite the findings of the Lawrence inquiry noted above).

Turning to research put out to tender to external researchers or organizations, it is now commonplace (and even more so under the current government) for consultancy firms as well as academic sociologists to undertake research on behalf of individual local authority departments. On the positive side (in terms of addressing social inequalities), researchers can often influence the research agenda significantly, given that the tenderer is often unclear as to the key issues. Problems for researchers often concern funding and the ownership of data (and associated publishing rights). The use of public money does not ensure public access to final reports and the authority can, and sometimes does, block the publication of a report in the case of disputes over content. Most academics, I suspect, know of cases where publication has been held up pending changes insisted upon by the sponsoring/funding body.

This, of course, raises one of the central ethical and political dilemmas for the researcher. Does one (in the interests of career progression) go along with the funding body's demands even if one believes them to be fundamentally unjustified? Does one, on the contrary, respond to the likelihood of such pressure being brought to bear by refusing such commissioned research, unless on the understanding of independent ownership of the data and full rights to publish (without a veto). Data rights are now more likely to be a problem with central, rather than local, government research, but sociologists are increasingly pressured into undertaking contract research, irrespective of the strings attached, as will be demonstrated later.

More important in practice is the disjucture between the research act and the policy act: the researcher is not in a position to effect policy change. They can only use the power of the written word (and in the context of the RAE-led academe of the 1990s, the written word in the appropriate place – preferably an international, refereed journal – is the only currency, beyond research income, which is valued).

The sociologist in academe

> There is a dangerous sociology abroad – a sociology of race relations, that is – and dangerous to the black cause that it seeks to espouse.... It purports to ameliorate the condition of the black minorities, and the black young, in particular, by appeals to enlightened capitalism.
>
> (Bourne, 1980, p. 331)

Although this remark was aimed at a particular research unit (the SSRC-funded Research Unit on Ethnic Relations at Aston University), it provides a useful focus for an appraisal of UK academic research more broadly. Bourne saw much of the profession as comprising 'cheerleaders and ombudsmen'. Gilroy (interestingly now a Professor of Sociology himself), in the same issue of *Race and Class*, saw them as simply 'managing the underclass' (Gilroy, 1980). Criticism from some quarters has continued unabated into the 1990s. For some, academe itself is the target, for others it is a question of *who* does the research, white researchers being the principal target (Robinson, 1983; Gutzmore, 1983; James and Harris, 1993). For yet others, the key issue is that of 'eurocentrism' (Gheverghese Joseph *et al.*, 1990) or eurocentrism compounded by the 'distortions' of white feminism (Carby, 1982; Bourne, 1983).

Probably the most effective way of examining the impact of sociological research is to set it in its institutional context with particular modes of funding. Two contexts will be considered; university-based researchers and research units, and independent research consultancies or institutes. This is admittedly a somewhat oversimplified characterization of the British scene but it will serve our present purposes.

University-based researchers and research units

The days of the large core-funded research centres in the field (such as the Centre for Research in Ethnic Relations), are now over. Since the termination of core ESRC funding in 1998, CRER has joined the ranks of those (such as the Ethnicity Research Centre at the University of Leicester and the Centre for Ethnicity and Racism Studies at the University of Leeds) which derive their income from disparate sources. They do little more than provide a focal point for groups of researchers working in the field.

It is worth reflecting here on Bourne's critique of RUER/CRER insofar as it relates to *structural* position. As an SSRC-funded organization (and thereby dependant on government funding), she saw it as part of a panoply of state racism (and would presumably have seen CRER in the same light). It would indeed be naive to suggest that the 'state' did not keep a close watch on its work. A blatant example of control from above was provided by an incident in the mid-1980s, when a CRER researcher published a paper containing the term 'Thatcherism'. Shortly after this had landed on the desk of the then head of the SSRC, the Director of CRER was summoned to London to explain how an SSRC publication could have been allowed to contain such an 'unacademic' term. The fact that the term was in common popular usage was not seen as sufficient reason. Academe was presumably required to retain a distance from what was in this instance open criticism of the government, that is, the holders of the SSRC's pursestrings and (perhaps more pertinently in this particular case) the political masters of its head!

One, possibly positive, feature of the change in status in 1984 from a unit funded by the ESRC to the status of a Designated Research Centre (DRC) might have been a freeing-up of centralized control. Unfortunately, however, there are two problems with this. For one thing, the requirement under the DRC mode to raise a proportion of funds from resources other than the SSRC, imposed extra day-to-day pressures on the Centre. In addition, as sources of such potential funding were relatively limited, the Centre was forced to consider those with possibly unacceptable strings attached. In the event, CRER remained remarkably free from succumbing to such temptation. It adopted a policy of accepting only those commissions which conformed to its published research programmes. The latter were never overtly 'radical', but nor were they 'dangerous to the black cause'.

The other units noted earlier have a much more free-floating role. Largely constituted by existing staff, as distinct from being generated by core (external) funding, they are free to act in much the same way as the individual sociologist. As noted earlier, the RAE regime now essentially drives current research effort, and universities have tended to encourage the formation of 'centres' and 'units' to increase the chances of funding.

In many ways, the key question for the current chapter is: What have these bodies achieved? Clearly they have informed academic debates. They have also contributed to national policy and, to a lesser extent, political debates. CRER, at least in its phase as a core-funded organization, saw itself as not only producing high quality research for an academic audience, but also informing a wider public, especially minority communities. Locally-based research into, for example, racial harassment and the need for a Muslim Community Centre, helped, but the aloofness of the university (Warwick), and its physical separateness from the city (Coventry) made its resources really only of use to a small (highly educated) section of the black population. Increasing public relations work and the development of media contacts (including the minority press) were helpful, but one has to accept that the overall impact in terms both of minority empowerment and in policy transformation was probably rather slight. As to the policy-makers, who listens 'when the party in power represents a benighted capitalism which is determined to dis-assemble the welfare state altogether'? (Bourne, op. cit., p. 351).

Were Bourne writing her paper today, some 20 years later, the analysis one suspects would differ in only one respect. The welfare state has been subjected to massive cutbacks over the intervening period – the election of the Blair administration in May 1997 merely slowing the pace. There is, however, a much greater willingness to listen to 'the people' (via focus groups), and a much more positive attitude towards (policy) research. Research centres of the type noted earlier are undoubtedly doing more research than hitherto on behalf of local authorities and central government. The problem is that the RAE places a higher value on Research Council grants, driving high status universities to seek such funding as a priority. This inevitably encourages research of a more 'theoretical' nature which is more likely to lead to international refereed journal articles than to material change on the streets of Brixton or Handsworth.

Difficult choices have to be made by contemporary sociologists. Research which they feel to be more worthwhile, in the sense of leading to the amelioration of living conditions or community empowerment, is likely to be poorly regarded within the current RAE rules (as, incidentally, is interdisciplinary work). In addition, the spirit of 'radical individualism' embodied in the assessment of research output (referred to in Chapter 1), devalues collaborative work and places a high value on the notion of 'principal investigator'. The atomization process also means that the direct cross-fertilization of ideas is made all the more difficult.

Within a generally difficult funding climate, some sources are clearly less difficult than others. Research geared to answering specific policy questions is relatively easy to fund, especially if it falls within the agenda of (say) a government department, or local authority. But, as noted earlier, this means that the profession is simply responding to the agenda of 'the state'.

Independent research bodies

The non-university research sector mushroomed dramatically during the 1990s. At the risk of oversimplification, one could suggest there are three broad groupings. There are generic policy research units and consultancy firms (which undertake commissioned work but may also solicit funding to support in-house projects). There are charitable organizations, which (except in the case of major players such as the Joseph Rowntree Foundation) dispense a relatively small amount of research funds and act as a pressure group for policy change. Then there is the Institute of Race Relations (IRR) which sees itself as providing a focus for political opposition to the forces of racial oppression, hence the subtitle of its in-house publication *Race and Class*, namely 'A Journal for Black and Third World Liberation'.

Amongst the first group, until its recent incorporation within the University of Westminster, is the Policy Studies Institute (PSI). Formerly Political and Economic Planning (PEP), this organization is often credited with direct involvement in the promotion and development of anti-discrimination legislation. Certainly, their 1966 study of the extent of racial discrimination in Britain (Daniel, 1968) was commissioned by the statutory bodies set up to administer the 1965 Race Relations Act and a further Act, taking into account many of the report's findings, did emerge in 1968. The 1972–75 PEP study (Smith, 1977), which was funded in large part by the Home Office, *did* point out many of the weaknesses of the 1968 Act and *was* followed by the Act currently in force (the 1976 Race Relations Act).

Against this evidence, one could point to the fact that the 1982 PSI research (Brown, 1984), once again funded largely by government departments, does not appear to have had a major impact on political debate, let alone action. Given that this report once again showed massive evidence of inequalities, pointing to the need for more comprehensive legislation, one can conclude that the key issue once again was the lack of political will. All previous Acts, flawed as they were, were passed by Labour administrations. As suggested earlier, the Thatcher governments had little sympathy for the cause of 'racial equality'. PSI met with some resistance when, in the early-1990s, they applied for funds to undertake a fourth national study. The Home Office refused to back the project, though on the grounds that it did not appear to offer much new data (taking into account the huge research budget). They argued that the 1991 Census provided ample evidence of 'racial disadvantage'. It was ultimately funded jointly by the ESRC and a number of government departments. Appearing as Modood *et al.* (1997), it was generally well received in the academic world, but as yet has had negligible impact on the broader political agenda.

One of the major concerns of all British governments since the late-1950s has been to reduce immigration and, more recently, to make efforts to evade responsibility for refugees wherever possible. The Thatcher government of the early-1980s also tried to block the CRE's investigation of the Immigration Service. It is in this context that organizations such as the Runnymede Trust can do extremely useful work. Set up in 1968 as a registered educational charity, the Trust defined its objectives as 'the collection and dissemination of information and the promotion of public education on immigration and race relations'. With the likes of Paul Gordon writing very effectively on the politics of immigration control and the 'New Right' (Gordon, 1985), and their association with the Radical Statistics Race Group, they have provided a very useful information service to those looking for political ammunition as part of the empowerment process. And they have done so without transcending the social democratic image of academic 'respectability' shared with action-oriented, issue-based organizations such as the Joint Council for the Welfare of Immigrants (JCWI). Their recent study of *Islamophobia* (Runnymede Trust, 1997) proved a highly useful document in both highlighting a serious problem and in undermining misconceptions about Islam.

The IRR is a different matter entirely. Born out of 'revolution' (Bourne, 1980; Mullard, 1985), it relies heavily on voluntary donations and income from its Journal *Race and Class*. Frequently sniping at mainstream academe, it has maintained a strident 'black' perspective. As such, it has been a useful corrective to the 'conservatism' of much academic sociology, providing a rallying point both for students (particularly black students) and young academics bemoaning the lack of black contributors to the sociology literature.

Conclusion: recent shifts in academic terrain and issues for the new millennium

It is impossible to do justice in such a brief chapter to all the nuances of constantly shifting academic debates in the area. We therefore focus here specifically on the major implications of these for social change processes. In this context, the first point to make is that the discipline has often been markedly out of touch with the everyday experiences of minority communities. Thus, Blauner (1971) in the US and Bourne (1980) in the UK argued that while theorists of the 1950s and 1960s were writing about 'the melting pot' and growing evidence of assimilation, urban streets were ablaze. A parallel tendency in the 1990s is the flirtation with postmodernism; a rejection of grand narratives and a focus of the unique and different (Westwood and Rattansi, 1996). Prominent black sociologists such as Hall and Gilroy now write less about combatting racism, becoming major players in the growth of 'cultural studies' within, some would say incursion into, sociology (Gilroy, 1993).

Not surprisingly, these developments are RAE-friendly. 'Theory' of whatever persuasion is highly regarded, thereby explaining a significant upturn in the number of refereed journals of this genre. In one sense, this is a positive development, in that crass, under-theorized and badly conceptualized work betrays the discipline. An obvious example is the widespread tendency to essentialize ethnicity. This is not only bad sociology, it can also lead to bad policy in the form 'ethnic managerialism' (Law, 1996). In addition, the focus on culture, and on processes of hybridization, both in theoretical monographs and in ethnographies (Back, 1996; Baumann, 1996), challenges the tendency towards pathologization by stressing the power of agency/empowerment. But the current author shares the concerns of many in the profession that the discipline may be losing its way, or being led astray (by the RAE), by undervaluing good, critical, theory-driven empirical research.

What, then, might an agenda for the new millennium look like? Despite the concerns just expressed, there is clearly a need for further historical/theoretical work on the reconstruction of 'black history and culture', untainted by the eurocentrism of many past accounts. This should also have the effect of continuing to render women visible in the sense of reflecting their role in the struggles against colonial domination and oppression.

As to empirical work, it is undoubtedly important to turn the spotlight firmly onto 'white racism' (rather than the 'problems' of minorities), including 'institutional racism'; widely recognized as a key issue since the publication of the Macpherson report in 1999. It also involves assessing the impact of government policy (national and local) on these communities. But it is also important, as implied by earlier remarks, to focus on strategies of empowerment (of 'down-up' policy-making), and on processes of (gendered) cultural change. All of this implies a greater engagement than hitherto with issues of importance to minority communities; rather than being chosen simply because they are 'interesting' to the curious academic mind. Whether this form of engagement with a (relocated) agenda leads to a significant (*and real*) change in material conditions is still open to conjecture: clearly the key issue is political will. But, it is undoubtedly disingenuous (and, arguably, 'unethical') for the sociologist to undertake funded policy research which they know is unlikely to be acted upon (whatever RAE considerations might dictate).

References

Back, L. (1996) *New Ethnicities and Urban Culture*, London, UCL Press.

Ball, W. (1990) 'A Critique of Methods and Ideologies in Research on Race and Education, paper presented to the XII World Congress of Sociology, Madrid, July.

Banton, M. (1985) *Promoting Racial Harmony*, Cambridge, Cambridge University Press.

Baumann, G. (1996) *Contesting Culture*, Cambridge, Cambridge University Press.

Ben Tovim, G. *et al.* (1986) *The Local Politics of Race*, London, Macmillan – now Palgrave.

Blauner, R. (1971) *Racial Oppression in America*, New York, Harper & Row.

Booth, C. (1894) *The Aged Poor in England and Wales*, London, Macmillan – now Palgrave.

Booth, C. (1897) *Life and Labour of the People of London*, 9 vols, London, Macmillan – now Palgrave.

Bourne, J. (with A. Sivanandan) (1980) Cheerleaders and Ombudsmen: the Sociology of Race Relations in Britain, *Race and Class*, Vol. XXI, No. 4, 331–51.

Bourne, J. (1983) Towards an Anti-Racist Feminism, *Race and Class*, 25(1).

Bradford Commission (1996) *The Bradford Commission Report*, London, HMSO.

Brown, C. (1984) *Black and White Britain: the Third PSI Survey*, London, Heinemann.

Bulmer, M. (ed.) (1978) *Social Policy Research*, London, Macmillan – now Palgrave.

Bulmer, M. (1982) *The Uses of Social Research: Social Investigation in Public Policy-Making*, London, George Allen and Unwin.

Bulmer, M. (ed.) (1986) *Social Science and Social Policy*, London, Allen and Unwin.
Bunting, M. (1990) 'Tighter race laws urged', *The Guardian*, 14/6/90.
Campbell, H. (1980) Rastafari: Culture of Resistance, *Race and Class*, vol. XXII(1).
Carby, H. (1982) 'White Woman Listen! Black Feminism and the Boundaries of Sisterhood' in CCCS, *The Empire Strikes Back*, Hutchinson, London.
CRE (1984) *London Borough of Hackney*, Commission for Racial Equality, London.
CRE (1988) *St Georges Hospital Medical School*, London, Commission for Racial Equality.
CRE (1994) *Environmental Health and Racial Equality*, London, Commission for Racial Equality.
Dale, A. and Marsh, C. (eds) (1993) *The 1991 Census User's Guide*, London, HMSO.
Daniel, W. W. (1968) *Racial Discrimination in England*, Harmondsworth, Penguin.
Engels, F. (1968) *The Condition of the Working Class in Britain in 1844*, London, Allen and Unwin.
Gheverghese Joseph, G. *et al.*(1990) Eurocentrism in the Social Sciences, *Race and Class*, 31(4)
(Lord) Gifford *et al.* (1986) *The Broadwater Farm Enquiry*, London, Karia.
Gilroy, P. (1980) Managing the 'underclass': a Further Note on the Sociology of Race Relations in Britain, *Race and Class*, vol. XXII(1).
Gilroy, P. (1987) *There Ain't No Black in the Union Jack*, London, Hutchinson.
Gilroy, P. (1993) *The Black Atlantic*, London, Verso.
Gordon, P. (1985) *Policing Immigration: Britain's Internal Controls*, London, Pluto.
Gutzmore, C. (1983) Capital, 'Black Youth' and Crime, *Race and Class*, 25(2).
Heffer, S. (1996) 'Cull this useless race', *Daily Mail*, 7 September.
James, W. and Harris, C. (eds) (1993) *Inside Babylon: the Caribbean Diaspora in Britain*, London, Verso.
Jenkins, R. (1987) Doing Research into Discrimination: Problems of Method, Interpretation and Ethics, in G. C. Wenger (op.cit.).
Karn, V. (ed.) (1997) *Ethnicity in the 1991 Census, vol. 4*, London, HMSO.
Law, I. (1996) *Racism, Ethnicity and Social Policy*, Hemel Hempstead, Prentice Hall.
Mayhew, H. (1862) *London Labour and the London Poor*, London, Griffin-Bohn.
Miles, R. (1982) *Racism and Migrant Labour*, London, RKP.
Miles, R. (1989) *Racism*, London, Routledge.
Miles, R. (1993) *Racism after 'Race Relations'*, London, Routledge.
Modood, T. (1988) 'Black', Racial Equality, and Asian Identity, *New Community*, 14(3), 397–403.
Modood, T. *et al.* (1997) *Ethnic Minorities in Britain: Diversity and Disadvantage*, London, PSI.
Moore, R. and Wallace, T. (1975) *Slamming the Door: the Administration of Immigration Control*, Oxford, Martin Robertson.
Mullard, C. (1973) *Black Britain*, London, Allen and Unwin.
Mullard, C. (1985) *Race, Power and Resistance*, London, RKP.
Pryce, K. (1979) *Endless Pressure*, Harmondsworth, Penguin.
Rainwater, L. and Yancey, W. L. (eds) (1967) *The Moynihan Report and the Politics of Controversy*, Cambridge, Mass., MIT.
Ratcliffe, P. (1988) Race and the Sociologist: the Case for a Research Agenda, paper presented to the ISA/CRES Seminar *New Frontiers in Social Research*, University of Amsterdam,

Ratcliffe, P. (ed.) (1994) *'Race', Ethnicity and Nation: International Perspectives on Social Conflict*, London, UCL Press.

Ratcliffe, P. (1996) *Ethnicity in the 1991 Census*, vol 3, London, HMSO.

Rattansi, A. and Westwood, S. (eds) (1994) *Racism, Modernity and Identity*, Cambridge, Polity.

Robinson, C. (1983) *Black Marxism*, London, Zed.

Rowntree, B. S. (1902) *Poverty: a Study of Town Life*, London, Longman.

Rowntree, B. S. (1941) *Poverty and Progress: a Second Social Survey of York*, London, Longman.

Runnymede Trust (1997) *Islamophobia: its Features and Dangers*, London, Commission on British Muslims and Islamophobia.

Sanders, P. (1998) Tackling Racial Discrimination, in T. Blackstone, B. Parekh and P. Sanders (eds), *Race Relations in Britain: a Developing Agenda*, London, Routledge.

(Lord) Scarman (1981) *The Brixton Disorders 10–12 April 1981: Report of an Inquiry by the Rt. Hon. The Lord Scarman OBE*, London, HMSO.

Sillitoe, K. (1978) Ethnic Origin: the Search for a Question, *Population Trends*, 13.

Sivanandan, A. (1976) Race Class and the State: the Black Experience in Britain, *Race and Class*, vol. XVII(4).

Smith, D. (1977) *Racial Disadvantage in Britain*, Harmondsworth, Penguin.

Solomos, J. (1989a) *Race Relations Research and Social Policy: a Review of some Recent Debates and Controversies*, Policy Papers in Ethnic Relations, No. 18, CRER, University of Warwick.

Solomos, J. (1989b) *From Equal Opportunity to Anti-Racism: Racial Inequality and the Limits of Reform*, Policy Papers in Ethnic Relations, No. 17, CRER, University of Warwick.

Solomos, J. (1993) *Race and Racism in Britain*, Basingstoke/London, Macmillan – now Palgrave.

Wenger, G. C. (1987) *The Research Relationship: Practice and Politics in Social Policy Research*, London, Allen and Unwin.

WING (1985) *Worlds Apart*, WING, London.

7
Research on Immigrant Ethnic Minorities in the Netherlands

Jan Rath

Introduction

No country in the world has such a high concentration of social scientists as the Netherlands, and this is particularly evident in those fields which are publicly recognized as 'problem areas'. Research into post-migratory processes is such a case. Up to, and throughout, the 1970s, only sporadic research was done, but this picture changed spectacularly after 1980. In that year the state accepted officially that 'guestworkers' from Mediterranean countries and 'fellow citizens' (*rijksgenoten*) from former colonial territories were in fact immigrants and not temporary visitors. At the same time the state judged it necessary to develop a coherent minorities policy in which the political goal of the integration of 'ethnic minorities' – as the people involved came to be called – should be achieved. This led to an explosive growth in what was called 'minorities research'. Many thousands of projects were started, and so far approximately 6000 to 7000 academic articles have been published, an average for the past two decades of almost one a day.[1] The totals are particularly high in the sectors comprising education, health, housing and employment.

The scale is not the only surprising thing about minorities research; the speed with which it was institutionalized is also striking. For example, in 1978, the Minister of Culture, Recreation and Social Work set up the Advisory Commission for Research into Cultural Minorities (ACOM), which gave a powerful spur to the emerging 'industry'. In 1983, the Minister of Education and Science established two new Chairs for the study of multiethnic societies, one in Amsterdam and one in Utrecht, soon to be followed by a series of other Chairs for inter-cultural communication, bilingualism and the like. The Netherlands Organization for Scientific Research (NWO) in 1988 gave official recognition to

137

the study group for the Social and Cultural Studies of Ethnic Minorities, which at the time had more than a hundred members, while the Netherlands Foundation for Legal Academic Research (NESRO) and the Foundation for Research in Theology and Religious Studies in the Netherlands (STEGON) also established specialized working parties and funding programmes. There are now a variety of academic institutes specializing in whole or in part on research into minorities, and since 1985 there has even been a specialist journal *Migrantenstudies*. Anyone aware of the speed with which this growth has occurred, must be impressed. There is no question that we are faced with an exceptionally active sector of the social science industry.

Paradoxically, the more reflective publications about minorities research adopt a predominantly sceptical and pessimistic tone. From the very beginning, minorities researchers – such as Van Amersfoort (1982a; 1983; 1991), Bovenkerk (1984; see also Bovenkerk, Miles and Verbunt (1991), Ellemers and Borghuis (1988), Köbben (1980), Penninx (1988b), Van Praag (1987) and Shadid and Van Koningsveld (1986), but also Van Doorn (1985), Gelling, De Jong and Schoemaker (1990), Jongkind (1992), Monsma (1987), Tinnemans (1991), Waardenburg (1986) and several others – complain particularly about the sparseness of theoretical results. In their judgement, the academic output has been mainly descriptive, not particularly high in quality, and has failed to lead to a significant accumulation of knowledge. There is little connection with theoretical writings in other countries, and insofar as researchers have dared to enter the territory of international comparative studies, they have made no real contributions to the advancement of theory. Van Doorn (1985, p. 75) described this condition as 'academic provincialism'.

In its generality, this diagnosis of minorities research is a fair one. There are certainly researchers who are interested in theoretical issues, but ultimately their analyses/observations have a low level of abstract thought, and limited significance. Yet the diagnosis is not a complete one. There is another serious shortcoming: minorities researchers often start from the same theoretical premises, so that their research concerns more or less the same aspects and processes, systematically failing to consider alternatives. This means that minorities research not only suffers from being theoretically superficial, but also from a one-sidedness in its conceptual framework. The fact that this weakness is ignored in almost all meta-analyses – except that of Bovenkerk (1984) – is a telling example. There may indeed be a general consensus about the epistemological foundations of the research, but as yet researchers have not shown much interest in debating these foundations.

As I have demonstrated in detail elsewhere (Rath, 1991, pp. 30–58; 1993; 1997), most minorities research falls within the 'ethnicity paradigm', as described by, among others, Omi and Winant (1986). This paradigm starts from the assumption that ethno-cultural distinctions are the most important social distinctions. Ethno-cultural differences are accepted as being differences of an essential nature, caused in this context by the arrival of people from foreign lands. The maintenance of ethnocultural characteristics is not without its obligations. After all, newcomers are living within the 'unitary Dutch culture' of the majority. Various researchers acknowledge cultural diversity within the native Dutch 'imagined community', but when it comes to the question of incorporating immigrant ethnic minorities, the dominant culture is generally regarded and treated as fairly homogeneous and fixed. By not adjusting to the pattern of the society surrounding them they are putting their social position at risk – so goes the argument. Their adaptation to this society is to be desired and in fact can hardly be avoided. Those who fail to adapt adequately and, in addition, have to contend with social disadvantages over a long period, are labelled 'ethnic minorities'. These minorities can only make up for their disadvantages in one way; by a process of integration controlled by the 'majority'. Van Amersfoort's book *Immigration and the Formation of Minority Groups* (1982) can in a sense be regarded as the theoretical sublimation of Dutch minorities research.[2]

Let me illustrate this with an example. Take research on immigrant entrepreneurship. Most researchers show a great deal of interest in ethnocultural characteristics and processes of ethnocultural incorporation (Rath and Kloosterman, 2000). Completely in line with Dutch ethnic minorities research, they regard entrepreneurship in *ethnic* terms, something which is illustrated by the indiscriminate and unthinking use of the term '*ethnic* entrepreneurship'. Exactly what distinguishes *ethnic* entrepreneurship from entrepreneurship in general – the origins of the entrepreneur, management strategies, personnel, the clientele, the products, or a combination of these? – is seldom, if ever, made (theoretically) explicit. Most researchers simply assume that there are real differences, just because they are dealing with immigrants. They subsequently search for ethnocultural traditions, ethnic moral frameworks, ethnic loyalties, ethnic behaviour patterns and ethnic markets and compare the entrepreneurship of different ethnic groups.

In so doing, they reduce immigrant entrepreneurship to an ethnocultural phenomenon existing within an economic and institutional vacuum. Little systematic attention is paid to the structural changes through which either the economy as a whole is going or which specific parts of the market are experiencing, or to the institutional framework of the welfare state within which entrepreneurs operate.[3] They thus behave as if the market is of little importance, as if bakers, garages, ice-cream parlours, clothing manufacturers and marketing bureaux operate under more or less identical market conditions, fall under the same regulations and institutions, demand similar entrepreneurial skills of the entrepreneurs, and produce similar trading results. Clearly this is not the case.

The strong rise of Turkish clothing firms in Amsterdam during the 1980s and the beginning of the 1990s, for instance, was very much associated with the changing consumption patterns and purchasing strategies of wholesalers and chain stores, and also the fairly tolerant attitude of the relevant authorities towards informal practices. The collapse of this industry in the mid-1990s was linked to the opening of new markets in Eastern Europe and more rigorous controls on illegal work and tax evasion. This illustrates the extent to which processes external to the entrepreneurs and their businesses, can boost or thwart entrepreneurship. The minorities paradigm, however, fails to appreciate these processes adequately.

The hegemony of the 'ethnicity paradigm' is overwhelming. The other two which Omi and Winant highlight are rarely encountered in the Netherlands. Only a handful of researchers take account of the 'nation paradigm' or the Marxist variants of the 'class paradigm'. It is this last which I would like to discuss here.

A comprehensive survey of the literature, comprising many thousands of books and articles about ethnic minorities in the Netherlands, reveals some two dozen which draw their inspiration from some version of Marxist theory.[4] This inspiration is not always expressed explicitly: sometimes it is a question of eclecticism, in many cases the theory is superficial. A salient feature is that most of these publications date from the 1970s, when the phenomenon of guestworkers was still relevant. They emphasized the asymmetrical development of international economies (as a cause of the guestworker phenomenon) and referred to the role of states in supporting the interests of the bourgeoisie: industry was only interested in the economic advantages of foreign labour, while the state stood by to provide solutions to the contradictions to which it gives rise. In this perspective, guestworkers were part and parcel of the working class, or of a new class beneath it. Most of the writers argued that the classic workers organizations, such as the trades unions and socialist parties, took too little account of the interests of immigrant workers, or even deliberately allowed the interests of the native-born section of the working class to take precedence. In practice, the much-praised ideology of international solidarity came to nothing. Only a few writers took a more finely-tuned theoretical position.

In the context of the international academic debate on the subject, especially in the 1970s and 1980s, the unpopularity of the class paradigm in the Netherlands is rather odd. At this time, many researchers in other West European countries, such as Great Britain, Germany and France, found their inspiration in Marxism (for overviews, see Solomos, 1986; Kalpaka and Räthzel, 1992). In their own countries, and also outside it, they carried on lively debates about the role of the state, about racism or about the interrelationships between race, ethnicity, gender, class and state. Although, in the early-1970s, some Dutch social scientists showed interest in these debates, most subsequently spurned them. De Jong's (1986) study illustrates this excellently: in his wide-ranging review of theories about interethnic relationships, Marxist theories were completely absent.

Various other researchers went even further: they explicitly and categorically rejected any arguments that tended towards Marxism. Interestingly, the most pronounced criticisms were advanced by academics who already for many years assumed positions of authority in minorities research. The critics were influential researchers who had to an important extent determined the shape of Dutch minorities research, and are still doing so. This fact gives their categorical rejection of Marxist theory extra significance.

For example, van Amersfoort (1982b, pp. 63–6) stated that 'the concept of class is, in general, difficult to use in the analysis of minority situations'. In his inaugural lecture (1987, p. 20) he was, if anything, even more firm: '[...] a Marxist class model [can] not be applied to the situation of immigrants in Western Europe, not even if one is prepared to modify the model drastically'. Van Doorn (1985, p. 80) was scornful about the stratificational and historically materialist reductionism of some theoretical tendencies, which failed to recognize ethnicity and ethnic groups as autonomous phenomena. Entzinger in his inaugural lecture (1987a, p. 9) stated that the adherents of what he called 'the antiracism model' engaged in 'moralizing', and wrongly tended to regard 'class and race differences' as 'of the same order' and as 'the result of [...] exploitation'. Hoppe (1987, p. 11) accused Dutch political science of grossly disregarding the politicizing of ethnicity by, among other things, 'explaining away ethnicity through subsuming it among "more general" social inequalities such as class or socio-economic status'. Penninx (1988a, pp. 40–1) in the 1980s, had – contrary to his views in the 1970s – little time for 'the Marxist approach' because 'in welfare states such as the Netherlands' 'its core concepts are not (or cannot) be accurately defined'. Finally, van Praag (1987, p. 170), referring to Marxist writers, sniffed at the 'tendencies in the British "sociology of race relations" in which people hardly did more than embodying the requirements of the capitalist system'.[5]

The key question is whether these social scientists were (once again) displaying academic provincialism? Or did they really have good academic grounds for consigning all Marxist theory to the dustbin? We demonstrate the ways in which prominent Dutch minorities researchers dismissed Marxist theory, and then assess the reasons for this negative attitude, and how far the stated objections are tenable. Finally, an attempt is made to find an explanation for the absence of Marxist theory in minorities research.

Categorical rejection of Marxism: the arguments

Van Amersfoort (1987, pp. 19–20), in his inaugural lecture, examined the settlement pattern of migrants in Amsterdam and for this purpose checked the practicability of several 'conceptual frames'. One of them was the concept of 'the city as a mirror of fundamental differences'. Pahl (1970), an exponent of this idea, argued in favour of an analysis of the basic conflicts between the haves and the have-nots. Van Amersfoort condemned Pahl on the grounds that he did not explain precisely how these classes had to be operationalized. Perhaps van Amersfoort might have ventured an attempt at this himself, but he chose to repeat his opinion that a 'Marxist class model' was not relevant to the situation in Europe. In a note, he referred the reader to the English edition of his dissertation (1982b, pp. 63–6; see also 1974, pp. 70–2). This contains his criticism of the unidimensionality of the Marxist tradition.

In his view, the adherents of this tradition only recognized 'one valid form of social inequality that divides all people [...] in two categories which assume contradicting positions'. The fundamental criterion for an industrial society is the labour market and, in particular, the ownership of the means of production; all other forms of inequality derive from this. The attempt by Dahrendorf – whom he curiously considered as representative of Marxism – to modify the theory, in part by suggesting that 'all bureaucratic personnel must be reckoned among the ruling class', was in Van Amersfoort's view no improvement. His main objection was that this sharp dichotomy did not do justice to the situation in which minorities find themselves, arguing that on the basis of a variety of criteria, they occupied a position in one or more continuous hierarchies.

He next launched a broadside at the American Marxist writer O. C. Cox. In 1948, Cox essentially saw the relationship between whites and blacks in the southern United States as one of class struggle and characterized 'racial prejudices as a manoeuvre by the white elite to keep poor whites from becoming aware of their real class position'. Cox was convinced that 'the Negroes' class position was the same as that of a section of the white population. Van Amersfoort thought it rather clumsy to regard the existence, and continuation, of differences within a single class as 'fake or unreal, or that they are a trick of the ruling clique'. He concluded: 'They apparently belong to the sort of contrasts that cannot be analysed with the class concept'.

Van Doorn (1985, pp. 76–82) based his judgement on a reference to Marx himself, who (according to Van Doorn) negatively evaluated the signification of nationality and ethnicity. Where a distinction arising from descent and local roots did occur, 'they are "accidental" and are not part of the "real" problem: that of the class society'. Both were crystal clear from Marx's own interpretation of the Irish question. Van Doorn thought that Marx was convinced that the problems in Ireland were economic in nature, and he rejected this reductionism.

According to Entzinger (1984, p. 249; see also 1987b, pp. 5–8), Marxists claimed that the entrepreneurial class took advantage of immigration to destroy the unity of the working class and thus their ability to oppose exploitation. The capitalists gambled on latent racism, and thus divided the immigrants as a sub-proletariat from the native-born proletariat. The interests of the capitalist production system were served by keeping the immigrants in a subordinate, exploited position. In Entzinger's inaugural lecture (1987a, p. 9), this caricature turned up again in a paragraph where he described 'the antiracism model'. He claimed that Marxists treated class and race differences as one, whereas they should in fact be distinguished from each other at an analytical level. He also poured scorn on the determinism in Marxism: 'Ethnic distinctions would be doomed to disappear [...] because these distinctions are overshadowed by class differences'.

Penninx's (1988a, pp. 38–41) rejection of the Marxist approach came in a paragraph about the 'discriminatory point of view', which according to him is one of the seven from which minorities researchers work in the Netherlands. He argued that this 'point of view' is relatively new both in the Netherlands and abroad, and had to an important degree developed in minority circles themselves. This observation prob- ably did not refer to Marxism but only to the theoretical positions involving 'institutional racism' or 'white racism' which Penninx 'for convenience' treated under the same heading. According to Penninx, they are, in fact, all concerned with power and the inequalities of power relationships between groups, and together they make the 'social and political position' of migrants more crucial than the 'ethno-cultural position'. The first comment is certainly true, but still not sufficient reason to consider these approaches as being of equal importance; it is a question of fundamentally different power relationships. And as for the second: Marxists paid particular attention to the dialectical relation- ships between both positions, and would never consider treating these positions as separate phenomena (cf Ng, 1989). Penninx, however, said about the Marxist approach that 'its adherents claim the "black pro- blem" originates in developments in capitalism, and emphasize the special role of the state and of government as the implementer and protector of the interests of capital'. Like van Amersfoort, Penninx maintained that the operationalization of the core concepts of the Marxist approach, such as that of class, is problematic, particularly in the modern welfare state.

Finally, van Praag (1987, pp. 168–73) slipped his criticism into a passage in which he commented on the demand for theory. He was referring to Britain when suggesting that minorities research was still at the stage of 'rival theories of oppression, which appear to be linked to ideological positions'. The basic pattern is a 'classical Marxist structural analysis', which cannot account for all the facts. As to which 'facts', Van Praag did not say. Later, he contrasted the assimilation theory of the German sociologist Esser (1980) with the Marxist tendencies in what he called the 'British sociology of race relations'. He characterized both as 'exploded attempts to form theories' and thus as reductionist. Hence, the Marxists would only regard people as pawns of capitalism.

Comment

Do these arguments, albeit at times perhaps rather briefly summarized, support the rejection of the whole body of Marxist theory? First, a small but still telling point: in his criticism of British Marxism, van Praag categorized the British sociologist Miles as an exponent of the 'sociology of race relations', referring to Miles' book *Racism and Migrant Labour* (1982). Now, if there is one writer who has repeatedly and bitterly inveighed against the sociology of race relations, and has consequently distanced himself from such a characterization, it is Miles. For instance, in the introduction to the book mentioned, Miles emphasized (ibid., pp. 1–6; see also 1984, 1989) with the greatest possible force that ideas like 'race' and 'race relations' have no analytical value.[6] The sociology of race relations is obsessed with 'race', and therefore systematically distorts our comprehension and analysis of the position of migrants, in Miles' view. Evidently, van Praag had not read this crucial passage properly, raising serious doubts about his criticism of the rest of the book. As will become clear, he is not alone in studying this frequently quoted book with too little care.

We will now examine each of the arguments against Marxism in turn. A regularly recurring argument was the unidimensionality of Marxists. They were accused of having a stereotyped vision of society and of reducing all social phenomena to social classes or to their function in economic processes. But is it in fact true that Marxists have reduced ethnic or racial relationships to class relationships, or that they regarded racism as a functional element of the process of economic accumulation? Van Amersfoort saw Cox as representing this tendency, and Entzinger and Van Praag referred to Castles and Kosack (1973) and to Miles. It is certainly the case that Cox, and Castles and Kosack, presented a somewhat reductionist and economic-determinist vision of reality. Cox's *Caste, Class and Race* (1948) is, however, more than 50 years old, and was already in the late-1970s no longer taken seriously in Marxist circles. The occasional references to Cox's early (and not so early) works exposed the one-sidedness and inadequacy of this mechanistic view and rejected it as a product of the time (see, for example, Gabriel and Ben-Tovim, 1978; George, 1984, pp. 139–44; Miles, 1980, and 1982, pp. 81–7; Solomos, 1986, pp. 87–8). Thus, Solomos stated that:

> the model of Marxism with which Cox was familiar was based on the conceptual baggage of "base" and "superstructure" and an instrumental view of the state as the agent of the capitalist class. [...] This adherence to such views runs counter to the main tendency of contemporary Marxist analysis, which in fact has evolved a number of competing schools of thought, and whose central concern is to question the tenability of the classical base-superstructure model as a conceptual framework.

He then referred to Przeworski (1977; see also Wright, 1980), who pointed out that the traditional separation between the economic definition of classes and the political and ideological determinants of class-formation is in fact quite misleading when it comes to the concrete analysis of the contradiction that arises either within or between social classes. Przeworski argued, and here he expressed a view shared by most Marxist writers in the 1980s, that it is not possible 'to separate the "objective" analysis of class from the totality of economic, ideological and political relations which organise, disorganise and reorganise social classes as a result of class struggles and historical transformations'. Solomos concluded that it would be 'quite mistaken' to suppose that modern Marxist writings about races and classes was derived from Cox.

Miles – who, as has already been said, was accused by some Dutch authors of economic determinism – had many times been sharply critical of Cox for his ... economic determinism. He demonstrated that Cox was misinformed and logically inconsistent, when he considered class and race as two specific types of the same phenomenon. Miles (1980, p. 186) said about Cox:

> If that formulation is to be regarded as a work of Marxist scholarship (I tend to the view that it should not), then it is most certainly inadequate but [...] the fault lies not in some inherent aspect of Marxism but in Cox's formulation of the concepts of political class and ethnic system. Herein lies a double challenge to those who believe that, in demolishing Cox's analyses, they have proven that Marxist theory cannot "cope" with race relations and to those Marxists who believe that Cox's analyses constitutes *the* Marxist analysis of an empirical epiphenomenon of the class struggle.

Here, Miles targeted Castles and Kosack who (in 1972) heartily endorsed Cox's 'superb work of Marxist scholarship' (Castles and Kosack, 1972, p. 16).

The most quoted work by Castles and Kosack, *Immigrant Workers and Class Structure in Western Europe*, first published in 1973, concerned the effects of migrant labour and the position of the migrant workers themselves. This classic text attracted praise in (neo-)Marxist circles, at least insofar as (in contrast to more conventional accounts) it made connections between the political, social and ideological demands of capitalism and migrant labour (Cohen 1987, p. 138) and criticized those studies which dealt only with the problems of assimilation of individual migrants (Miles and Satzewich 1990, p. 336). However, this left the most severe criticism untouched. Eleven years after this publication, Castles (with Booth and Wallace, 1984) presented a more balanced view, having seemingly taken into account some of the criticisms of the earlier text. This shift had evidently escaped Entzinger (1987a), who in fact was the only one to mention this more recent book. Like van Praag (1987), he referred to Castles and Kosack in the same breath as Miles, and claimed that they all embraced the discredited and stereotyped Marxist opinions to the same degree.

The failure to differentiate between these writers is remarkable because Miles was one of those who expressed fairly severe criticism of the views of authors like Castles and Kosack. Even more, this criticism led to the development of a whole new perspective in the field. In *Racism and Migrant Labour* (1982; see also Miles and Satzewich, 1990), Miles argues that, like Cox and writers such as Nikolinakos and Sivanandan, Castles and Kosack claim that migrant work fulfilled an economic and sociopolitical function for capitalism, as a fresh reservoir of labour and as a means of dividing the working class. They further located the origin of racism in capitalist expansion only. Miles (ibid., pp. 81–7; pp. 152–3; pp. 165–6; see also 1989), however, rejected the functionalism implicit in this explanation.

In his view, racism did not originate in a conspiracy by capitalists any more than racism was the privilege of the ruling class, or limited to the idea of white supremacy over blacks. In Castles and Kosack's view, working class racism was not an independent phenomenon but only the product of the divide-and-rule policy of the bourgeoisie and its agent, the state. Miles suggested, in contrast, that the ruling class gained no benefit from conflicts within the working class and that neither the capitalists nor the state had an interest in stirring up racism. In his view it was a mistake to look for the origins of racism in the simultaneous growth of capitalism and colonialism. Miles also opposed the assumption that the development of racism had been linear. Racism is a far from homogeneous phenomenon, and anyone who, like Castles and Kosack, maintained that this is the case, ignored the specific character that racism assumes in different situations.

This occurred, Miles continued, because Castles and Kosack applied an economistic definition of class, and took too little account of the influence of current political and ideological relationships on the process of class formation, including the more autonomous role of the state. The result is a rather linear concept of class relationships. Castles and Kosack made it seem as if the working class once formed a homogeneous *bloc* against the bourgeoisie, but that after the immigration of migrant workers it was split in two purely and simply because the natives and the immigrants occupied different economic positions. Miles rejected this view and maintained that the working class was fragmented long before there was any immigration. It should be noted that Miles (as a neo-Marxist), was putting forward precisely the same arguments, plus a few additional ones, to those which Entzinger and van Praag used to fulminate against 'Marxism'. How they had managed to achieve such a negative judgement about the *whole* of Marxist theory, and particularly about Miles, is unclear – especially as they acknowledged Miles (1982) as their source.

A further argument against Marxism was the operationalization of the concept of class (van Amersfoort, 1987; Penninx, 1988a). Definition of classes by objective criteria is always a problem, said Penninx, but on the grounds of subjective ones (class consciousness), it is hardly possible to do so meaningfully, particularly so in modern welfare states. Penninx offered no proof for this statement, or even the beginning of a clarification, but it is possible to suspect 'where the shoe pinches'. Before the coming of the welfare state, things were quite simple. In the nineteenth century – say, in the time of Marx and Engels – it was easy to describe relationships of production. Those who owned the means of production belonged to the entrepreneurial class, and everyone else to the working class. Workers could only generate income in one way, and that was by selling their labour to the entrepreneurs. They, in turn, could generate capital by creaming off the surplus value of the work. The state played no significant role in this process; the little the state did was to protect the interests of capital.

With the rise of the social or Christian democratic welfare state in the course of the twentieth century, this picture changed dramatically. The state began to intervene in the economic, social and political life of its citizens, and in an unprecedented way. It invested on a large scale, redistributed financial resources and provided an income for a substantial part of the population, either by taking them into their service (the state became, in fact, the largest employer), or by subsidizing institutions in whole or in part, or by giving them a straightforward remittance. It instituted numerous measures, influencing not only the process of economic accumulation, but also social and political relationships and the prevailing ideology. Also, or perhaps rather *because*, the state imposed such a powerful stamp on society, and no longer acted just as the agent of capital, the simple nineteenth-century concepts of working class and bourgeoisie were no longer adequate.

If these were the objections to applying Marxism to the minorities issue, they were not in the least convincing, because these were exactly the issues which were being addressed by many Marxists in the 1980s: what is the post-industrial mode of production, how does the process of class formation develop, and what is the role of the state in this? Van Amersfoort (1982b) paraphrased Dahrendorf who maintained that the state bureaucracy is *de facto* part of the ruling class, or in any case acts as the accomplice of capital. His attempt to remove in this way the concept of class, among other things, from its historical context, was considered unsatisfactory in van Amersfoort's eyes. But was Dahrendorf's theory really a good model for modern Marxism? Far from it. This is not to claim that operationalizing presents no problems.[7] But the point here is that Van Amersfoort and Penninx pushed the problem of operational-ization to the forefront, without seriously considering what contempor-ary Marxists had to contribute on the subject.

In conclusion, we can say that the categorical rejection of Marxist theory by Dutch minorities researchers was not based on tenable argu-ments. The critics based their rejection mainly on a few (hopelessly) outdated studies which they wrongly believed were representative of 'the Marxist approach'. Although their criticisms of these studies were justifiable in places, they had little relevance to the overall tendency and even less to neo-Marxist schools of thought. The critics had completely overlooked the fact that Marxists had made more or less the same criticisms; and had overlooked this fact in some cases even after claim-ing to have studied the literature involved. Their judgement therefore said more about their failure to understand the modern literature than about Marxist theory itself.

The political nexus

Why was it that minorities researchers in the Netherlands had been so little inspired by theory, and above all wanted to have so little to do with Marxist theory? The answer lies in the tradition of Dutch social science research which is embedded in the way in which the nation-state has developed. Historically, the Netherlands became a society in which religion and philosophies of life were the most important social deter-minants, and in which the struggle for resources took the form of a struggle between social groupings which emerged on this basis. These social groupings constituted 'pillars': more or less closed communities within which all social life–from the cradle to the grave – took place (Lijphart, 1975; van Schendelen, 1984). Each group had its own institutions, from hospitals, daily and weekly newspapers, broadcasting systems, schools, universities, sporting clubs, to (trade)unions and political parties. There was very little social interaction between them, with the exception of those at the top who took responsibility for the accommodation that occurred between pillars. Political leaders consulted and debated amongst themselves, settled possible conflicts and looked after the interests of their pillar well, thereby taking account of the feelings of other pillars and ensuring that each would get an equal slice of the pie. In the developing welfare-state the 'pillarized' organizations were closely involved with the formation and implementation of government policy and, not least, with the distribution of social goods and services to citizens – an activity which sanctioned their *raison d'être*. These activities were not only firmly anchored in social and political practice, but also in rules and regulations. This system contributed to social stability in a society that was otherwise marked by sharp cleavages between the various religions and philosophies of life.

Within this system, it was common practice not to make a 'hot issue' of something: sensitive subjects were usually resolved by a technocratic compromise. In that process, experts had acquired a dominant, if instrumental, role. Hence a type of social science research had arisen with strong politically-directed traits, and a type of researcher who saw their task primarily as one of 'service to the community'. Academic work tended to conform to the political theory which was agreeable to the state and to the political parties (Gastelaars, 1985). To paraphrase the criminologist Fijnaut (1990, p. 269), researchers allowed themselves to be 'intellectually domesticated'. These circumstances, occurring in a society in which religious and philosophical divisions blurred class divisions, seemed not to offer a favourable culture for the sustained development of an academic tendency based on Marxism.[8]

This is precisely what happened in the case of minorities research. As has already been noted, it only really mushroomed after the state had developed their own minorities policy. In the mid-1970s, the Minister of Culture, Recreation and Social Work (CRM) – the main promoter of the minorities policy – came to the conclusion that providing welfare to guestworkers and fellow citizens from former colonial territories would not really alleviate their problems with regard to employment, housing, education or legal security. Other ministries had to assume their responsibilities and address the issue as well. However, the others remained to be convinced that this was really necessary for people who – in their view – would anyway return to their homelands.

The Ministry of CRM then embarked on a kind of missionary project in order to persuade the other ministries to take on board the new paradigm, that guestworkers and fellow citizens actually constituted ethnic minorities on whose behalf a coherent 'ethnic minorities policy' should be developed. At the time, van Amersfoort's dissertation (1974; 1982) was circulated widely within the ministry, and one of its then public officials, Entzinger (1975), published a paper in which he pleaded for a minorities policy to 'avoid the formation of minorities groups as described by van Amersfoort'. By 1976, public officials of the Ministry of CRM had called on the services of academic researchers, whose reports showed the gravity of the situation. Their activities gained offic- ial status in 1978, when the Minister set up the Advisory Commission for Research into Minorities (ACOM) with minorities researchers such as van Amersfoort, Bovenkerk, Ellemers, Entzinger, Köbben, Penninx and van Praag among its leading members. The main task of the Commis- sion was now to advise the government with regard to its research programme on ethnic minorities. Its very first advice turned out to be particularly influential (ACOM, 1979). ACOM presented its view on the situation, including a definition of 'ethnic minorities', a description of the social groups that were deemed qualified for this label, and the kind of processes within which they were supposedly embedded. The theore- tical basis for this advice was, once again, van Amersfoort's dissertation (1974; 1982), thus highlighting the congruity of state and social science research.

Particularly in the late 1970s and 1980s, the time when the ethnic minorities policy was still 'under construction', the *communis opinio* among leading politicians was that immigration and the incorporation of immigrants was too sensitive to make a 'hot issue' of it. So they reverted to the traditional ploy; resolving the issue by developing a technocratic compromise, in the process of which social scientific researchers acquired a dominant role. For a long time, the majority of sponsored researchers, and remarkably also independent researchers – all mostly natives[9] – had unhesitatingly put their academic work at the service of the minorities policy (which was supported by all political parties), thereby taking the advisory reports of ACOM as the starting point for their research (Rath, 1990, p. 227; 1991; 1993; 1997; see also Penninx 1988b, pp. 34–44). In this process, they were able to exert considerable influence on the formation of state policy (Penninx, 1988b).

This congruity of state and social science research was enhanced by the continuous exchange of personnel: researchers were appointed as public officials, and public officials became researchers. It was, more- over, visible in the researchers' choice of one specific paradigm, the ethnicity paradigm, the bases of which display an interesting parallel with that of the minorities policy. Bovenkerk (1984, p. 35) rightly says that the development of political–economic theory on guestworkers in the Netherlands was quite suddenly interrupted, precisely at the moment that the state incorporated researchers into the bureaucratic apparatus and initiated wide-scale funding for 'politically relevant' research. Penninx (1988a, p. 249), in his popular review of minorities research, cautiously suggests – even burying the remark in a footnote – that the absence of 'the Marxist analytical model' in the Netherlands 'probably' 'in part' is connected with the strong domination of policy-linked research in areas involving minorities.

Conclusions

So-called 'ethnic minorities studies' are an active sector of social science in the Netherlands. Despite great productivity in terms of volume, however, theoretical sophistication has been rather lacking. As the Dutch sociologist Van Doorn (1985, p. 75) puts it, the problem is 'academic provincialism'. Especially in the 1980s, minorities researchers mainly worked within the ethnicity paradigm, ignoring, and even rejecting, the Marxist class paradigm. Comparing this situation to that in countries such as France or Britain, it seems rather odd. In this chapter, it is shown how prominent Dutch researchers 'disposed' of Marxist theory, while showing extremely little knowledge about it. In their view, Marxist theory would only offer stereotyped and economistic explanations for social phenomena, is built on a simplistic division between two sharply distinguished social classes, sees racism as the product of the ruling class who use it to undermine the position of the working class, ignores ethnic loyalties (or at best makes them subordinate to class loyalties), regards the state as the agent of capital, and so on. Adherents of Marxist theory would, in addition, abjure empirical work and work primarily ideologically. Critics of Marxist theory based their rejection entirely on a limited number of rather outdated studies, particularly those of Cox (1948) and Castles and Kosack (1973) which they wrongly believed to be representative of the whole of Marxist theory. In this way, they presented a rather static and one-dimensional view of a theoretical tendency which has, in contrast, displayed a high degree of dynamism and acceptance of new insights – for example, those derived from semiotics – and which currently stands for a multiplicity of different, and sometimes mutually competing, schools of thought.

The lack of interest among minorities researchers in Marxist theory is not an isolated phenomenon. It is connected to the specific nature of Dutch social science, which is highly oriented to the prevailing political climate and to policymaking, and in which the state has a remarkable amount of influence. That minorities research has not looked seriously into what the latest Marxist literature has to offer is hardly scholarly, and casts some doubt on the quality of the social sciences in the Netherlands.

Moreover, ignorance of this research genre has practical implications. Precisely because of the close connection between policy-making and social science, researchers have contributed to a political climate in which ethno-cultural processes have been heavily overstated while political and economic processes have been underplayed. It is obvious that symbiosis has paved the way to specific kinds of policy measures that do not necessarily address the issues adequately.

This state of affairs is even more regrettable since neo-Marxist literature offers (non-reductionist) insights into the relation of the subject to its social environment; into the formation of identities and societies; into processes of social division; into the role of the state; into ideologies such as racism; and into the interrelationships between race, ethnicity, gender, class and state. These are, in fact, precisely those areas which concern researchers into post-migration processes. We would propose that researchers draw up a detailed agenda/programme based on modern (and postmodern) variants of Marxist theory; focusing, for example, on the ways in which, at specific historical junctures and within specific social contexts, certain groups of people – whether migrants or natives – have been ideologically problematized and excluded from certain resources (cf Bovenkerk, Miles and Verbunt, 1991). In view of the tendency of many Dutch social scientists to form a symbiotic relationship with the state, such a programme should also allow scope for research into the role of the social sciences in these processes.

Notes

1   This includes books as well as journal articles and edited volumes. In fact, the library of the Leiden Institute for Social Research (LISWO), which since 1992 has absorbed the library of the former Advisory Commission for Research into Minorities (ACOM), at this moment possesses no less than 11 000 titles, including a number of policy documents and MA dissertations.
2   For an elaboration of this view, see Penninx (1989).
3   This is, for example, the case in the work of Choenni (1997) who – instead of drawing on theoretical insights from economics or economic sociology –

sought refuge in culturalist notions and in van Amersfoort's thesis (1982) on the formation of ethnic minority groups.

4   In the *Nesbic Bulletin* in 1971, Heemskerk discussed the extent to which guest workers were a consequence of inequalities in economic development. In the centres of capitalism they made up a reserve army of labour, completely at the service of the bourgeoisie which only used their productive power. The bourgeoisie paved the way for racism and other 'false doctrines' by exaggerating the differences between groups of workers. All in all, guest workers led to a considerable weakening of the working class. These kinds of argument are also found in the *Sunschrift* by Lucassen *et al.* (1974; see also Lucassen, Penninx and Zwinkels, 1973a, 1973b and 1973c), and by Penninx and Van Velzen (1977), in a thesis by Marshall-Goldschvartz (1974), the *Ars Aequi* special issue on 'Gastarbeiders à la Carte' by Brummelhuis *et al.* (1975), the *Studium Generale* articles by Feddema (1979) and Nieuwstadt (1979), in Carchedi (1979) and to some degree in Theunis (1979) and Van Twist (1977). The position of the classical interest group of the working class, the trades union, is the subject of studies by Van de Velde and Van Velzen (1978), Feddema (1984) and De Jong, Van der Laan and Rath (1984), the last work also inclining towards the ethnicity paradigm. Other researchers describe the proletarian status of 'foreign workers' (Bovenkerk, 1985) or 'minorities' (Ellemers, 1978) using it to underline the historical similarities between these categories and native-born workers. Köbben and Godschalk (1985) emphasize the ethnic differentiation of this working class, while Gowricharn (1987) particularly refers to class differences within the immigrant population. Bader (1985) and Hira (1985) discuss the connection between racism and capitalism. Hisschemöller (1985; 1988b) sets out the relationships between internationalism, nationalism, the antiracist struggle and class solidarity, and criticizes the way in which 'classical' Marxist theorists approach the phenomenon of racism. De Boer (1982) describes and analyses state intervention and the role of immigrant interest groups. Among more recent works are Bovenkerk (1984; 1989; see also Bovenkerk, Miles and Verbunt, 1990 and 1991), Rath (1990; 1991a; 1991b and 1993) and Schuster (1992) who concentrate on the role of the state and on its role in the construction of problem groups. They condemn the orthodox economic analyses in which the state is exclusively portrayed as buttressing capital.

5   There were other criticisms. Strijbosch (1992, p. 37) stated that 'many Marxists and neo-Marxists have a sense of superiority', while Junger (1992, p. 335) saw the expansion of neo-Marxist views as a 'danger'. Both, however, made these suggestions without further explanation.

6   Whether this is really so, is in any case a moot point in British social sciences. Marxist-oriented researchers such as Anthias, Gilroy and Solomos do indeed hold that 'race' is a social construct, but believe that this concept – because of the significance that people give to it in daily life – does have a certain value for analysis.

7   The conceptual problem is by no means unique. What should one think of such concepts as 'ethnic groups (or groupings)', 'ethnic minorities' or 'integration'? Van Amersfoort (1990, p. 263) comments on this in another article, but did not in this case go so far as to reject completely his theoretical approach.

8 The distinguished Dutch sociologist Goudsblom (1967, p. 63) made a similar
point. In a later article he accuses Marxist sociologists of scholasticism, and
suggests that they have a strong tendency towards preaching and denunci-
ation (1974, pp. 83–4).
9 The share of immigrant/minority researchers is gradually increasing. It
remains to be seen whether this will make a difference in the matter discussed
here, as most have adopted the dominant paradigm.

References

ACOM (Adviescommissie Onderzoek Minderheden) (1979) *Advies Onderzoek
Minderheden*, The Hague, State Publishing Office.
van Amersfoort, J. M. M. (1974) *Immigratie en Minderheidsvorming. Een Analyse van
de Nederlandse Situatie 1945–1973*, Alphen aan den Rijn, Samsom.
van Amersfoort, J. M. M. (1982a) Immigrant en samenleving. Een terreinverken-
ning, in J. M. M. van Amersfoort and H. B. Entzinger (eds), *Immigrant en
Samenleving*, Book issue, Mens en Maatschappij 57, Deventer, Van Loghum
Slaterus, pp. 7–19.
van Amersfoort, H. (1982b) *Immigration and the Formation of Minority Groups: the
Dutch Experience 1945–1975*, Cambridge, Cambridge University Press.
van Amersfoort, H. (1983) Migratie-onderzoek, overheidsfinanciering en beleid.
Aantekeningen van een participant, *Grafiet*, 4, pp. 130–54.
van Amersfoort, J. M. M. (1987). *Etnische Woonpatronen. Vier Benaderingen van
Woonsegregatie Toegepast op Amsterdam*, inaugural lecture, Amsterdamse Sociaal-
Geografische Studies 8, Amsterdam, University of Amsterdam, Institute of
Social Geography.
van Amersfoort, J. M. M. (1990) Leve het positivisme!, in F. Bovenkerk, F. Buijs
and H. Tromp(eds.), *Wetenschap en Partijdigheid: Opstellen voor André J. F. Köbben*,
Assen/Maastricht, Van Gorcum, pp. 255–66.
van Amersfoort, J. M. M. (1991) Van gerepatrieerdenzorg tot allochtonenbeleid.
Wetenschap en beleid met betrekking tot immigranten in Nederland, *Socio-
logische Gids*, 38(1), January/February, pp. 24–36.
Bader, V. M. (1985) Nieuw racisme of neonationalisme?, *Komma*, 5(1), March,
pp. 109–43.
Boer, A. de (1982) Over de positie van buitenlandse arbeid(st)ers in Nederland,
Komma, 3(2), September, pp. 33–63.
Borghuis, M. G. M. (ed.) (1988) *Etnische Minderheden in Nederland: Een Geselecteerde
Bibliografie van Sociaal-Wetenschappelijke Publikaties 1945–1986*, Muiderberg,
Coutinho.
Bovenkerk, F. (1984) Rassen of klassen? De politieke economie van de gastarbeid,
Intermediair, 20(47), 23 November, pp. 35–41.
Bovenkerk, F. (1985) Over een oud en een nieuw immigranten-proletariaat, *De
Gids*, 148(3–4), May, pp. 271–8.
Bovenkerk, F. (1989) *Er zijn Grenzen*, inaugural lecture, Arnhem, Gouda
Quint.
Bovenkerk, F., Miles, M. and Verbunt, G. (1990) Racism, Migration and the state
in Western Europe: a Case for Comparative Analysis, *International Sociology*,
5(4), December, pp. 475–90.

Bovenkerk, F., Miles M. and Verbunt G. (1991) Comparative studies of migration and racism in Western Europe: A critical appraisal, *International Migration Review*, 25(2), Summer, pp. 375–91.

Brummelhuis, J., Cassé, P. Eppings, F. *et al.* (1975) *Gastarbeiders à la Carte: De Gaarkeuken van de Nederlandse Overheid*, Maarsen, Ars Aequi Libri.

Carchedi, G. (1979) Authority and foreign labour: Some notes on a late capitalist form of capital accumulation and state intervention, *Studies in Political Economy*, 2, pp. 37–74.

Castles, S., Booth, H. and Wallace, T. (1984) *Here for Good: Western Europe's New Ethnic Minorities*, London, Pluto Press.

Castles, S. and Kosack, G. (1972) The Function of Labour Immigration in Western European Capitalism, *New Left Review*, 73, May–June, pp. 3–21.

Castles, S. and Kosack, G. (1973) *Immigrant Workers and Class Structure in Western Europe*, London, Oxford University Press.

Choenni, A. (1997) *Veelsoortig Assortiment: Allochtoon Ondernemerschap in Amsterdam als Incorporatietraject 1965–1995*, PhD dissertation, University of Amsterdam.

Cohen, R. (1987) *The New Helots: Migrants in the International Division of Labour*, Aldershot, Gower.

Cox, O. C. (1959) *Caste, Class, and Race: a Study in Social Dynamics*, New York, Monthly Review Press (first published, 1948).

van Doorn, J. A. A. (1985) Het miskende pluralisme: Een herformulering van het minderhedenvraagstuk, in G. G. Cain, *et al.*, *Etnische Minderheden. Wetenschap en Beleid*, Meppel, Boom, pp. 67–96.

Ellemers, J. E. (1978) Minderheden en beleid in Nederland: De opkomst van een 'nieuw proletariaat', *Intermediair*, 14(13), 31 March, pp. 1–7, 55, 59.

Ellemers, J. E. and Borghuis, M. G. B. (1988) 'Inleiding bij de bibliografie', in M. G. M. Borghuis (ed.), *Etnische Minderheden in Nederland: Een Geselecteerde Bibliografie van Sociaal-Wetenschappelijke Publikaties 1945–1986*, Muiderberg, Coutinho, pp. 7–12.

Entzinger, H. B. (1975) Nederland immigratieland? Enkele overwegingen bij het overheidsbeleid inzake allochtone minderheden, *Beleid en Maatschappij*, 2(12), pp. 326–36.

Entzinger, H. B. (1984) *Het Minderhedenbeleid: Dilemma's voor de Overheid in Nederland en Zes Andere Immigratielanden in Europa*, Meppel, Boom.

Entzinger, H. B. (1987a) Een kleine wereld, *Migrantenstudies*, 3(4), pp. 2–20.

Entzinger, H. B. (1987b) Race, Class and the Shaping of a Policy for Immigrants: the Case of the Netherlands, *International Migration*, 25(1), March, pp. 5–20.

Esser, H. (1980) *Aspekte der Wanderungssoziologie. Assimilation und Integration von Wanderern, Ethnische Gruppen und Minderheiten: Eine Handlungstheoretische Analyse*, Darmstadt/Neuwied, Luchterhand.

Feddema, R. (1979) De organisatie van de ontwikkeling in de thuisregio, in M. van Nieuwstadt *et al.*, *Gastarbeid*, Eindhoven, Technische Hogeschool Eindhoven, Studium Generale, pp. 31–40.

Feddema, R. (1984) De buitenlandse arbeider en de vakbond in de tang, *Dunk*, 2, Summer, pp. 17–26.

Fijnaut, C. (1990) Ideologie en misdaad in de justitiële beleidsplannen, *Tijdschrift voor Criminologie*, Special Issue 'Justitieel beleid in beweging', 32(4), pp. 268–77.

Gabriel, J. and Ben-Tovim, G. (1978) Marxism and the Concept of Racism, *Economy and Society*, 7(2), May, pp. 118–54.

Gastelaars, M. (1985) *Een Geregeld Leven: Sociologie en Sociale Politiek in Nederland 1925–1968*, Amsterdam, Sua.

Gelling, M., de Jong, G. and Schoemaker, E. (1990) Minderhedenbeleid, wetenschap en politiek: Over de verhouding van wetenschap en politiek bij de totstandkoming van het minderhedenbeleid in Nederland, *WO Nieuwsnet*, Special Issue, 'Sociaal-culturele wetenschappen: Wetenschappelijke essays', pp. 5–26.

George, H. Jr. (1984) *American Race Relations Theory: a Review of Four Models*, Lanham, University Press of America.

Goudsblom, J. (1967) *Dutch Society*, New York, Random House.

Goudsblom, J. (1974) *Balans van de Sociologie*, Utrecht/Antwerp, Het Spectrum.

Gowricharn, R. (1987) *Migranten en het Arbeidsvraagstuk in Rotterdam*, Stafrapport No. 3. Rotterdam, Stichting KROSBE.

Heemskerk, C. (1971) De (gast)arbeid, *NESBIC Bulletin*, 6(10–11), October/November, pp. 1–144.

Hira, S. (1985) *Racisme en Fascisme: Ontstaan en Bestrijding*, Weesp, Wereldvenster.

Hisschemöller, M. (1985) Oude tradities en nieuwe obstakels: over nationaal antifascisme en nieuw antiracisme, *Komma*, 5(1), March, pp. 85–108.

Hisschemöller, M. (1988) Ras, klasse en natie, in M. Hisschemöller (ed.), *Een Bleek Bolwerk: Racisme en Politieke Strategie*, Amsterdam, Pegasus, pp. 27–42.

Hoppe, R. (ed.) (1987) *Etniciteit, Politiek en Beleid in Nederland*, Politikologische Studies VU 5, Amsterdam, Free University Press.

de Jong, W. (1986) *Inter-Etnische Verhoudingen in een Oude Stadswijk*, Delft, Eburon.

de Jongh, R., van der Laan, M. and Rath, J. (1984) *FNV'ers aan het Woord over Buitenlandse Werknemers*, Issue No. 16, Leiden, University of Leiden, Centre for the Study of Social Conflicts (COMT).

Jongkind, F. (1992) Ethnic Identity, sSocietal Integration and Migrants' Alienation in Sstate-Policy and Academic Research in the Netherlands, *Ethnic and Racial Studies*, 15(3), July, pp. 365–80.

Junger, M. (1992) Review of Jan Rath, Minorisering: de sociale constructie van 'etnische minderheden', *Mens en Maatschappij*, 67(3), August, pp. 334–35.

Kalpaka, A. and Räthzel, N. (eds) (1992) *Rassismus und Migration in Europa*, Beitrage des Kongresses 'Migration und Rassismus in Europa', Hamburg, 26–30, September 1990, Argument-Sonderband AS 201, Hamburg/Berlin, Argument Verlag.

Köbben, A. J. F. (1980) Het heilig vuur. Moeilijkheden en mogelijkheden bij onderzoek inzake minderheden, *Intermediair*, 16(49), 5 December, pp. 1–7.

Köbben, A. J. F. and Godschalk, J. J. (1985) *Een Tweedeling van de Samenleving?* OSA-Voorstudie no.10, Leiden, University of Leiden, Centre for the Study of Social Conflicts (COMT).

Lijphart, A. (1975) *The Politics of Accommodation: Pluralism and Democracy in the Netherlands* (2nd edn 1968), Berkeley, California, University of California Press.

Lucassen, J., Penninx, R. and Zwinkels, A. (1973a) Trekarbeid van Middellandse Zeegebieden naar West-Europa: Een bibliografisch overzicht I, *Kroniek van Afrika*, 13(1), pp. 12–38.

Lucassen, J., Penninx, R. and Zwinkels, A. (1973b) Trekarbeid van Middellandse Zeegebieden naar West-Europa: Een bibliografisch overzicht II, *Kroniek van Afrika*, 13(2), pp. 85–118.

Lucassen, J., Penninx, R. and Zwinkels, A. (1973c) Trekarbeid van Middellandse Zeegebieden naar West-Europa: Een bibliografisch overzicht III, *Kroniek van Afrika*, 13(3), pp. 190–235.

Lucassen, J., Penninx, R. van Velzen, L. and Zwinkels, A. (1974) *Trekarbeid. Van de Middellandse Zeegebieden naar West-Europa: Een Bibliografisch Overzicht*, Sunschrift 84, Nijmegen, Socialistische Uitgeverij Nijmegen (SUN).

Marshall-Goldschvartz, A. J. (1973) *The Import of Labour: the Case of the Netherlands*, Rotterdam, University Press Rotterdam.

Miles, R. (1980) Class, race and ethnicity. A Critique of Cox's Theory, *Ethnic and Racial Studies*, 3(2), April, pp. 169–87.

Miles, R. (1982) *Racism and Migrant Labour*, London, Routledge & Kegan Paul.

Miles, R. (1984) Marxism Versus the Sociology of 'race relations', *Ethnic and Racial Studies*, 7(2), April, pp. 217–37.

Miles, R. (1989) *Racism*, London, Routledge.

Miles, R. and Phizacklea, A. (1984) *White Man's Country: Racism in British Politics*, London/Sydney, Pluto Press.

Miles, R. and Satzewich, V. (1990) Migration, Racism and 'Postmodern' Capitalism, *Economy and Society*, 19(3), August, pp. 334–58.

Monsma, G. (1987) *Programmering in de Praktijk: Een Reconstructie-Onderzoek naar Researchprogramma's in het Minderhedenonderzoek in Nederland*, SCO-Rapport No.97, Amsterdam, University of Amsterdam, Centre for Educational Research (SCO).

Ng, R. (1989) Sexism, Racism and Canadian Nationalism, *Socialist Studies/Etudes Socialistes*, A Canadian annual, 'Race, class, gender. Bonds and barriers', 5, pp. 10–25.

van Nieuwstadt, M. (1979) Achtergronden en oorzaken van de gastarbeid, in M. van Nieuwstadt *et al.*, *Gastarbeid*, Eindhoven, Technische Hogeschool Eindhoven, Studium Generale, pp. 3–10.

Omi, M. and Winant, H. (1986) *Racial Formation in the United States: From the 1960s to the 1980s*, New York, Routledge & Kegan Paul.

Pahl, R. (1970) *Whose City?*, London, Longman.

Penninx, R. (1988a) *Minderheidsvorming en Emancipatie: Balans van Kennisverwerving ten aanzien van Immigranten en Woonwagenbewoners*, Alphen aan den Rijn, Samsom.

Penninx, R. (1988b) *Wie Betaalt, Bepaalt? De Ontwikkeling en Programmering van Onderzoek naar Migranten, Etnische Minderheden en Woonwagenbewoners, 1955–1985, met Speciale Aandacht voor de Rol van de Overheid*, Amsterdamse Sociaal-Geografische Studies 13, Amsterdam, University of Amsterdam, Institute of Social Geography.

Penninx, R. (1989) Ethnic groups in the Netherlands: Emancipation or Minority Group-Formation?, *Ethnic and Racial Studies*, 12(1), January, pp. 84–99.

Penninx, R. and van Velzen, L. (1977) *Internationale Arbeidsmigratie: Uitstoting uit 'Thuislanden' en Maatschappelijke Integratie in 'Gastlanden' van Buitenlandse Arbeiders*, Sunschrift 124, Nijmegen, Socialistische Uitgeverij Nijmegen (SUN).

Praag, C. S. van (1987) Onderzoek naar etnische minderheden in Nederland, *Sociologische Gids*, 34(3), May/June, pp. 159–75.

Przeworski, A. (1977) Proletariat into Class: the Process of Class Formation from Karl Kautsky's 'The class struggle' to Recent Controversies, *Politics and Society*, 7(4), pp. 343–401.

Rath, J. (1990) De overheid en het 'minderhedenonderzoek', in F. Bovenkerk, F. Buijs and H. Tromp(eds.), *Wetenschap en Partijdigheid: Opstellen voor André J. F. Köbben*, Assen/Maastricht, Van Gorcum, pp. 225–40.

Rath, J. (1991) *Minorisering: De Sociale Constructie van 'Etnische Minderheden'*, Amsterdam, Sua.

Rath, J. (1993) La construction sociale des minorités ethniques aux Pays-Bas et ses effets pervers, in M. Martiniello and M. Poncelet (eds.), *Migrations et Minorités Ethniques dans l'Espace Européen*, Bruxelles, De Boeck, pp. 17–41.

Rath, J. (1997) Das strenge Gesicht von Frau Antje: Die andere Seite des nieder-ländischen Modells für die Integration ethnischer Minderheiten, *Neue Praxis*, 26(6), December, pp. 479–94.

Rath, J. and Kloosterman, R. (2000) Outsiders Business: a Critical Review of Research on Immigrant Entrepreneurship in The Netherlands, *International Migration Review*, 34(3), Fall, 657–60.

van Schendelen, M. P. C. M. (ed.) (1984) Consociationalism, Pillarization and Conflict-Management in the Low Countries, *Acta Politica* (Special Issue), XIX January, pp. 1–178.

Schuster, J. (1992) The State and Post-War Immigration into the Netherlands: the Racialisation and Assimilation of Indonesian Dutch, *European Journal of Inter-cultural Studies*, 3(1), pp. 47–58.

Shadid, W. A. R. and van Koningsveld, P. S. (1986) Minderheden in de gezond-heidszorg. Evaluatie van recent onderzoek, *Migrantenstudies*, 2(4), pp. 54–63.

Solomos, J. (1986) Varieties of Marxist conceptions of 'race', Class and the State: a Critical Analysis, in J. Rex and D. Mason (eds.), *Theories of Race and Ethnic Relations*, Cambridge, Cambridge University Press, pp. 84–109.

Strijbosch, F. (1992) Hoe heilloos is nu eigenlijk minorisering, *Migrantenstudies*, 8(3), pp. 34–43.

Theunis, S. (1979) *Ze Zien Liever Mijn Handen Dan Mijn Gezicht: Buitenlandse Arbeiders in Ons Land*, Baarn, Wereldvenster.

Tinnemans, W. (1991) Minderhedenonderzoek. Meer politiek dan wetenschap, *Intermediair*, 27(13), 29 March, pp. 45–53.

van Twist, K. (1977) *Gastarbeid Ongewenst: De Gevestigde Organisaties en Buiten-landse Arbeiders in Nederland*, Baarn, In den Toren.

van de Velde, B. and van Velzen, J. (1978) De Nederlandse vakbonden, interna-tionale solidariteit en buitenlandse werknemers. Ideologie en werkelijkheid, in F. Bovenkerk (ed.), *Omdat Zij Anders Zijn: Patronen van Rasdiscriminatie in Neder-land*, Meppel/Amsterdam, Boom, pp. 166–88.

Waardenburg, J. D. J. (1986) Iets over onderzoek betreffende de islam bij etnische minderheden, *Migrantenstudies*, 2(1), pp. 39–48.

Wright, E. O. (1980) Varieties of Marxist Conceptions of Class Structure, *Politics and Society*, 9(3), pp. 323–70.

8

Is There a Belgian School of Ethnic and Migration Studies?[1]

Marco Martiniello and Hassan Bousetta

Introduction

In Belgium, as in many other European countries, migration and the social problems allegedly generated by this process have in recent years gained an increasingly high profile in media and political debates. Social questions linked to asylum, immigration, interethnic relations and so on, have undoubtedly assumed a higher profile within the public consciousness. Significantly, this process has tended to associate '(im)migration' with 'social problems'. In the last couple of years, Belgium has been faced with several cases which gave rise to passionate public debates and controversies on matters related to migration processes – either 'upstream' involving the movement of people or 'downstream' with issues linked to the management of multi-ethnic and multicultural relations.

Among these debates was the Semira Adamu case, in September 1998. This related to a young Nigerian refugee, who died from suffocation while she was being brutally expelled from Belgian territory by the police. Among the consequences of this dramatic event was the resignation of the federal Minister of the Interior. The Semira Adamu case also helped to bring to light the practical consequences of the very restrictive refugee policy implemented by Belgium, and more generally by most European Union member states. At the same time, it gave a wider media presence to the mobilization of undocumented migrants, who organized several politically motivated acts such as hunger-strikes and the occupation of churches.

A few months earlier, in November 1997, urban violence broke out again in Brussels; a significant number of youngsters of foreign descent were involved. As happened in the early 1990s, an impressive volume of press coverage was devoted to the issue (Martiniello, 1991; Rea and Brion, 1992). All these developments, and the public debates surrounding them, seriously perturbed the country's political elite. In many ways this is not surprising given that support for racist political parties of the extreme right (especially in Flanders and Brussels) had, since 1987, made significant strides.

To say that debates about migration, in the public and political spheres, are highly contentious is a gross understatement. In fact, since the early 1980s, this social phenomenon has become the focal point for passionate debates and controversies on a regular basis. The fear of an 'invasion' of Europe by cohorts of poor people has been propagated, while the issue of the co-existence between nationals and migrant communities has become increasingly interpreted in terms of social tensions and problems (criminality, drugs, unemployment, school drop-out, insecurity, etc.) In these circumstances, social scientists find themselves caught in a very difficult position, even more so if they interpret their role as elaborating and developing a body of 'objective' knowledge, free from passions and fears. Their work in effect runs the risk of unwittingly reinforcing the excessive dramatization surrounding migratory phenomena. Even when they assign themselves precisely the opposite goal, they are not always immune from distorted interpretations of their work within the public sphere.[2] This ambiguity, linked to the social and political use of academic knowledge, has not, however, during the course of the last 15 years, precluded researchers from being highly prolific.

The large-scale development of sociological research on migration and ethnic relations in Belgium, and in continental Western Europe,[3] is in fact a recent phenomenon, essentially starting in the early 1980s. The expansion of social science research, and the sociopolitical dramatization of this topic, are processes which actually began almost at the same juncture. Before that, the study of migration was almost exclusively the province of economists and demographers. Traditionally, migration is a key area of study for the discipline of demography. As far as economics is concerned, the discipline has quite logically developed an interest in this field. Until the oil crisis of 1973, the economic aspect of migration was actually assumed to be the most obvious – and most – 'natural', dimension of the process, usually being portrayed in terms of movements of the labour force (Castles and Kosack, 1973; Martiniello, 1992a).

The objective of this chapter is not to present a definitive, state-of-the-art portrayal of the sociology of migration and ethnic relations, something which would consist of yet another literature review. This work has already been done several times, and has given rise to many publications in different countries.[4] In Belgium, there are a myriad of publications which give an idea of the development of the Belgian sociology of migration and ethnic relations. Others try at the same time to provide an assessment of it (Martens, 1972; Campioli, 1975; Sybidi, 1985; Brion and Rea, 1990; Martiniello, 1992a; Sybidi, 1993[5]). Instead of repeating what has already been said, it seems more fruitful in this context to articulate a number of arguments which aim to lay the groundwork for a sociology of the sociology of migration and ethnic relations, and which shed light on the problems and difficulties facing the constitution of this particular field of knowledge. In other words, the objective is to establish a broad, qualitative assessment of social science research in the field and to present a number of reflections which may ultimately explain its current state.

Three further introductory remarks

First, even though a locus of debate between social scientists interested in migration and ethnic relations has slowly emerged as the volume of research has increased, it is hard to talk of a sociology of migration and ethnic relations as a firm and coherent theoretical corpus. In other words, this field of research has not yet reached the status of a branch of sociology in its own right. It can hardly pretend to compete academically with more established branches of sociology, largely because of its major theoretical weakness: its theoretical fragmentation.

Secondly, the sociology of migration and ethnic relations has for a long time been marginalized in academic circles and universities. As already underlined in France by Sayad (1984) and Lorenzo (1989), it has long been an undervalued field of research. As a consequence, it has remained unattractive for academic researchers.[6] In France, as in many other European countries – and we should add here that the influence of the French intellectual tradition in French-speaking Belgium is usually very significant – the leading figures of sociology were until very recently not interested in these phenomena. When they did show an interest, they did it in a way which was once characterized by Lorenzo as marginal, periodic and brief (Lorenzo, 1989).

This situation has evolved significantly in the course of the 1990s. The French intellectual tradition, which had hitherto developed independently from that of the American and British, entered the international debate with substantial contributions to the study of nationalism (Balibar and Wallerstein, 1997), racism (Wievorka, 1991; 1992; 1993; 1998), ethnicity (Wievorka, 1993; Taguieff, 1994; Tribalat, 1996), and citizenship (Schnapper, 1991; 1994; Withol de Wenden, 1988). Although theoretical divergence within the French field concerning the relevance of ethnicity as a mobilizing social and political force – which is, in other words, close to disagreement on the integrative function of the French assimilatory citizenship – remains important, a form of de-compartmentation and de-marginalization is undoubtedly at work. From either analytical angle, migration has become a key issue in the social analysis of contemporary France, and the same holds true for Belgium and other continental West European countries.

In terms of education, if French universities and high schools provide postgraduate training opportunities and several curricula linked to migration research, this is absolutely not the case in Belgium. Indeed, the teaching of the sociology of migration in Belgian universities is almost non-existent. In the early 1990s, the State University of Liège was one of very few universities to provide a course entitled 'sociology of migration processes and ethnic relations' in the final year of the sociology curriculum. Several other universities have followed this path but with important restrictions. Indeed, the opening up of university curricula to this discipline remains dependent on the availability of an academic expertise in this field. In Belgium, academic experts exclusively specializing in the field of migration and ethnic relations are not numerous. Moreover, this theme has been overlooked and treated contemptuously for too long. Therefore, it is usually introduced as secondary subject-matter within mainstream sociological disciplines, representing at best one topic in courses on sociological methods, urban sociology, education sociology, electoral analysis, and so on.

In the main, then, research and teaching in this field have for a long time remained poorly valued. As a consequence, the subject has, of course, not been very rewarding in terms of academic prestige. Investing time in developing these themes has not been the most direct way forward for those wishing to join the elite of social science research. As a respondent of Lorenzo put it: 'You don't make a career in academia with immigration' (Lorenzo, 1989, p. 9). The Franco-Algerian sociologist Abdelmalek Sayad once asked the very uneasy question: 'is the science of the "poor", of the "small people" (socially) a poor science, a small one?'[7] (1984, p. 20). The answer was, for him, not in doubt: the sociology of immigration is seen as a very minor topic within the discipline of sociology. Moreover, it seems that immigration and ethnic relations have almost exclusively been studied by researchers who are in one way or another *complaisant* regarding the subject.

In Belgium, many researchers in the field are either migrants them-selves, or are of migrant descent. The same narrow relationship between personal experience and research experience is observable among auto-chtonous researchers. The latter often have a 'special relationship' with the immigrant population – either through marriage or friendship. In other cases, they have close links with the migrants' countries of origin. It should also be added, however, that most of these researchers, both autochtonous and migrants, occupy precarious and unstable positions within the academic world, and are often wholly dependent on external funding. One could contend that in the (social) scale of academic pres-tige, the sociology of migration is in the hands of 'second class' research-ers. The latter evaluation, of course, has nothing to do with an assessment of scientific competence. It simply emphasizes that, because of their social and national backgrounds and the resultant weakness of their position in the profession, they do not generally qualify for the most academically-valued positions.[8] Moreover, it is often expected that ethnic minority researchers should work on ethnic and migration issues, just as it is often considered 'natural' that Womens's Studies is first and foremost 'women's business'.

In the course of the 1990s, though, research in the field of migration has undergone a process of change and de-marginalisation. An important development is the growth of non-academic expertise in this area. The development of integration policy frameworks at various levels of power (European inter-governmental, European Union, National, Regional, etc.) has created a demand for strictly policy-oriented expertise. At this level, social scientists, who were not collectively organized in research centres, networks, and so on, have been by-passed by a readily mobiliz-able expertise among sizeable advocacy groups. As far as the key issue of funding and intellectual legitimacy are concerned, social scientists found themselves in fierce competition with this growing 'non-academic' expertise, which is most often linked to organizational interest-groups such as trade unions, churches, business corporations, and so on.

So much for these three important introductory remarks. In the fol-lowing, we focus on three major set of problems and difficulties – dis-tinct but to a large extent interdependent – facing the development of the sociology of migration and ethnic relations. The issue at stake is to identify the obstacles that must be overcome in order to reflect upon and to make sense of current, and likely future, global and national developments. In this sense, we consider that a critical reflexive analysis is a prerequisite if we are to consolidate a space for knowledge in the area of migration and ethnic relations.

The uneasy development of a sociology of migration and ethnic relations in Belgium

Migration and ethnic relations are destined to remain key issues of concern for the future of European societies (Martiniello, 1992b). Most experts agree on this. The idea that Europe may freely decide to grow as a closed and isolated space, impermeable to new human movements and new migratory inflows, is a myth that contradicts all empirical observations. There are many potential reasons for the consolidation of Europe's role as a continent of immigration, most notably wars, geo-political troubles, uneven demographic and economic growth, simplified means of communication, and so on. These factors may well give the twenty-first century the hallmark of a century of mobility.

As a result, European populations will undergo a dual process of regeneration and diversification, as has already been the case in past decades. Modification of the social, economic, ethnic, cultural and religious fabric of Western Europe will maintain its pressure on the still-dominant form of political organization, the nation-state. Indeed, it has been shown that the regulation of power within the political unit of the nation-state has failed to come to terms with issues of migration and ethnic diversity. Therefore, it becomes clear that migration and post-migratory societal issues will stand prominent on the agenda of the European Union in the next century. Given the vast number of societal issues raised by migration processes – *phénomène social total* to use the vocabulary of Marcel Mauss – the social sciences must re-evaluate their intellectual categories and conceptual frameworks. Without this, there will be little scope for the development of a coherent body of knowledge. By the same token, social scientists must address the challenge of maintaining the immunity and integrity of this subject-matter in the face of constant threats in the guise of 'intellectual expediency', where agendas are invariably driven by decision-makers, politicians and the mass media.

The first obstacle to the constitution of an autonomous research field on migration and ethnic studies is what may be called the problem of the epistemological break (Bachelard, 1983; Bourdieu, 1973). More precisely, we would argue that a major problem in the sociology of migration and ethnic relations is the absence of any epistemological break, which is often a result of a combination of the sort of intellectual expediency just discussed together worth the social conditions of production of sociological work. As noted earlier, a biased media generates a form of 'common sense' knowledge which conceives of immigration in terms of economic, social and political 'problems': insecurity and criminality, unemployment, poverty, urban decay, violence, religious and ethnic conflicts, the dilution of the nation, and so on. Since 1973, this mosaic of 'folk representations' has become widely diffused in the public mind.

Perhaps surprisingly, the social sciences in general, and sociology in particular, has failed to challenge these interpretations. Sociologists have actually begun to categorize the social experience of migrant populations into distinct domains, and to elaborate these as specific social problems to be studied and resolved. In fact, it is notable that the construction of the sociological *problematique* of migration and ethnic relations in the early phase of the discipline simply mirrored the intuitive theories of migration present in the wider public consciousness. This led to the development of a literature which is rife with binary perspectives such as 'immigrants and housing', 'immigrants and school', 'immigrants and criminality', 'immigrants and security', 'immigrants and health', 'immigrants and culture', 'immigrants and the labour market', and so on. A large volume of research has been, and is being, undertaken in all of these sub-fields of research. In the worse cases, these have been either narrowly empiricist or unfruitful because of their redundancy and of their lack of theoretical and methodological innovation.[9] This, to a large extent, accounts for the relative theoretical stagnation of the field.

It is almost as if the sole *raison d'être* of the sociology of migration and ethnic relations was to contribute to solving the social problems associated with a phenomenon which remained predominantly perceived as a threat to the social order (Sayad, 1984). Insofar as it tends to answer more or less directly a 'social demand', the sociology of migration has been constrained to internalize the problematized and dramatized perception of the common-sense, which is itself largely determined by the concern for social order. In this situation, it is quite difficult to establish a positive assessment in terms of the scientific value of the works produced. As noted by Michel Oriol: 'in their concern to solve concrete problems quickly, they (the researchers) can only raise problems in terms comparable to those of public opinion. It therefore becomes more difficult to break with ideology in order to establish a properly scientific approach' (1981, p. 6).[10] This helps to explain the weaknesses of the sociology of migration processes and ethnic relations, and also the predominance in the field of the narrowest form of empiricism (Noiriel, 1989).

But why do sociologists of migration have so much difficulty in breaking away from these external social demands? Is it the case that we are dealing with 'second class' researchers from the point of view of competence (as well as of status)? We do not accept this as a valid explanation. Their incapacity to reach autonomy should rather be explained by the social, economic and political circumstances in which they have to function. This problem is not immune from the more general problem of the place of the university in our societies. Indeed, the social demands we referred to are often echoed by decision-makers and politicians. Contrary to other European countries, such as the United Kingdom where one finds an Economic and Social Research Council relatively free from partisan political affiliation (but see Chapter 6 in this volume), sociological research in Belgium is largely controlled by political authorities, which have over a number of years cut the budgets and drastically reduced the possibilities of autonomous funding within universities and from the National Fund for Scientific Research. As far as social sciences and the study of migration is concerned, the establishment of a new research programme in the late 1980s, managed by the Service of Programmation of Scientific Research (SPPS) at the national level, gave a new impetus to work in the social sciences. It included policy-oriented projects such as a sub-programme aimed at providing a scientific rationale to governmental decision-making (*Recherche universitaire d'aide à la décision politique*). However, this policy did not last long enough to produce results of any long-term significance. The SPPs has become the Federal Services for Scientific, Technical and Cultural Affairs (SSTC) and has launched a new research programme on social cohesion in which migration issues are extensively dealt with.

Many researchers in the social sciences are all too often constrained to 'chase' funding and research contracts from the various ministries and governmental agencies. It is important to note that the completion of the federal structure of the Belgian state in 1993 has given wide power and competencies to the authorities of the regions and communities. Alongside the devolution of powers, there is also a very effective transfer of budgets which allow the governments of the regions and communities to develop research programmes independently from those developed by the federal Ministry of Scientific Research. In Flanders, the more healthy budgetary situation has provided many more research opportunities than in the French-speaking part of the country. Moreover, in a policy report drafted by the Flemish Ministry of Welfare, Family and Culture, local authorities are explicitly recommended to build their integration policies on scientific policy reports.

However, the fact that immigration-integration has in the course of the last 20 years remained a very contentious issue (and a very sensitive one from an electoral point of view), has had various consequences. Most often, elected politicians holding executive offices are particularly careful in selecting those research projects which may be directly useful in terms of policy-making. In this respect, the title of the aforementioned SPPS[11] project could not be more explicit. In other cases, preference is given to those research projects which provide an academic 'alibi' – often of a quantitative nature – to policies which have already been agreed upon. In other words, politicians in executive office have a strong tendency to intrude upon academic debates by imposing the 'legitimate' research *problematiques* and themes without taking into account the researchers' own 'independent' scientific concerns and agenda. In recent years, one can observe that among the themes which were deemed to be worthy of financial support were the control of flows of asylum-seekers and refugees flows, the control of external borders, criminality, insecurity and (un)employment among migrants.

The scarcity of funding sources and the 'contractualization' of research do not easily accommodate the theoretical concerns of researchers. The weak autonomization of the academic field, which is a precondition for an effective epistemological break, has another perverse and harmful consequence for the sociological debate.

Because of the scarcity of available funding, the struggle for access to public resources often takes precedence over healthy scientific debate. Rather than a 'community' of researchers in theoretical convergence or divergence, the sociology of migration and ethnic relations is characterised by intense confrontations and quarrels, which are generally harmful to the progress of research.[12] This may not be unique to this field of research. Others may also contend that the pathway to the elaboration of knowledge is often unpredictable. Pierre Bourdieu argued from the viewpoint of his theory of practice and conceptualization of practical reasoning, that the search for properly social and/or symbolic recognition is in itself a powerful driving force for scientific discovery and the generation of scientific knowledge (Bourdieu, 1992). Although the theory is questionable in the sense that it builds on a very cynical picture of the scientist – seen as a self-interested person merely driven by the accumulation of symbolic social goods and profits – it provides one dimension of the explanation of why, on the whole, in spite of the huge obstacles it confronts, the Belgian sociology of migration and ethnic relations has not gone adrift into an irrelevant or low quality literature (or why it did not simply vanish). The perseverance of a number of individual researchers in various disciplines (sociology, law, anthropo-logy, political science, geography, criminology, social psychology, lin-guisitics, and so on) has proved without any possible doubt the existence of a relevant opus of Belgian research in the field.

The fascination for the Americas of European social scientists

The second problem confronting migration and ethnic studies derives from the introduction, without sufficient care, of conceptual and the-oretical elements developed in other social and national contexts. As observed by Oriol, 'Sociology has known the same enthusiasm as the people for the Americas and searched there for its paradigms while seek-ing fortune' (1981, p. 24).[13] In fact, a wide variety of theoretical con-structs in the European sociology of migration have been imported from the United States. The Chicago School and structural-functionalism have, for example, provided European researchers with a huge stock of concepts; most notably, assimilation, adaptation, marginality, inclusion and integration. The abundance of theoretical imports seems to stem, on the one hand, from a fascination with the United States (as noted by Oriol) and, on the other hand, from the fact that the study of migration by American sociologists was far more advanced than in Europe when this theme became topical among European researchers. Acknowledging the richness and relevance of the American conceptual legacy should not prevent us from expressing explicit reservations in terms of the very questionable way in which these concepts have been applied by Eur-opean researchers.

A major problem lies in the fact that the divergence in terms of the historical, social and economic background of Europe and the United States has been underestimated. This divergence should, at the very least, have triggered a sense of caution in transferring concepts from one context to the other. Indeed, historical and spatial contexts never correspond in every respect, and therefore it is somehow illusory to use theories and concepts developed for explaining and accounting for the situation in one context to the other. Before they can be introduced in a given context, theories and concepts external to a social formation should first undergo a critical and thorough examination. They must be deconstructed and reconstructed in order to be applied satisfactorily to a new context. This has not been done in the substantive field of interest here, especially with regards to the appropriateness/portability of the American intellectual tradition. Moreover, the intrinsic problems of these imported concepts and *problematiques* were not definitively solved even in the American context. Therefore, by introducing them uncritically in Europe, theoretical difficulties have also been unwittingly imported. This factor may in itself account for the uneasy development of a European sociology of migration and ethnic relations.

The problems stemming from theoretical and conceptual imports (especially from the US), may be illustrated briefly through the example of the late introduction and development of concepts linked to 'ethnicity'[14] and multiculturalism (Martiniello, 1997) in continental Europe. It is unquestionable that these external influences on European debates can potentially reinvigorate this field of research. However, imported concepts must be used carefully. For example, can we assert that the concept of 'ethnicity' refers to the same intellectual representation in a society which has always conceived of itself as a country of immigration, and which has been influenced by the powerful ideology of the 'melting pot', and in countries with historically entrenched national(-ist) traditions which have over a sustained period regarded migrant populations as a temporary labour force? This crucial question has often been neglected by European researchers. Furthermore, sociological debates about 'ethnicity' in the United States gave rise to the creation of competing schools of thought. Today, the advocates of a substantialist conception of 'ethnicity' seem to be very much in a minority as a result of the extensive critiques of their position in the early 1960s and even more so after the publication of the influential works of Nathan Glazer and Daniel Moynihan (Glazer and Moynihan, 1972). Now, among European researchers who employ the concept of ethnicity in the sociology of migration, some adopt an ambiguous position on substantialism; a tendency which threatens to drive back the theoretical debate by decades.

The influence of economicist paradigms on the sociology of migration

The third difficulty encountered by our discipline is related to what may be called the imperialism of economicist and utilitarianist paradigms in the social sciences. More or less sophisticated *problematiques* derived from economic 'cost-benefit analysis' have permeated the sociology of migration and ethnic relations, just as in sociology more generally. As underlined by Sayad, the fundamental question that researchers were led to raise, especially in the early phases of this sub-discipline, may be stated as follows: 'how can a given society maximize the advantages (mostly economic) of immigration while lessening to the greatest extent the 'costs' (mostly social and cultural) involved in the process and imposed by the permanent presence of migrants?' (Sayad, 1979, p. 6). In our opinion, this kind of *problematique*, which is very likely to seduce decision-makers and politicians, is far from being the most relevant sociologically.[15]

Conclusion

This qualitative assessment of the current state of the sociology of migration and ethnic relations may appear very critical. It is also clear from our analysis that many of the crucial problems and difficulties discussed here are not amenable to simple solutions. It reveals the difficult position faced by this area of research and, more generally, by sociology as a discipline, in the context of societies unwilling to listen to analytical discourses which are not confined to purely economic, budgetary and financial concerns. Sociology and political science currently suffer from a crisis of credibility and legitimacy: sociologists and political scientists are usually only heard when they provide an academic 'alibi' to decision-makers and public authorities.

Moreover, it is undoubtedly the case that recent societal evolution has challenged many of the classical theoretical frameworks of sociology. Most researchers feel the necessity to re-evaluate the intellectual terrain and conceptual frameworks developed and deployed during the last three decades in order to reach a better understanding of increasingly rapid and complex shifts in social milieux.

In Belgium, this has given rise to new kinds of academic cooperation partly breaking away from the 'academic war' paradigm. In the case of migration and ethnic relations studies, in both Dutch-Speaking and French-Speaking Belgium, the editing of collective works has multiplied impressively in the last couple of years (Collective, 1997, Foblets and Hubeau, 1998 a,b; Foblets, 1998; Frantzen, 1999; Swyngedouw, Phalet and Deschouwer, 1999; Martiniello and Poncelet, 1993; Rea, 1998). This development points out to a relative demarginalization. Research opportunities for academics in this field are currently multiplying, mainly under the umbrella of mainstream disciplinary branches. A form of decompartmentalization between disciplines is also observable. Migration and ethnic relations have indeed become topical beyond the social sciences and humanities. These are emergent processes and are not firmly established. What we cannot claim is that they are indicative of clear-cut qualitative progress at a theoretical level.

In the specific case of sociology, however, it remains imperative to turn away from the state of intellectual expediency and excessive empiricism which we have witnessed over the last two decades. By giving more centrality to the work of theoretical elaboration, it would be possible to give birth to the sort of novel intellectual frameworks and conceptual schema which are currently lacking. Our assessment emphasized the enormous internal challenges facing the future development of the field of migration and ethnic relations in Belgium. There are also a number of challenges linked to the place of knowledge within society and to the relationship between academics, politicians and social actors. Without endorsing a simplified view of academics as prophets of the social world, it is clear that academics cannot simply avoid discussions about the social and political use of academic knowledge. It seems that, so far, the impact of Belgian academic research on changing institutionalized patterns of interaction between the state and immigrant minorities has been minimal, and at best it has performed a legitimizing function for decisions already taken by policy-makers.

There are some reasons for optimism though. First, the internationalization of research through several networks and programmes (for example, within the framework of the European Union scientific research programmes), can provide an impetus to the development of fresh theoretical orientations. Undoubtedly, immense conceptual and methodological problems still have to be solved (Lloyd, 1995) and there are few opportunities to develop vital research activities such as data collection and standardization on an international level. However, there are currently wider possibilities offered to European researchers to meet on a more or less regular basis and to exchange ideas via collaborative research projects.

Secondly, the rise of the extreme-right in Belgium, as in other European countries, gave fresh impetus to the study of racism (perhaps most notably in France). The success of the corpus of research on racism led in France by Pierre André Taguieff (1988; 1991) and then by Michel Wievorka (1991; 1992; 1993; 1998) gave a real impetus to the sociology of migration and ethnic relations. In Belgium, it was also the case that increases in overt racism and political extremism (unintentionally) fostered the scientific study of racism and its links to political behaviour and attitudes. It is in this respect important to note the creation in 1991 of a research centre at the University of Leuven, the ISPO, systematically collecting data on elections and political behaviour, and notably on racism and political extremism (Swyngedouw, 1992; 1995; 1996; 1997).

The future of research in this field will largely depend on the capacity of researchers to convince politicians and policy-makers that our societies have never needed theoretical sociology more than they do currently. A fundamental issue at stake is to convince decision-makers that short-term social problems may not be solved without the investment over the longer term in theoretical work. Indeed, only by making such an investment can we hope to build innovative projects for our societies; something we all expect irrespective of whether we are decision-makers, intellectuals or ordinary citizens.

Notes

1 This is a fully revised version of a contribution initially published in Dutch in E. Deslé, R. Lestaeghe and E. Witte (eds) (1993) 'Denken over Migranten in Europa', Brussel, VUB Press, Balans No. 2.

2 In French-speaking Belgium, this may be more often the case when theories of ethnicity are used to account for the social realities of immigrant groups. This conceptual apparatus, Anglo-American in origin, is regarded somewhat sceptically by those who still associate it with the racial theories of the nineteenth century. This is discussed later in the chapter, and in Martiniello, 1996.

3 The same holds true for the interest in migration which emerged among historians even more recently. In this respect, the pioneering works of Gérard Noiriel in France and of Anne Morelli and Frank Caesteker in Belgium deserve special attention.

4 One can mention here a number of publications which testify to the uneasy development of the sociology of migration and ethnic relations in the European and Canadian context. Although slightly outdated, these works bear witness to the period in which they were written. Among these works is the special issue of *Current Sociology*, edited by Mirjana Morokvasic, which offers a comprehensive analysis of the field in different European countries (Morokvasic, 1984). In French sociology, one can mention the works of Michel Oriol (1981) and of François Dubet (1989). The Italian case has been analysed by Maria-Immacolata Macioti (1990). As far as Québec is concerned, Danielle Juteau (1990) and Mikhaël Elbaz (1990) have a few years ago attempted to synthesize the most significant contributions to the field.

5 This document is an update of the literature review edited by Felice Dassetto and Greta Sienap, and published by Sybidi in 1985.

6 This is mainly the case in continental Europe. In the United States, and to a lesser extent in the United Kingdom, things are different. In the first case, the professionalization of sociology happened in the context of a country conceiving of its history as an history of immigration. It comes therefore as no surprise to see that the discipline has grown while retaining immigration as a central concern. For instance, research in this field stimulated growth of the Chicago School and contributed to its reputation worldwide.

7 Free translation of 'La science du "pauvre", du "petit" (socialement) est-elle une science "pauvre", est-elle une "petite science"?'.

8 Pathways to academically-valued positions for ethnic minority researchers certainly exist within the Belgian academic world, but not generally in the field of ethnic and migration research. As argued above, this remained a structurally undervalued field of research.

9 As a pointer to this reality, one should note that innovative approaches turning the problematization of immigrants on its head and throwing into question issues linked to the majorities (for example, Flemish nationalism, the internal cohesion of Belgian society and the very problematic issue of Belgian national identity) were slow to emerge.

10 Free translation of: 'Par souci de résoudre vite des problèmes concrets, ils (les chercheurs) ne peuvent guère les poser que dans les termes où l'opinion publique les reconnaît. Il sera alors d'autant plus difficile de s'arracher à l'idéologie, pour essayer de fonder une démarche proprement scientifique...'.

11 The SPPS has now become the SSTC (Scientific, Technical and Cultural Services) and has lost a significant part of its budget in the process of federalization.

12 The fact that a field is not structured along theoretical ideas with competing schools of thought does not necessarily render it immune from intense confrontations and 'academic wars' on non-academic battlefields. In this latter case, the competition may be even more intense.

13 Free translation of 'la Sociologie a connu la même fascination que les peuples pour les Amériques et vint y chercher ses paradigmes tandis qu'ils y quêtaient fortune'.

14 We could also have mentioned the concept of citizenship which has emerged in the European sociology of migration and ethnic relations in the course of the 1980s.

15 There is no space to develop this theme in detail. We will limit ourselves simply to emphasizing that utilitarianism is the focal point of vigorous theoretical debates in contemporary sociology.

References

Bachelard, G. (1983) *La formation de l'esprit scientifique*, Vrin, Paris.

Balibar, E. and Wallerstein, I. (1997) *Race, nation, classe*, Paris, La Découverte, new edition.

Bastenier, A. (1990) *Cycles migratoires et fixation des populations d'origine étrangère en Belgique*, Louvain, Université Catholique de Louvain, Collective PhD in Sociology, co-authored by F. Dassetto.

Bourdieu, P. *et al.* (1973) *Le métier de sociologue*, Paris-La Haye, Mouton.

Brion, F. and Rea, A. (1990) *Les jeunes d'origine étrangère: Aperçu de quelques recherches et pratiques en communauté française*, Bruxelles, Synergie Research Report.

Campioli, G. (1975), De la sociologie des immigrés à la sociologie de l'immigration, *L'Année Sociologique*, 26, pp. 43–56.

Castles, S. and Kosack, G. (1973) *Immigrant Workers and Class Structure in Western Europe*, London, Oxford University Press.

Collective, (1997) *La Belgique et ses immigrés: les politiques manquées*, Bruxelles, De Boeck Université.

Dubet, F. (1989) Trois processus migratoires, *Revue Française des Affaires Sociales*, 3, pp. 7–28.

Elbaz, M. (1990) Les sciences sociales et la question des étrangers, in I. Simon-Barouh and P-J. Simon (eds), pp. 13–22.

Foblets, M.-C. and Hubeau, B. (1998) (eds) *Nieuwe burgers in de samenleving*, Leuven, ACCO.

Frantzen, P. (1999) (eds) *Nederlandstalige Brusselaars in een multiculturele samenleving*, Brussel, VUB Press.

Hubeau, B. and Foblets, M.-C. (1998) (eds) *Politieke Participatie van allochtonen*, Leuven, Acco.

Glazer, N. and Moynihan, D.P. (1972) *Beyond the Melting-Pot*, Cambridge/London, MIT Press, 2nd edn.

Juteau, D. (1990) L'étude des relations ethniques dans la sociologie québecquoise francophone, in I. Simon-Barouh and P-J. Simon (eds), pp. 23–41

Leman, J. (1991) *Intégrité, intégration, innovation pédagogique et pluralité culturelle*, Bruxelles, De Boeck Université.

Lloyd, C. (1995) International Comparison in the Field of Ethnic Relations, in A. Hargeaves and J. Leaman (eds), *Racism, Ethnicity and Politics in Contemporary Europe*, Aldershot, Edward Elgar, pp. 31–44.

Lorenzo, P. (1989) *Approche qualitative des recherches sur l'immigration en France*, Paris, Centre de recherche et d'études d'anthropologie et d'urbanisme, 1989.

Maciotti, M-I. (1990) Un aperçu de la recherche sur les migrations en Italie, *Revue Européenne des Migrations Internationales*, 6(2), pp. 173–7.

Martens, A. (1972) Travailleurs immigrés: critique de quelques études, *Recherches sociologiques*, 3(1), pp. 3–21.

Martiniello, M. (1991) Turbulences à Bruxelles (mai 1991), *Migrations-Société*, 18(3), pp. 19–28.

Martiniello, M. (1992a) *Leadership et pouvoir dans les communautés d'origine immigrée*, Paris, Ciemi-L'Harmattan.

Martiniello, M. (1992b) L'immigration: menace pour l'Etat-Nation ou révélateur de son caractère obsolète?, *Revue Suisse de Sociologie*, 18(3), pp. 657–73.

Martiniello, M. (1996) *L'ethnicité dans les sciences sociales contemporaines*, Paris, PUF 'Que sais-je?'.

Martiniello, M. (1997) *Sortir des ghettos culturels*, Paris, Presses de Science Po.

Martiniello, M. and Poncelet, M. (sous la direction de) (1993) *Migrations et minorités ethniques dans l'espace européen*, Bruxelles, De Boeck Université.

Morelli, A. (1992) *Histoire de l'immigration et des étrangers en Belgique*, Bruxelles, EVO-CBAI.

Morokvasic, M. (1984) Migrations in Europe: Trends in Research and Sociological Approaches: Perspective from the Country of Origin and Destination (1960–1983), Part 1 and 2, *Current Sociology*, 32(2 and 3).

Noiriel, G. (1989) Enjeux: une histoire sociale du politique est-elle possible?, *Vingtième Siècle*, oct.-déc., pp. 81–96

Oriol, M. (1981) *Bilan des études sur les aspects culturels et humains des migrations internationales en Europe Occidentale 1918–1979*, Strasbourg, Fondation Européenne de la Science.

Rea, A. (sous la direction de) (1998) *Immigration et racisme en Europe*, Bruxelles, Editions Complexe.

Rea, A. and Brion, F. (1991) La construction médiatique et politique des 'émeutes urbaines', *L'Année sociale*, pp. 282–305.

Roosens, E. (1989) *Creating Ethnicity: the process of Ethnogenesis*, London, Sage.

Sayad, A. (1979) Qu'est-ce qu'un immigré?, *Peuples Méditerranéens*, 7, pp. 3–23.

Schnapper, D. (1991) *La France de l'intégration: Sociologie de la nation en 1990*, Paris, Gallimard.

Schnapper, D., (1994), *La communauté des citoyens. Sur l'idée moderne de nation*, Paris: Gallimard.

Simon-Barouh, I. and Simon, P.-J. (eds) (1990) *Les étrangers dans la ville. Le regard des sciences sociales*, Paris, L'Harmattan.

Sybidi, Document II (1985) *L'immigration dans les sciences sociales: Bilan des recherches en Belgique*, Louvain-la-Neuve, UCL, Sybidi, October.

Sybidi, Document VII (1993) *L'immigration et la recherche en Belgique (1930–1991)*, Louvain-la-Neuve, Académica-Sybidi.

Swyngedouw, M. (1992) National Elections in Belgium: The Breakthrough of Extreme Right in Flanders, *Regional Politics and Policy*, 2(3), pp. 62–75.

Swyngedouw, M. (1995) Les nouveaux clivages dans la politique belgo-flamande, *Revue Française de Science Politique*, 45, pp. 775–90.

Swyngedouw, M. (1996) Re-defining the Social Space: a Case-Study of the Construction of the 'Immigrant Threat' in Flanders, 1930–1980', in M. Cross (ed.), *The Threatening Minority: Racial Violence and Political Extremism in Europe*, Ercomer, Utrecht.

Swyngedouw, M. (1997) *Les motivations électorales en Flandre: 21 mai 1995*, Bruxelles, Courrier Hebdomadaire du CRISP.

Swyngedouw, M., Phalet, K. and Deschouwer, K. (1999) *Minderheden in Brussel*, Brussel, VUB Press.

Taguieff, P.-A. (1988) *La force du préjugé: Essai sur le racisme et ses doubles*, Paris, La Découverte.

Taguieff, P.-A. (ed.) (1991) *Face au racisme, vols 1 and 2*, Paris, La Découverte.

Tribalat, M. (1996) *De l'immigration à l'assimilation: Enquête sur les populations d'origine étrangère en France*, Paris, La Découverte-Ined.

Wievorka, M. (1991) *L'espace du racisme*, Paris, Seuil.

Wievorka, M. (1992) *La France raciste*, Paris, Seuil.

Wievorka, M. (eds) (1993) *Racisme et modernité*, Paris, La Découverte.

Wievorka, M. (1998) *Le racisme: une introduction*, Paris, La Découverte.

Withol de Wenden, C. (1988) *Les immigrés et la politique*, Paris, Presses de la FNSP.

Part IV

Eastern Europe: Socialist and Post-Socialist Societies

9
Social Change and Sociological Research on the 'Nation' Issue in Yugoslavia

Milena Davidovic

This chapter focuses on how Yugoslav sociologists have interpreted the social reality in which they live, and more importantly to what extent they wished, and/or were able, to influence *changes* in that reality. Before its collapse in 1991, Yugoslavia was a socialist society. As such, it is inevitable that in the *sociologist-state-social change* nexus the weakest link would be that between sociologist and state; far more important is the relationship between sociologist and *party*. Although there were occasional demands from 'the highest places' for sociologists to explain, propagandize about, or check new policy initiatives geared to promoting social change, 'in practice', in most cases, the initiator has been the party. The sociologist's role was simply to promote 'planned' changes by 'justifying' them.

It is difficult to analyse the causes of the cataclysmic forces of 'social change' in Yugoslav society at the beginning of the 1990s. The war (1991–95) still appears unreal and incomprehensible to the majority of people, though the effects are constantly with them. Yugoslav sociologists failed to *predict* the war. Indeed, they failed even to *anticipate* that the result would be interethnic killing on a massive scale. The obvious question is 'why?' How did Yugoslav sociologists conceptualize national and interethnic relations, conflicts and interests, and how did they theorize *social change* and *social inequalities* resulting from the centrality of *'nation'*?

The chapter will first address the theoretical and methodological development of Yugoslav sociology in relation to the national issue. Then, we will try to demonstrate substantively how this phenomenon has been researched. Thirdly, we summarize the principal results of surveys that explore this issue. Finally, we focus on the war period, and the immediate post-war years, to assess whether there have been any significant changes in sociological studies of Yugoslav society and inter-ethnic relations.

Theoretical and methodological trends in the development of Yugoslav sociology

Immediately after the second world war, as the new socialist state was being created, sociology was banned on the grounds that it represented 'bourgeois science', the ban remaining in force until 1959. There were lengthy debates about 'science' versus 'ideology', whether the new socialist state needed to create an entirely new 'socialist' or 'Marxist' sociology (or just partially abandon the old 'bourgeois' sociology), and whether historical materialism and sociology could be equated. The outcome was an explicit agreement that the theoretical basis of Yugoslav sociology would be Marxist social theory. This largely remains the case. Yugoslav sociologists either (uncritically) adhere to Marxist social theory or attempt to incorporate (into the Marxian paradigm) marginal elements of contemporary sociological theory (Davidovic, 1985; 1988).

One of the most distinctive characteristics of Yugoslav sociology was the presence from the outset of a specific group of intellectuals who, as communists and WWII partisans or post-war members of the Yugoslav League of Communist Youth, were supporters of the ideal of interethnic reconciliation for Yugoslav peoples. Their task was to provide the conditions for 'fraternity and unity' leading to a development of a collective 'Yugoslav spirit'. They brought a genuine internationalism into the discipline and all post-war generations of sociologists shared this 'spirit'. In contrast to other groups of intellectuals – writers, economists and historians – where insidious forms of nationalism surfaced from time to time, in sociological/philosophical circles there were no traces of these ideas. The latter were among the founders of the well-known Korcula Summer School (*Praxis-philosophy group*). Praxis-group members could not, by definition, be nationalist (although there were some striking exceptions in the early 1990s).

Yugoslav sociology was grounded in a rejection of value neutrality. This arguably led to the establishment of a discipline which was not able to deal with real problems of social life. It could certainly not promote fundamental social change, nor offer a competent theoretical and methodological framework leading to a better understanding of the type of society in which they lived. Various methodological attributes ('cre-

ative', 'anthropological', 'humanistic', 'revolutionary', 'critical') were claimed by sociologists in an attempt to distinguish their approach from
dogmatic Marxism.

As the Berlin Wall came down, they were still writing about 'humanistic' socialism as a vision that was yet to come, and about how to realize such a vision. But their work contained no substantive evidence,
apart from extracting elements of everyday practice, which, they
claimed, demonstrated a contribution to the 'humanization of Yugoslav
socialism'. A prime example would be workers' self-management. However, many of the *praxis-sociologists* who wrote about this had never set
foot in a factory. What they envisioned was a form of humanistic
socialism for Yugoslavia which would be radically different from existing socialist societies. While the Soviet Union lived in 'real socialism',
with its Gulags, Kolimas and other forms of repression, leading Yugoslav
sociologists were trying to prove how *Yugoslavia had never lived in socialism!*

Influence of the Party on research agenda

From this analysis it is clear why Yugoslav sociologists have not
attempted to address the phenomenon of the national/nation. There
were, however, many events which made interethnic and international
relations (and in particular the social inequalities arising from them) to
be studied, reluctantly. This reluctance is demonstrated clearly by the
fact that there are no analyses of the complex interethnic relations in
Kosovo. Only at the end of the 1980s (too late), was a book about
Serbian migration from Kosovo and Metohija published (Petrovic and
Blagojevic, 1989). Poor relations between Serbs and Albanians are represented by mutual accusations: that Albanians hold lower social positions
solely because of their national origin while, although 'on their land',
Serbs are in jeopardy because they are of a different national origin.

A key point is that studies of interethnic relations were rarely done by
individuals motivated by their own intellectual curiosity or desire to
effect changes in social reality. An analysis of the literature in former
Yugoslavia reveals that it is dominated by Yugoslav politicians, national
or regional (Janjic *et al.*, 1987). Hence, national problems were discussed
by those who were in a sense compelled to; in most cases by the dictate
of the party, a party committee or (later) so-called Marxist Centres where
they were paid to do only that kind of work.

The typical product of Party writers, especially of the youngest generation, is an enormous amount of pseudo-scientific analysis but with

no conclusion, no message about the real quality of interethnic relations. A major focus has been on the appropriate *definition* of a nation. The problem is that, by quoting hundreds of definitions of the concept, it becomes impossible to spot the wood for the trees (Janjic, 1993). Other publications report the current view on national politics from the Party's standpoint. These authors could have used the material to influence debates on 'nation' and create the conditions for social change. Instead, like quasi-scientists, they have simply regurgitated well-known phrases accompanied by numerous quotations from authors sharing the same theoretical and ideological position. Relations between nations are described, and solutions to ethnic conflict are seen as involving a 'self-managing pluralism of interests' or the need to eliminate 'national bureaucracies'. Importantly, the term 'national' does not reflect power relations in that it treats all kinds of nationalism as 'the same thing'.

Theoretical and practice difficulties

Two factors contributed to the 'conspiracy of silence' surrounding the vital issue of nationalism. On the one hand, sociologists were conscious that in such a repressive society entering into such a debate was extremely risky. One could never know which 'nationalism' might lead to prison. Mihailo Djuric, a professor of sociology at the Belgrade Law School, was imprisoned for one year because of views expressed in a public debate about amendments to the 1974 Constitution (these were declared as 'great Serbian nationalism'). His punishment can be seen as a clear warning to anyone thinking of discussing the issue of nationalism publicly.

In the country where a so-called *national key politics* was applied, one could be rewarded by great privileges or, equally, brutally punished, for it was never really learned when and how the 'right' moves needed to be made. The national key politics produced a proportional number of 'nationalists' across the country . If it was announced that a 'group of Muslim nationalists' were put on trial in Bosnia one week, it was almost certain that, the next week, a group of Serbian or Croat 'nationalists' would be discovered. [As is well known, some of today's presidents or party leaders in Croatia, Bosnia and Serbia, spent years in prison as 'nationalists' before the collapse of Yugoslavia.]

Yugoslav sociology was also silent about 'nation' (and religion) on *cognitive-theoretical* grounds. In Marxist social theory, there was no place for analyses of such phenomena . There was no general Marxist 'theory of nations' and, even more importantly, what Marx and Engels *had* written about nations presented highly unpleasant facts which needed to be concealed from the public. If all the problems concerning 1948 and the fate of Inform Bureau members in Yugoslavia (i.e. the way in which the official policy of the Yugoslav leadership 'broke off' with Stalin) are added, it becomes clear that neither Stalin's understanding of the national issue, nor his definition of a nation could have any future in Yugoslav social sciences.

Throughout former Yugoslavia, until its collapse, every student of sociology or social science had to know Edvard Kardelj's definition of a nation by heart. As a young Slovenian communist, he wrote it under the influence of Stalin's definition in 1938, but changed it after the Inform Bureau and the 'break' with Stalin, in 1959. The briefest version was: 'Nation is a specific people's union created on the basis of the social distribution of labour in the capitalist era, on a compact territory, and on a common language frame and close ethnic and cultural relations' (Kardelj, 1960, p. 104).

After the break with Stalin, young Yugoslav sociologists/Marxists sought to replace the dogmatism of historical materialism with an anti-dogmatic, humanist view drawn from Marx's *Early Works*. In the context of nation or national issues, though, it appeared that Marx and Engels were not a good source. The main problem lay in the distinction they drew between historical (revolutionary) and non-historical (counter-revolutionary) nations. In such a scheme, roughly speaking, historical nations were those representing the spirit of Western Europe (English, French, German, etc.), while non-historical nations included, amongst others, Serbs, Croats, Slovenians and Albanians. These non-historical nations were seen as lacking the 'capability and energy' to establish their own states; their role in world history already played and in any case insignificant. In the future development of Europe, the fate of these nations was to be swept away by the 'revolutionary development of great, civilized European nations': the progress of the latter being far more important for the proletariat than a struggle for independence of these 'small, crippled and powerless nations' (Meznaric, 1984, pp.140/149). The social theory adopted by Yugoslav sociologists, and regarded as inviolable, saw Serbs, Slovenians and Croats as conflictual because of a deep hatred between Austrian and Turkish Slavs; 'they have known each other for centuries as pickpockets and bandits, and they hate each other in spite of the fact that they are kindred'.

An unwavering belief in the socialist project

Today, when we look back, especially after the 1991 interethnic war in former Yugoslavia, it could be argued that the biggest tragedies of Yugoslav sociology lay in its unwavering commitment to socialism and its failure to predict the threat of national conflicts. One of the last major sociological projects planned for 1985–95 also bears witness to this. The *Encyclopedia of Contemporary Socialism* involved more than 200 authors from Yugoslavia and other countries (including 'the inner circle of Yugoslav authors of Marxist orientation'). It aimed to demonstrate that 'despite the crisis and defeats of some socialist projects or their limited realization, socialist projects are still attractive today as an alternative to the state of permanent crisis, conflicts and nuclear self-destruction threats' (Sekulic, 1985, p. 115).

Although workers' self-management, urban and rural sociology, and the sociology of the family were well researched, studies of Yugoslav social structure took greatest prominence. The last major research project organized by the so-called Consortium of Institutes of Social Sciences (which released initial results just before the outbreak of war in 1991), was titled *The Structure of Yugoslav Society*, that is, *The Class Entity (Structure) of Yugoslav Society.*

In the 1980s, a great number of sociologists concluded that it was a classless (or one-class) society for all its elements constituted an 'integral part of the working class', which is 'unique, and the only, class'. Thus, all are 'working people' and the state is only an instrument of 'working people'. Yugoslav socialism has been seen as 'a class society in disappearance', more precisely 'a society with the class structure in disappearance'. In the spirit of *praxis*, this concept followed the idea that socialism has only one social class, that is, working class, which is defined as 'a revolutionary subject with its awareness of the historical purpose'. So, Yugoslav society is classless because everyone in it belongs to 'working people'. The message is already crystal-clear: if there is only one 'working people' in a society, and if that society is classless, then it is probably *nationless* as well.

Research on interethnic relations failed to detect the increase in 'ethnic distance' between some of Yugoslavia's peoples until the very last moment. *Ethnic stratification*, which would have illuminated the crucial interdependency of class origin and ethnicity, was nowhere to be found.

One long-term project on interethnic relations

Uniquely, Belgrade's Institute of Social Sciences studied the national phenomenon until the disintegration of the country. An independent scientific institution founded in 1957, the Institute could be said to have played an important role in the development of Yugoslav sociology. Its Centre for Sociological Research hosted a project entitled *Inter-Ethnic Relations in Yugoslavia and SR Serbia* as early as 1965. In retrospect, it is clear that the project's roots lay in the Eighth Congress of the Yugoslav League of Communists where, *for the first time*, it was acknowledged at the highest level that *nationalism was an issue in Yugoslavia*.

The project started with a review of some constitutional issues regarding the position of the country's various peoples/nationalities. Later, it encompassed the history of 'the national question', the origins and formation of the Serbian nation, the resolution of the national issue during the War of National Liberation in WWII, and contemporary problems relating to the social and economic inequality of peoples/ nationalities within Yugoslavia. Until 1975, five of the Centre's associates were engaged in the project, but from 1976 the status of the project was changed. It appeared that none of the researchers with 'scientific' status wanted to work on the project.

From the very beginning, it had not been financed by the Republic's Council of Science (or some other independent client) as was the case with all other projects in the Institute: it had been financed by the Central Committees of the League of Communists of Yugoslavia and Serbia. Associates at the Institute had the autonomy to decide whether or not to work on a particular project. Here, in order to retain funding, two associates (without scientific status) were under the supervision of a politician appointed as external associate. He acquired funding to employ a large group of external associates. Although possessing scientific titles, most were not members of the Sociological Association. The annual *Bulletin on Inter-Ethnic Relations*, which they produced, dealt with questions of interethnic relations under the Constitution and other principal laws. Over the period 1976–82, that same group prepared a *Bibliography on the National Issue and Inter-Ethnic Relations in Yugoslavia from 1945–1977* (which never appeared in its entirety).

As if this topic had not already been exhausted, the same sponsor funded, in 1985, *The Relation between Nations and Nationalities*. This focused on two issues: the historical development of social thought on interethnic relations, and problems of interethnic relations in Yugoslavia (Serbia) after WWII, principally the question of creating a 'self-managing political system as a framework for establishing more complete equality of nations and nationalities in Serbia and Yugoslavia'.

The collapse of Yugoslavia in 1991, accompanied by one of the most horrifying inter-ethnic wars, caught this group of *experts on the national question* researching the following topics:

1. Serbian social democracy and the national question in Serbia before unification in 1918;
2. Communists and the national question in Yugoslavia between the two world wars;
3. The War of National Liberation, revolution and the national question in Yugoslavia, 1941–1945;
4. System of political self-management and relations between peoples and nationalities in processes of uniting labour and resources;
5. Large systems (production, transport, finance, communication) and current questions concerning realization of national equality;
6. Interethnic relations and problems of federalism; and
7. Relations between Yugoslav nationalities and emigration processes before and after WWII.

The fall of the Berlin Wall in 1989 caused great political changes in Yugoslavia. By a spectacular withdrawal from the joint session of the Central Committee of Yugoslavia, the Slovenian communists, among other things, initiated the disintegration of a number of Party institutions; most notably, various Committees of the Communist League, some politicians' cabinets, Marxist Centres (and many others employing large numbers of Party intellectuals). As these institutions disintegrated in the early-1990s, at a federal, republic and regional, communal and urban level, some of the displaced people were transferred to scientific institutes. Even after the outbreak of war in 1991, work on the Belgrade Institute's 'interethnic relations' project continued, though now the focus, not surprisingly, was on the position of minorities and war refugees *within Serbia*.

Beginning of the 1990s: weak ethnic distance

Despite the profession's general emphasis on social structure and class relations, the last major research project with the prefix 'Yugoslav' (from the Consortium of the Institutes of Social Sciences) *Social Structure and Quality of Life in Yugoslavia* did address interethnic relations. [Its findings were presented at a scientific meeting in Zagreb in June 1991.]

Research carried out in Croatia and Bosnia-Herzegovina by Katunaric (1991) revealed some interesting results. Although levels of authoritarianism suggested the possibility of new ethno-political conflict, there was no evidence of major social inequality between the 'strategically' most important groups, and ethnic 'preferences' were mildly stated (although by the end of 1989 some changes were being felt in Croatia; 'self-preference' increasing among major groups and a greater distancing from 'Yugoslavs' (ibid., p. 383)).

In a Croatian survey, people were asked whom they would most like to work with. Croats favoured members of their own nationality most (92.2 per cent), followed by Serbs, Yugoslavs and Muslims. Serbs, however, preferred Croats (!) (59 per cent), to members of their own nation (27.3 per cent). Yugoslavs also preferred Croats most, ahead of Yugoslavs and Serbs. Comparing these findings with his 1985 study, Katunaric (1991, p. 378) suggests that 'self-preference' of Croats has increased while that of Serbs and Yugoslavs has declined in favour of Croats. This is seen as the result of a major political campaign (at the end of 1989) aimed at the 'rehabilitation of ethnic and political Croatism'.

As regards the empirical studies, Katunaric points to certain methodological problems; most notably, rather weak measures of 'socio-ethnic distance' and high refusal levels to these questions (around 60 per cent). He concludes that this type of research cannot determine the causes of ethnic conflict: these are rooted in 'political processes before and after the first multiparty elections. These take the form of nationalist movements...under the formula "one nation-one state". It is a formula from nineteenth-century Europe, and it usually leads to the outbreak of local wars' (ibid., p. 384).

Public opinion on the national question: increasing national homogenization

Arguably, studies of national consciousness between the mid-1960s and late-1980s provided the clearest evidence of worsening interethnic relations. These studies were, however, poorly regarded within Yugoslav sociology as simply representing non-theoretical 'snapshots' of public opinion (and thus more befitting of social psychology). Of course, in totalitarian regimes, studies of public opinion are often shunned or, being sponsored by the Party and its organs, are greatly distrusted. In this case, public opinion surveys were carried out under immense ideological and political pressure by the sponsors so the results when publicized were obscured by over-complex language. This was particularly so when the field of inquiry was 'sensitive' (for example, national or religious beliefs). Even though researchers deliberately used an elusive discourse, results of these surveys in retrospect undoubtedly point to an *increasing national homogenization*.

In spring of 1989, the Institute of Social Sciences' Centre for Public Opinion Research carried out research into *Public Opinion of Yugoslav Youth on Current Social-Political Issues*. Based on a sample of 5000 young people (aged 15–27) within the Socialist Federal Republic of Yugoslavia, the results were delayed for a year because the sponsors (the Conference of the Socialist Youth League of Yugoslavia) were 'preoccupied by its own disappearance'. One review of the book argued that 'if the research was to be repeated today, the results would be different: what was just a slight indication a year ago, today it is a reality which we're living!'

The survey points out that interethnic relations became an 'unavoidable subject' of all Yugoslav public opinion research only in the late-1980s (Bacevic, 1990, p. 147). It emphasized, for the first time, the necessity of studying the *crisis* of interethnic relations, the roots of which lay in the conflicting economic interests of republics and nations. Furthermore, even though this could have been anticipated in the early-1960s, and was 'seen, felt and experienced' in 1971 and 1981, the crisis of the late-1980s was unique in that it *reached every part of the country and every social group*.

This study demonstrated that national identity among the young generation was projected through the sense of belonging to a particular republic, so identification with a nation was under-developed (with the exception of young Slovenians and, to a lesser extent, Albanians). Secondly, data on 'ethnic distance' in relation to possible marriage and friendship revealed that Yugoslav youth in the late-1980s differed from that of the early-1960s. [There was still some reluctance to form social ties, but this was less than in many other countries.] Thirdly, the acceptability/unacceptability of particular nations could be discerned. Slav peoples were more acceptable than non-Slavs, and the salience of religion was evidenced by a greater social distance between all nations and Muslims. Many attitudes were mutual: young Albanians demonstrated least acceptance of other nations/nationalities in respect of possible marriage, but not in respect of friendly relations. Finally, the study demonstrated the strong influence of situational factors, that is, current events, in that the mutual distance was higher between nations who were currently in political conflict.

Unlike young Croats and Albanians, for young Slovenians, the Yugoslav spirit of togetherness 'had lost its meaning', being equated with 'centralism and unitarianism'. Research in 1990 by the Consortium of Yugoslav Institutions for Public Opinion Research (with research centers in Belgrade, Sarajevo, Ljubljana, Zagreb and Skopje), coincided with a period of deep social crisis experienced by most people. It showed that an astonishing percentage of citizens (87 per cent) evaluated inter-ethnic relations in Yugoslavia as 'bad' (46 per cent) or 'very bad' (41 per cent). A majority of those in the latter group were from central Serbia (56 per cent), and the least from Croatia (23 per cent). Of major sig-nificance was the fact that poor interethnic relations were rarely inter-preted at workplace or neighbourhood level; more frequently featuring broader spheres of republic, regions or Yugoslavia (Miljevic and Popla-sen, 1991, pp. 155–7).

Astounded by the outbreak of war

A study of the development of Yugoslav sociology (Bogdanovic *et al.*, 1990) talked of several phases: a time of enthusiasm and extensive growth during the 1960s; deep crisis and repressive intolerance in the 1970s, followed by a period of de-marginalization and professional reaffirmation. Today, it is quite clear that sociologists have failed to demonstrate competence in the face of social reality.

By the late-1980s a 'scientification of politics' was argued to have taken place. Academics were more prominent in political meetings, and increasingly lent their signatures to political documents. Kraigher's Commission (Slovenia) prepared a 'Long-term Plan of Economic Sta-bilization' in which around 200 scientists participated. Vrhovec's Com-mission (Croatia), involving 250 scientists, produced a 'Critical Analysis of the Functioning of Socialist Self-Management Political Systems'. It was then announced that more than 300 social scientists would take part in Mikulic's 'Commission for Economic System Reform' (Bosnia). Taken together, these should have provided the catalyst for major social change. But they failed to do so. One of the participants in all three Commissions claimed that this was because their work was informed by outmoded theoretical ideas and, by operating in isolation, they in any case missed the bigger picture (Letica, 1989).

The generally accepted, and highly simplified, explanation of con-flicts in former Yugoslavia is that it suited the political elite *to translate social tensions into national(ist) tensions*. Indeed, the complex relationship between *democracy* and *nation*, is still not an object of sociological study and, of course, the Resolution of the UN Security Council on sanctions against Serbia and Montenegro means that sociologists from Croatia,

Slovenia and Bosnia are forbidden to enter any scientific/expert collaboration or take part in joint/international research projects, meetings or publishing ventures with sociologists from Serbia or Montenegro.

In the middle of the war, the editors of the journal *Sociological Review* invited the views of sociologists on *responsibility* for the absence of more precise diagnoses for, and predictions of, social reality. One of the rare direct answers came from one of the *praxis-group* founders:

> I think that we, sociologists, are far more responsible than other intellectuals because of the tacit tolerance (although it doesn't necessarily mean the acceptance) of the increased nationalism with all its tragic consequences, since we were the most competent to explain the reasons for current historical events, and our knowledge about the nature of a social system oblige us the most to make it transparent and to point out the widespread illusion that the present system would be able to deal with the catastrophe it had caused. We cannot excuse ourselves like the rest of the population, that we didn't know, that we were misled, that poverty and hunger forced us to compromise with the authorities, for it would mean that we admit sociology not to be a profession which assumes the capability to critically clarify social causes of historical events and to rise above ideological manipulations, but only a craft which serves us to make a living.
>
> (Golubovic, 1993, p. 48)

1991 war and immediate post-war years

The brutal warfare in the former Yugoslav republics of Croatia and Bosnia-Herzegovina produced a culture of hatred, the demolition of material and cultural foundations of communal life, masses of displaced people, and the permanent separation of children and parents, husbands and wives, and friends. In the 'rump' Yugoslavia (Serbia and Montenegro) a period of poverty ensued; economic collapse; hyperinflation; international sanctions; and the influx of almost a million refugees. It was a time of collapsing ethical value systems, and a complete moral vacuum where the brutalization of everyday life and simple struggle for survival led to massively increased criminality. It is no longer possible to talk about normal life, work or research. As to the development of sociology, I am now forced to confine comments to Serbia and Montenegro . To use the term 'Yugoslav' is something of a misnomer. No Serbian sociologist has undertaken research in Croatia, nor has a Croatian in Serbia. War refugees are still not returning either to Croatia or Serbia. There are no new debates about ethnicity or ethnic relations, let alone about different perspectives and the possibility of new approaches to these phenomena.

The first sociological study of the 'post-communist period' (within 'rump' Yugoslavia) was carried out by a group of researchers under the supervision of Mladen Lazic in November to December 1993. [It was financed by the Soros Foundation whose work would subsequently be banned.] Conducted in extremely difficult circumstances, *Destruction of Society: Yugoslav Society in Crisis of the Nineties* aspired to find stability amid 'deep and relatively rapid social change'. A short chapter entitled 'Research in a time of sanctions' describes in detail problems researchers were facing in the field. This was a time of hyperinflation, non-functioning telephones, and a collapse of the traffic system with many smaller towns and villages completely cut off. As to the study's explanatory focus, Lazic's (1994, p. 19) views are revealing: 'In a time marked by civil war on national (also, partly on religious) grounds, the study had to *at least partially pay attention to inter-ethnic relations*, especially because nationalism in its present manifestation is complementary to other patterns of conservative mind' (italics added).

This signalled an important development. Social psychologists now dominated research into nationalism, the 'national phenomenon' and 'national distance'. Sociologists continued to avoid these issues, despite the drastic upheavals and rapid social change wrought by interethnic war. Even after the war, we still cannot find a single new, innovative theoretical-methodological approach to these phenomena. What we do find looks more like 'going through the motions'; being driven more by a sense of professional duty than inspired by an intellectual, ethical or scientific curiosity to explain fundamental social change. The causes are numerous and not difficult to understand.

In addition to the obvious lack of funding, there is undoubtedly an overwhelming sense of sadness, and exhaustion of both soul and mind. Human indolence should not be ignored either: most sociologists have simply continued to deal with the same topics as before the war. In some ways, however, this may be better for the discipline. The recent sociological literature has reflected some efforts to interpret social reality, but these have been heavily influenced by strong personal views of a *nationalist* nature: Something which will be covered in more detail below.

So, what are the results of the first survey conducted in Serbia and Montenegro? In the 1980s, 'ethnic distance' (from other nations) was not high except in the case of Albanians. After several years of civil war, it is no longer a question of *whether* ethnic distance has increased generally, *but by how much.* Using a modified Bogardus-type attitude measurement scale, very high levels of distance have been found, especially towards Albanians. However, common factors of social distance (education, social status, place of birth/residence) and social-psychological characteristics (value orientation and character traits such as authoritarianism and traditionalism), were not highly correlated with the distance towards different nations living in the territory of former Yugoslavia. That leads to the conclusion that factors relating to *social situation*, that is, political conflict, the disintegration of Yugoslavia, and civil war determined the ethnic distance.

Xenophobia, ethnocentrism and group psychological closure are widespread. There is a high correlation between distances for different nations: the lowest correlation being for Gypsies/Slovenians (0.60) and Gypsies/Croats (0.60), and the highest for Albanians/Muslims (0.88) and Croats/Slovenians (0.87). So, there is *a tendency towards general distancing.* The conclusion is that, in addition to authoritarianism and ethnocentrism, xenophobia is going to represent a significant socio-psychological obstacle to the consolidation and development of a modern civil state (Lazic,1994, pp. 238–40).

Post-communist transition

Silvano Bolcic is one of those rare authors who provided a *sociological* analysis of the 'new historical period'; the so-called transition from socialist to post-socialist society in the early-1990s. Bolcic is by no means alone in arguing that the word 'transition', misleadingly, suggests a neutral and benign process: something disappears to make way for something new, created simultaneously. In the case of Serbia, *disappearance* is the only recognizable feature of social change: the only transition being towards a state of physical and social desolation, reflected in everyday routine.

In its standard meaning, 'society' doesn't exist any more:

> For the moment, people believe that laws, lawmakers and law enforcers still exist, that a social order that should be adhered to still exists, that there is a certain 'legitimate' social relation of an individual with other individuals and an individual with the 'state', that institutions which represent and assure that social order exist . . . . people sometimes still act in 'yesterday's manner': they 'go to work', although most of them don't work on anything meaningful at that

'job'; they wait to get their paycheck or pension, although they cannot pay for almost anything with what they get; they save money, although they just lower their purchasing power by that; go to the shops, although there's hardly anything in them to sell; write petitions and complaints to institutions which are dealing with their 'rights' although all 'rights' have practically become irrelevant for their everyday life. What exists in this country today is just a reminder of a long created 'society' on this territory that like a scattered meteorite still emits the residual 'radiation'.

(Bolcic, 1994, p. 144)

To understand everyday life in Serbia at the beginning of the 1990s, it is very important to recognize the demolition of its basic institutions, not only those of the state. Others ceased to exist in their true sense. In companies which were 'institutions of business life', normal business activities have ceased, to be replaced in some cases by inappropriate tasks such as delivering goods procured by the state or 'laundering' illegally-acquired money. Actors go to the theatre, and scientists to the institutes to collect sacks of flour or pork joints instead of their salaries. There are more and more factories that 'manufacture' nothing, shops which sell nothing, banks without money, schools without lessons, scientific institutes without scientific studies, courts without court verdicts, state services without real state activities. 'Transition' in Serbia is characterized by *a culture of survival and deficit*. Between this and the culture of the modern industrial, or postindustrial, society is an enormous chasm, yet East European societies, Serbia among them, are expected to make this 'transition'. This will take time (ibid., p. 146).

The nationalized society

A year later, at the annual meeting of the Serbian Sociological Association, Bolcic posed the question of 'transition' as a dilemma: transition or nationalization as a characteristic of *the nationalized society?* By this he means the ethnocratic constitution of the new global societies emerging from the ruins of the former, multiethnic, Yugoslav society. 'Nationalization' is a process which strives to mould society into the 'property' of a certain nation (*ethnos*). The basic identity of that society, its fundamental social order and social goals, are established so as to realize and protect the interests of the nation which has 'adopted' it. So, the 'ethnocratically' constituted society is primarily structured on an ethnic basis. Power is distributed to enable realization of the systematic interests of the ruling 'ethnos', from the constitution to other social spheres, especially cultural ones. As the system operates in the interests of the ruling 'ethnos', basic human values are devalued. This provokes widespread law-breaking, increased criminality and a decline in morality, coupled with hostility towards members of other nations (whether or not they are nominally citizens of the same country). Bolcic concludes that from the early-1990s new societies in the territory of the former Yugoslavia initiated the nationalization of society and not 'transition' (Bolcic, 1996).

He places major emphasis on the relationship between nationalism and increased criminality, arguing that, although criminality has also risen sharply in Russia and elsewhere in Eastern Europe, in the nationalized society it is probably more enduring. This is because it has the support, or tacit consent, of public opinion or majority society. Hence, Yugoslav criminality is not simply pathological, it is central to the establishment and maintenance of the nationalized society. Nationalization is seen as the most important feature of the society (Bolcic, 1995), in that it has left an indelible mark on all aspects of life.

Social character, social change and national conflicts

Social Character and Social Changes in View of the National Conflicts (Golubovic *et al.*, 1995) was based on research undertaken in October 1993. Its premise was that the vacuum created by the crash of communism has been replaced by the alternative ideologies of nationalism and populism. It specified an authoritarian political system relying on the cult of the leader, a mythologized view of the past, a strong ethnic identity (and intolerance towards other ethnic groups), anti-modernism and anti-individualism. A particular *social character* is deemed appropriate for such a society: subordination to the leader, distorted and inflexible mode of thought, reaffirmation of 'traditional values', intolerance towards 'the Other', and collectivism. The authors see the current political system in Serbia, and its authoritarian 'social characters', as firmly tied by a mutual dependency: the system produces the character that later nourishes it by its inertia (Golubovic, 1996, p. 17).

The term *nationalism* is interpreted as an exclusivist view in which a strong identification with one's own nation involves a negative attitude towards other nations. When nationalism is observed as an element of social character, it is seen as conditioned more *situationally than structurally* (endorsing the conclusions of Lazic's work discussed earlier). National political elites employed nationalism so as to maintain or win power, and the expansion of nationalist views were then exacerbated by *situational factors*, for example, the interethnic war.

The authors compare their results with those of the Consortium of the Social Science Institutes, from 1989 (mentioned above). This final sociological survey spanning the whole Yugoslav territory showed that the great majority of people disagreed with the statement that every nation should have its own state. Now, over half of the respondents supported the idea of the 'national' state. The attitude towards mixed-nation marriages had also changed: from 53 per cent positive in 1989 to 34 per cent in 1993. This trend of increased national exclusiveness can be described as *a reactive nationalism* as it was strongly inspired by *social-situational factors*. 'Nation' becomes a source of unquestionable authority and power, this nationalism being externally induced via official nationalist ideology. If social forces continue to act in the same way, nationalism may be affirmed as an element of social character (ibid., 1995, p. 349).

The 'rapid increase in nationalist orientation' is also stressed: only 25.5 per cent of the participants declared themselves as non-nationalists while 33.8 per cent expressed a firm nationalist conviction. In autumn 1993, 74.6 per cent of those surveyed in Serbia stated that 'the nation's fate had to be identified with its own fate' and 73 per cent accepted the necessity of loyalty toward the state (fatherland) and its prioritization over individual values: 'patriotism and loyalty toward one's own nation are the most important tasks of a good citizen'. More than half agreed that it was necessary to fight the 'national traitors' and took the view that 'Although my nation isn't perfect, our cultural tradition is better than others'. Over two-thirds felt than 'every nation without a leader is like a man with no head', and more than a half that in every society, there had to be a *political authority* that was *trusted completely* and whose decisions should be executed without question (Golubovic *et al.*, 1995, p. 158).

The survey also revealed an increase in ethnic distance, especially regarding Albanians (58.1 per cent), Muslims (52.8 per cent) and Croats (51.9 per cent). At the same time, absolute distrust is most noticeable towards Albanians (77.8 per cent), Muslims (73.1 per cent), Croats (69.1 per cent) and Germans (68.3 per cent); these nations constituting the current perception of 'the Enemy' of Serbia. More than half saw Albanians as primitive, and 61 per cent even concurred with the view that Croats have a tendency toward genocide on Serbs (ibid., pp. 197–8, 206).

Public opinion surveys point to the same conclusion. Once positive images toward nations of former Yugoslavia (Albanians apart) have radically changed for the worse. According to Pantic, these perceptions almost constitute *mass xenophobia*, albeit of a *temporary, reactive and situational nature*. The Dayton agreement has reduced levels of xenophobia, though not towards those nations considered responsible for the collapse of Yugoslavia (Pantic, 1996, p. 561).

On the dangers of the superficial

There have been surprisingly few serious analyses of the causes of the rise in nationalism. Every author mentions some *en passant*, but they are frequently rather banal. Thus, Golubovic *et al.* (1995, p. 335) cite three significant social events:

- *stormy and sudden changes caused by the breakdown of a social system* ('real socialism') which lasted for seven decades and maintained a balance of power between the two opposed superpowers;
- *collapse of the Yugoslav state* causing the mass migration of people; leading ultimately to
- *the civil and multiethnic war in former Yugoslavia.*

As noted earlier, these authors (for example, Golubovic) had not previously even acknowledged the existence of socialism in Yugoslavia. Now, it has not only crashed, but has also caused the emergence of nationalism. There are no attempts to answer the question as to whether the 'civil and multiethnic war in former Yugoslavia' is a cause or a consequence of the hidden and suppressed nationalism already evident. The superficiality of the 'analysis' is alarming. All results of previous studies from communist Yugoslavia have been 'taken for granted', the generally accepted belief being that before the 1991 war there had been no nationalism in Yugoslavia. Hence the war, a 'situational factor', had caused it.

Popovic (1996) argues that the eruption of nationalism was not a consequence of spontaneous conflict between Yugoslav peoples, but rather a result of the nationalist polices of republic leaders and their mutual conflicts. He concludes that two polar forms of nationalism have occurred; *aggressive and defensive nationalism* (for example, the aggressive Croatian and defensive Serbian, in the Croatian context).

Such a one-sided and simplified explanation is surprising, in that it contains propagandist views embodied in the official policy of the Serbian regime. As many other social scientists concur with his views, we present his account of these different types of nationalism in a little more detail:

New Croatian government has immediately come forth in aggressively nationalist manner not only restoring the former national symbols from the Independent State of Croatia (NDH), but also using greatly the assistance of former refugees, *ustashas*, who were coming in large numbers to Croatia helping it politically and financially. Certain continuity with the former Independent State from World War II has been established. This was openly stated in one of the election speeches by president Tudjman who then said that the NDH had been an expression of historical national aspirations of the Croatian people for liberation and creation of their own state. Immediately, a large number of Serbs were thrown out of public services, especially from executive positions. It all produced great fear of Serbian people who couldn't but revive their memories of the ustashas' bloody terror during the Second World War and who began to *organize themselves in self-defense*. As a reaction to the *aggressive Croatian nationalism*, which was imposed 'from above', *the defensive nationalism of Serbian people in Croatia* began to manifest, first as great fear and distrust toward new Croatian state and then, as hatred toward such a state and, consequently, toward Croatian people itself.

He wants to demonstrate that Serbian nationalism is *defensive* and so uses the findings of sociological research which fit his argument:

That this is true, that until the foundation of a new state, Serbian people in Croatia haven't been showing hatred toward former Croatian republic, and even less toward the Croatian people, is illustrated by the results of several sociological studies that were carried out during 1989, just before the collapse of the former state and in earlier years as well.

(Popovic, 1996, pp. 233–4)

In Serbia today, there are many sociologists and philosophers who openly express a 'hard-line' nationalism. The potential material effects of taking such a position are clear. Unfortunately, however, those who avoid an explicitly nationalist stance tend to comment on contemporary events hurriedly and without a willingness to reflect upon, and properly analyse, the phenomenon of the national, truly and reflexively (for example, in their own context).

The protest: 1996/1997

During the demonstrations in Serbia (November 1996 to March 1997) caused by vote rigging, a group of sociologists undertook research on civil and student protest. The survey revealed the Protest to be *a broadly-based revolt of citizens* far beyond the supporters of the 'Zajedno' ('Together') Coalition. Members and supporters of the latter constituted more than a half of the protesters (51.5 per cent), but almost a third (30.4 per cent) claimed that they were neither members nor sympathizers of any political party.

The world media focused on the strong 'nationalist colour' of the protesters (which the student leaders persistently denied). The research found that 27 per cent of students saw national affiliation as 'very important' (and 31 per cent 'important') to them: only 11 per cent saw it as not important at all. National affiliation is more significant to this group of student-demonstrators than it was to the participants of the similar student protest in 1992. On this criterion, students of the 1996/97 Protest are closer to the general population of Serbia questioned in Autumn 1993 (Golubovic *et al.*, 1995), even closer than the general student population of Serbia, questioned in that same year.

One further detail shows the significance of national affiliation to the 1996/97 students. They were asked to mark which of five given social groups was most important to them. Most chose 'the nation' (43 per cent), then 'a professional group' (16 per cent), 'generation' (14 per cent), while only 5 per cent chose 'class or social status' and 3 per cent 'religious group'. The researchers conclude that this does not mean they are predominantly nationalists or chauvinists: it was an 'element of patriotism' for most of them. They argue that protest has undoubtedly been directed towards the democratization of society, and 'the fact is that certain groups with intense national and nationalistic feelings were participating in it' (Grupa autora, 1997, pp. 59–60).

Squaring the circle

In many former socialist countries, a collapse of that system induced enormous social change. Here I have tried to show why a particular element of social change (interethnic relations) went largely unrecognized by Yugoslav sociology, despite massively violent resolution. Today, it is hard to tell what collapsed first: a state, a society or nations. What is called 'Yugoslav society' today is a deeply divided people who live in a certain bordered geographical region without a true, law-based state and social community. Parallel societies exist, and parallel social lives go on, much as once a 'parallel' life was organized in Kosovo. In the middle of Serbia, the Kosovo Albanians had succeeded in organizing their own extra-state, institutions, for example, in education. In Serbia itself, society has gradually atomised to such an extent that anyone can develop their own 'parallel life', independent from the rest of the society.

After the war (and the Dayton Agreement), there were no great changes in the socio-political landscape of Serbia (hardly surprising as, according to the official propaganda, Serbia has never even been in a war). The population is completely exhausted mentally, spiritually and economically. An estimated 300 000 young and highly educated people have left the country.

After the war, no significant changes occurred in the academic world either. The country remains subject to UN sanctions. Research funds are rare. Few are interested in the phenomenon of the national; it is an 'outlived' and 'defamed' topic. It is as if everything has already been said about it, in both public and political discourse. The state media only talk of *the national minorities* in Serbia: focusing on minor issues such as air-time on local TV for the Hungarian minority so as to convince people that the national problem in Serbia (and in all other ex-Yugoslav republics) has been solved. The term 'Serbian national minority' is avoided, as is a recognition of the fact that Serbs constitute a national minority somewhere, for example in Macedonia or Croatia.

Sociology is stagnant: sociologists continue to work on the same problems as before. Those who start to work on new topics are rare. The national issue awaits a new generation of researchers and favourable social conditions. But, that is where the circle is going to close. A primary question is what direction Yugoslav sociology will take in the future and whether sociologists will have enough organizational and professional strength to influence social change. An entirely new generation of sociologists, educated in a completely different theoretical-methodological tradition, will have to appear: a generation not physically and spiritually isolated from the rest of the world by wars and sanctions.

References

Bacevic, Lj. (1990) 'Nacionalna svest omladine', u Srecko Mihailovic i drugi, *Deca krize: Omladina Jugoslavije krajem osamdesetih* ('The National Awareness of Youth', in S. Mihailovic *et al., Children of Crisis: Youth of Yugoslavia in the Late*

Eighties), Institut drustvenih nauka, Centar za politikoloska istrazivanja i javno mnenje, Beograd.

Bogdanovic, M. *et al.* (1990) *Sociologija u Jugoslaviji: Institucionalni razvoj (Sociology in Yugoslavia: Institutional Development)*, Institut za socioloska istrazivanja Filozofskog fakulteta u Beogradu, Beograd.

Bolcic, S. (1994) *Tegobe prelaza u preduzetnicko drustvo: Sociologija 'tranzicije' u Srbiji pocetkom devedesetih (Difficulties of Transition to Entrepreneurial Society: Sociology of 'Transition' in Serbia in the Beginning of the Nineties)*, ISI FF, Beograd.

Bolcic, S. (1996) 'Osobenosti "nacionalizovanog" drustva', u *Jugoslovensko drustvo krajem devedesetih* ('Characteristics of the "Nationalized" Society', in *Yugoslav Society in the Late Nineties*), Sociolosko drustvo Srbije, Beograd, pp. 59–70.

Davidovic, M. (1985) 'Istrazivanja drustvene strukture u radovima jugoslovenskih sociologa: pravci razvoja teorijsko-metodoloskog pristupa' ('Research on Social Structure in Yugoslav Sociology: Development of Theoretical and Methodological Approach'), *Socioloski pregled*, Beograd, Vol. XIX (1–2).

Davidovic, M. (1988) 'Sociologija izmedju "integrativne" i "kriticke" uloge', u *Teorijski pluralizam u sociologiji* ('Sociology Between "Integrative" and "Critic" Role', in *Theoretical Pluralism in Sociology*), Sociolosko drustvo Srbije, Beograd, pp. 5–30.

Golubovic, Z. (1993) 'Od dijagnoze do objasnjenja "jugoslovenskog slucaja"' ('From Diagnosis to Explanation of "Yugoslav Case"'), *Socioloski pregled*, Beograd, 1–4.

Golubovic, Z., Kuzmanovic, B. and Vasovic M. (1995) *Drustveni karakter i drustvene promene u svetlu nacionalnih sukoba (Social Character and Social Change in View of National Conflicts)*, Institut za filozofiju i drustvenu teoriju i 'Filip Visnjic', Beograd.

Golubovic, Z. (1996) 'Drustvene promene devedesetih i drustveni karakter – primer Jugoslavije', u *Jugoslovensko drustvo krajem devedesetih* ('Social Changes of the Nineties and Social Character – an Example of Yugoslavia', in *Yugoslav Society in the Late Nineties*), Sociolosko drustvo Srbije, Beograd, pp. 17–29.

Grupa autora (1997) *'Ajmo, 'ajde, svi u setnju!: Gradjanski i studentski protest 96/97, (Let's All Go For a Walk: Civil and Students Protest 96/97)*, Medija Centar & ISI FF, Beograd.

Janjic, D. (with V. Tasic and V. Vujic) (1987) *Moderno drustvo. Drzava. Nacija. Prilog za bibliografiju, 1869–1986. godine (Modern Society. State. Nation. Contribution to the Bibliography, 1869–1986)*, Marksisticki Centar Gradskog Komiteta Organizacije Saveza Komunista u Beogradu, Beograd.

Janjic, D. (1993) *Nacija – sta je to? (A Nation – What is That?)*, Radnicka stampa, Beograd.

Kardelj, E. S. (1960) *Razvoj slovenackog nacionalnog pitanja (Development of the Slovenian National Issue)*, Kultura, Beograd.

Katunaric, V (1991) 'Uoci novih etnopolitickih raskola: Hrvatska i Bosna i Hercegovina' ('On the Eve of New Ethno-political Conflicts: Croatia and Bosnia and Herzegovina'), *Sociologija*, Beograd, 3 (July–September).

Lazic, M. (ed.)(1994) *Razaranje drustva. Jugoslovensko drustvo u krizi 90–ih (Destruction of Society: Yugoslav Society in Crisis of the '90s)*, Filip Visnjic, Beograd.

Letica, S. (1989) 'Znanstvenici o krizi' ('Scientists about Crisis'), *Nase teme*, Zagreb, 1–2.

Meznaric, S. (1984) ' "Teorija nacije" i kako je steci: Neomarksisticki pristupi sociologiji nacionalizma' (' "Theory of a Nation" and How to Realize It: Neo-Marxist Approach to Sociology of Nationalism'), *Kulturni radnik*, Zagreb, XXXVII (5).

Miljevic, M. and Poplasen, N. (1991) 'Politicka kultura i medjunacionalni odnosi', u Lj. Bacevic i drugi, *Jugoslavija na kriznoj prekretnici* ('Political Culture and Interethnic Relations', in Lj. Bacevic *et al.*, *Yugoslavia at the Crisis Turning Point)*, IDN, CPIJM, Beograd.

Pantic, D. (1996) 'Changes in Ethnic Stereotypes of Serbs', *Sociology*, Belgrade, XXXVIII (4), October–December, pp.561–83.

Petrovic, R. and Blagojevic, M. (1989) *Seobe Srba i Crnogoraca sa Kosova i iz Metohije: Rezultati ankete sprovedene 1985–1986 godine (Migrations of Serbs and Montenegrins From Kosovo and Metohia: Results of the 1985/86 poll*), Srpska akademija nauka i umetnosti, Demografski zbornik, Knjiga II, Beograd.

Popovic, M. V. (1996) 'Autoritarnost i nacionalizam u prelaznom drustvu' ('Authoritarianism and Nationalism in the Transitory Society'), *Sociologija*, 2, pp. 225–46.

Sekulic, G. (1985) 'Enciklopedija savremenog socijalizma', Informacije o projektu, ('Encyclopedia of Modern Socialism', Information on the project), *Gledista*, Beograd, 9–10.

10

The State and Social Science Research in Russia

Vicki L. Hesli and Brian L. Kessel

An important question that can be asked of any set of scholars is the degree to which their work is linked to the needs and demands of the state. Arguably, social scientists, like all creative intellectuals, can never be fully controlled. Thus, sometimes the work of social scientists falls beyond the dictates or the preferences of the state and may actually serve to undermine state legitimacy. At other times, however, the work of social scientists may be used to legitimize or authenticate state policy or state action. This close connection between the pursuit of state goals and social research is dramatically demonstrated by the critical role played by social scientists, most notably the public opinion researchers, in legitimizing the Soviet state – and, later, in undermining that same Soviet state.

The goal of this chapter is to evaluate the changing role that the sociological establishment has played in both Soviet and post-Soviet society. To this end we will describe the transformed nature of social science research as well as the new uses of this research. We will also discuss the implications of these changes for the future development of social science research and for the future development of democratic government in Russia. We begin by discussing how sociology was used by the state to legitimate its actions and authority during the Soviet era. Then we examine how Gorbachev's efforts to stimulate reform by encouraging sociologists to openly publish their findings contributed to the demise of the Soviet state. The published findings revealed to the public for the first time the high levels of discontent with the regime, as well as the mass support for popular independence movements within the Soviet Union's constituent republics. Within this context we also examine the problems and prospects of social science in the post-Soviet period. We conclude the chapter with a review of how social science has adjusted to changing circumstances by analysing the content of articles published in three academic journals during the 1970s, 1980s and 1990s. We find that the sociological establishment has addressed and has influenced a number of important societal and political issues. The independence of social scientists clearly increased during the late 1980s and 1990s. At the same time, the loss of Marxism-Leninism as a unifying ideology has forced social scientists to seek out new methodologies and to reassess their own role in society.

The changing role of the sociological establishment

Although the beginning of the history of social science in Russia cannot be marked by a specific date, the publication of sociological sketches in the 1840s and 1850s might reasonably be selected as a starting point for discussion. A notable example is P. Vistengof's *Essays on Moscow Life*. Russian literary geniuses such as Tolstoy and Dostoyevsky also contributed greatly to the exploration of human relationships. The first university sociologists in Russia were N. I. Kareev (*Introduction to the Study of Sociology*, 1887), S. N. Iuzhakov (*Sociological Studies*) and M. M. Kovalevskii (*An Essay on the Development of Sociological Theories*, 1906). The methodologies and structures of the sociological establishment experienced several transformations since a Department of Sociology was established at Petrograd University in 1918 under the leadership of P. A. Sorokin (Zdravomyslov, 1994, pp. 37–9).

After the revolution and during the 1920s the discipline registered numerous early contributions to the study of such diverse subjects as labour management relations, rural sociology, marriage, family, prostitution and suicide (Shalin, 1990, p. 1019). Scientists travelled abroad in the 1920s in order to study and to attend research conferences. Sociological literature from the West was discussed in the pages of Soviet journals. Following the rise of Stalin, however, Soviet social science went into a hibernation phase. All scientists and corresponding institutes were required to submit annual and five-year plans for research. In part the motivation was control, but this also represented an effort to reduce duplication in the research effort. In addition, under the policy of *vydvizhenie*, 'workers' without appropriate qualifications, were brought into positions of responsibility because of the presumed loyalty associated with their class origins. In 1934, this policy was scaled back because of the problems involved. Yet quota systems remained and opportunities for advanced training were frequently reserved for those scientists with a party affiliation. Other methods of control included cooptation and the coercion of the purges (Josephson, 1992, pp. 599–600). All social scientists who were suspected of independent thought were removed from their jobs.

It was after Nikita Khrushchev's famous de-Stalinization speech, given at the Twentieth Party Congress, that the Soviet Sociological Association (SSA) was established. Although empirical studies were once again conducted, the political ideology of the regime and the orientation of the leadership at the time left a clear imprint on the choice of topics and the thoroughness of study. Although the Soviet leadership needed accurate and reliable information about the implementation and effectiveness of government programmes – in order to make progress toward the stated goal of modernization – the authorities were reluctant to publicize too much information for fear that certain findings would highlight the failings and weaknesses of socialism (Shlapentokh, 1987, pp. 5–6).

The most sensitive areas, from the perspective of the leadership, were those that had to do with their own ability to maintain power. Their maintenance of power depended to a certain extent upon coercion, but also upon the degree of popular support for the Communist Party and for the other major institutions of the state. As long as most people believed that the regime was accepted as legitimate by a majority of their fellow citizens, thoughts of rebellion or opposition were rarely expressed openly. But should the dissemination of the results of public opinion polls reveal a widespread distrust and/or dissatisfaction with the leadership, citizens who were previously passive in their acceptance of political authority might come to question their own levels of support. Thus, even after the death of Stalin, the study of public opinion was treated with the greatest possible caution in the Soviet Union. Empirical investigations had to be legitimated within the framework of the official doctrine (Zdravomyslov, 1994, p. 44). For a project to receive official sanction, scholars had to present 'their research as related to economics and divorced from politics and ideology' (Shlapentokh, 1987, p. 18).

Nonetheless, the 1960s did see the creation of the Institute for Applied Sociological Research within the USSR Academy of Sciences and the beginnings of intensive study of public opinion. Researchers worded their questions cautiously and tended not to touch on subjects which were deemed to be politically sensitive (Shlapentokh, 1987, pp. 34–8). In 1968, a special department dealing with public opinion studies was established within the Institute for Applied Sociological Research (later renamed the Institute for Sociological Research, now the Institute of Sociology). The establishment in 1969 of an All-Union Council for the Study of Nationality Problems (headed by Yulian Bromlei) gave high visibility to empirical social research into ethnic processes (Lapidus, 1984).

Although authoritative pronouncements of the Soviet state continued to paint a picture of ethnic harmony and convergence of many nations into one internationalist whole, research about ethnic processes and relations intensified in the mid-1960s and ethnosociological surveys began to be published. Officially, the 'merging' of nations was to create a new historic community of people. Migration, intensified economic and social interactions, interethnic marriage, the universal knowledge of the Russian language, and the creation of new Soviet traditions would all serve to submerge ethnic and religious boundaries and create an all-Soviet consciousness. Materials published in *Pravda* and similar outlets idealized interethnic relations and were meant to serve as guides to party functionaries and to the populace. Studies tended to be preoccupied with the processes that promote ethnic integration, and the research focused on urban and industrial centres while de-emphasizing divergent rural or ethnic patterns (Karklins, 1986, pp. 10–13).[1] According to Iurii Arutiunian (1980, p. 73), 'The nationality aspects of Soviet rural life [were] virtually ignored ... on both the scholarly and the practical level'.

The most rigorous ethnosociological research (least hampered by ideology) occurred between 1969 and 1972, after which a crackdown occurred (Karklins, 1986, p. 14). But even under the best conditions, research could not contradict official rhetoric about the converging of the nationalities. The goal of research was to provide guidelines for the management of ethno-sociological processes. A primary concern was the effect of multiethnicity on workplace relations and productivity. Soviet researchers did ask their respondents to evaluate interethnic contacts – including both marriage and job contact – and related the answers to socioeconomic characteristics (Kholmogorov, 1970; Arutiunian, 1969). The desirability of interethnic marriage was specifically addressed and correlated with age, occupation and gender. Migration patterns and family structures were also the subject of study, most notably in relation to Islamic cultural influences, and given the labour surpluses in the Central Asian regions and the simultaneous labour needs of the economies in the more industrialized regions of the Soviet Union (Arutiunian, 1980; Filimonov, 1974). In these early studies, researchers did establish a relationship between higher educational levels and increased national consciousness (Karklins, 1986, p. 222).

During this period, sociologists primarily studied means of increasing labour productivity, such as by investigating training methods and employee job satisfaction. Sociologists were also called on to make recommendations on the size, layout and location of apartment complexes as the authorities tried to address problems related to increasing urbanization (Zemtsov, 1985, pp. 23–4). The work of sociologists had to be ideologically acceptable. A massive study of Soviet young people was scrapped when it indicated, for example, that moral alienation and hopelessness were important causes of juvenile delinquency, and that rejection of Soviet social norms extended to even the children of the privileged strata of Soviet society (Zemtsov, 1985, p. 47).

After the period surrounding the Prague Spring of 1968, the leadership developed a deep-seated suspicion of the motives and loyalties of many prominent intellectuals. The party tightened its control and the proportion of party personnel working within the sociological research institutions was purposefully increased (Shlapentokh, 1987, pp. 119–20). Entire areas of sociological study were discontinued and many scholars were forced to leave the Institute of Sociological Research of the USSR Academy of Science (Shalin, 1990 p. 1020). Some work continued, but sociology as a discipline was disjointed and made only limited progress.

During the 1970s, the results of sociological research were published mainly in specialized scientific journals with a narrow circulation (and very rarely in the public press). Political authorities used parts of the data (mostly those showing 'achievements of socialism in the USSR', positive attitudes toward various aspects of the Soviet way of life, and mass support of Soviet foreign and domestic policy) in various state and communist party documents, including official reports and speeches by political figures. Data characterizing negative attitudes toward Soviet society, however, were not incorporated into official documents. Rather, the official documents and speeches were aimed at reinforcing the climate of 'social optimism'. All major surveys were 'under the close supervision of the local party authorities of the regions in which the analysis [was] to be performed – local party committees [monitored] the data collection process' (Shlapentokh, 1987, p. 119).

Only with the death of Brezhnev did regime hostility towards social science begin to diminish, and the new posture filtered slowly through to the sociological establishment. Although Mikhail Gorbachev was elevated to the position of General Secretary of the Communist Party in March 1985, the real turning point for Soviet social science did not occur until a path-breaking speech was made in November 1986 by the newly-elected president of the Soviet Sociological Association, Tatyana Zaslavskaya. Zaslavskaya challenged Soviet social scientists to move beyond their previously circumscribed role of 'reiterating, explaining, and approving party resolutions' and urged them to take an active part in 'renewing society' (Zaslavskaya, 1988, p. 267).[2] Significantly, Zaslavskaya urged social scientists to function as agents of social and political change. She commanded scientists to 'warn society in good time about the difficulties which await it, work out alternative solutions, and substantiate the choice of the best [solution]' (ibid., p. 268). Social scientists held responsibility for providing managers and decision-makers with the 'full, accurate, and truthful information' that they needed in order to make necessary reforms (ibid., p. 268). She even defined the most important questions for study, particularly with regard to improving productivity and efficiency in the economic sector and with regard to alleviating the apathy and alienation that had come to characterize Soviet society. She called for improved methodologies, higher professional standards and better training for researchers. She entreated scientists to produce more and better data in such neglected areas as crime, alcohol and drug use, suicides, migration patterns, disease rates and ecological problems. The implication was clear: Soviet social scientists were not just to study problems within society, they were also expected to play a central role in solving the problems themselves.

The turnaround that occurred with the new thinking of the Gorbachev era encountered some resistance from the people in the sociological establishment who had come to power in the 1970s, and the transformation of the discipline followed a step behind the radical and critical reorientation of the media. Zaslavskaia was not alone as a social critic and as an exception to this institutional resistance.[3] Iu. A. Levada had much earlier (in the late-1960s) articulated a view that sociology should be fully separated from the orthodox constraint of historical materialism (Zdravomyslov, 1994, p. 45). In December 1987, pro-reform social scientists openly challenged the Communist Party when they publicly opposed the election of the known ideologue, M. N. Rutkevich, to full membership in the USSR Academy of Sciences. The incident revealed to the entire academic establishment that party ties were no longer a guarantee of regime support (Shalin, 1990, p. 1021).

Starting in late-1987, the articles published throughout Soviet social science tended to be highly critical of the dogmatism that had pervaded the sociological establishment in the past. Articles also criticized bureaucratism, intolerance and the lack of democracy. A series of articles published in 1987 and 1988 offered analytical self-reflection on the topic of Stalinism. An attempt was made to understand the socio-psychological roots of Stalinism, that is, an attempt was made to explain the state of mind that would allow for mass approbation of such horrible crimes.[4]

As *glasnost* (openness) unfolded with Gorbachev's blessing, the scope and range of topics covered through public opinion research expanded. By encouraging new lines of inquiry, as well as social critique by intellectuals, Gorbachev hoped to obtain a better understanding of why the Soviet economy was faltering and why new policy initiatives were ineffective. The goals were not only to realize radical economic reform (specifically, a shift to a market economy), but also to accomplish a political renewal by ending the monopoly of political power held by the Communist Party and encouraging the emergence of new political parties and organizations. *Glasnost* and democratization were intended to raise the level of political participation (and effectiveness) of the masses, while concurrently creating a lawful state.

In spite of the progress made in the pursuit of *glasnost*, however, some taboos remained. For example, editors would not publish articles which directly targeted the privileges enjoyed by the *nomenklatura*. Many of the links between the state and the social sciences remained intact. Social scientists served on government-sponsored task-force teams and the data gathered by social scientists provided the justification for formulating new social policies and for the authorization of new legislation (Shmelev, 1985; Tsypko, 1986). Social scientists were elected to positions of leadership in both the government and the party apparatus (Shalin, 1990, p. 1024).

Social science research provided a valuable tool for the Communist Party in the pursuit of its political agenda. The data gathered by social scientists demonstrating the failures of the Soviet system justified the party's proposed social and political transformation. As had historically been the case in the Soviet Union, sociological studies were being used to prove a point: that *perestroika* was necessary. Nevertheless, as *glasnost* progressed, public opinion surveys first went several steps and then quantum leaps beyond their traditional role of servicing the party line. As time passed and economic and political conditions worsened, surveys became a mouthpiece for public discontent, not only with the economy, but with the political leadership, government institutions, and even *perestroika* itself.

As it emerged from the Brezhnev era, the Institute of Sociology within the USSR Academy of Sciences had as its mandate the study of economic and social issues, such as labour productivity and divorce rates. During the 1980s, these same methodologies and structures were deployed (extended) for the study of politics. The subject matter of the surveys conducted in the late-Soviet period included the overtly political, and could even be considered as oppositional, as attitudes towards *perestroika*, *glasnost*, democratization, and individual political leaders became fair game. Researchers conducted studies without fear of demonstrating the marked decline in the popularity of important political figures. Soviet surveys tapped attitudes toward models of a market economy, the newly emerging political parties, and various drafts of the negotiated all-union treaty. Topics which were rarely discussed in public (and, if discussed, were limited to a single, 'official' view) were suddenly the focus of interview questions.

Overall, the processes of *perestroika*, democratization and *glasnost* in the Soviet Union gave rise to a proliferating publication of public opinion studies. The year 1988 ushered in an entirely new phase in the study of Soviet politics, when the Institute of Sociology began assisting with joint USSR-Western polling projects. Soon numerous institutions, agencies, departments and 'cooperative' (or private) firms were conducting survey research within the USSR. In response to the rising demand for survey-based information about the views of the people, the network of sociological services expanded throughout the country. One of the immediate manifestations was the establishment of the All-Union Centre for Public Opinion Studies of Social and Economic Problems, sponsored by the Trade Unions Council and the State Labour Committee and headed by Tatyana Zaslavskaia. When it was first established, the main purpose of the Centre was to serve the process of *perestroika* (according to Zaslavskaia) and to that purpose, survey results released by the Centre were often spotlighted in the mass media. Some of the more prominent research centres that began to operate on a commercial basis were Vox Populi (Professor B. A. Grushin) and the Institute of Independent Research (V. M. Voronkov).

Social science research goes public

Central to the capacity of the sociological establishment to have an impact on society was the opportunity to freely disseminate research results to the public. *Glasnost* made this possible. On 12 June 1990, President Gorbachev signed an All-Union law that abolished prior censorship and forbade the authorities from interfering in the work of journalists. The law confirmed that the print media had gained unprecedented freedom of expression. The print runs of the major subsidized newspapers, such as *Izvestiya* and *Pravda* were extremely high by Western standards, and the popularity of periodicals such as *Nezavisimaya gazeta*,

Literaturnaya gazeta, and *Moskovskie novosti* was on the rise. Although television is the main source of information for most Russian citizens, it was common practice in the late *perestroika* period for urban residents to read several newspapers each day. *Moskovskie novosti* (*Moscow News*), together with other Russian periodicals that are referenced below, regularly published the results of sociological surveys. Reporting the results of public opinion surveys became an important component of the weekly and monthly news. During the period between 1988 and 1991, the media had an extraordinary impact upon citizens. The media set a new tone for public discourse and played a crucial role in shaping the people's willingness to express opposition to the Soviet state. Because the messages being conveyed by public opinion polls were so vital to the transformation of the Russian state, we have reproduced below a sample of the kinds of survey results that were appearing in the Russian language newspapers.

The economy was one of the first areas of dissatisfaction tapped by Soviet researchers. In the 'End of the Year Poll (1990)', 86.9 per cent of Muscovites said that the economic situation as a whole was getting worse (68.4 per cent said much worse). In a January 1991 poll, respondents were asked what the Soviet Union had given its people. Two-thirds mentioned deficits, shortages, queues and poverty.[5] An All-Union survey held in August 1991 asked respondents what societal problems bothered them most. Sixty-nine per cent indicated increasing prices, 40 per cent noted shortages of products and goods, and 28 per cent mentioned increasing crime.[6] A November survey revealed that 70 per cent of Russians were upset by the lowering of the standard of living and 45 per cent by the disintegration of the economy.[7]

Surveys conducted by Soviet sociologists went beyond an evaluation of social and economic concerns and also reported attitudes towards government leaders and institutions. Immense dissatisfaction manifested itself not only through disenchantment with government leaders but also through frustration with the institutions of government that formed the foundation of the Soviet state. Although the early surveys of the late-1980s showed great support for Mikhail Gorbachev, by March 1991, only 22 per cent evaluated Gorbachev's performance as satisfactory.[8] The legitimacy of government institutions themselves was put into doubt by the lack of faith exhibited by poll respondents. The same March 1991 survey referenced above revealed that only 31 per cent of people trusted government to some degree and a majority (56 per cent) did not trust government structures at all. Residents of the Russian Federation (RSFSR) were asked which organizations and institutions they did trust. The military (63 per cent) and the church (57 per cent) inspired the most confidence. The USSR Supreme Soviet (36 per cent) and the President of the USSR (35 per cent) were trusted least.[9] A July 1991 poll showed that 69 per cent of Russians believed that the CPSU completely discredited itself during its years in power; only 10 per cent disagreed.[10]

In a sense, a national learning process took place. The evidence for systemic weakness and nationalist strength mounted – and had as one of its primary sources the research work of the sociological establishment. No other organization – official or unofficial – had the organizational resources or the network of field workers to chronicle the *perestroika* process. *Glasnost* served to expose corruption: it allowed discussion of serious social and economic ills, and provided a forum for criticism of the elite. Although euphoric at first about the possibility of change, such revelations demoralized the people and contributed to a crisis of legitimacy. The policy of *glasnost*, in allowing sociological research to explore previously uncharted territory, together with ·the open policy of publication, also provided an outlet for the expression of latent and suppressed nationalist tendencies and fuelled the building of a new national awareness. Thus, an important ingredient in the success of popular front movements in the republics was the work of Soviet sociologists.

Popular fronts in Lithuania, Ukraine and Russia

Popular front movements within the Soviet republics grew in strength as citizens sought to take advantage of the new spirit of *glasnost* emanating from Moscow. The pioneers in this regard were the Baltic republics. An example is the Lithuanian Movement for Reconstruction (*Lietuvos Persitvarkmyo Sajudis*), founded in June 1988. In the 1989 elections for the USSR Congress of People's Deputies, Sajudis candidates ran in 39 of 41 electoral districts, winning 36. In the February 1990 elections to the Lithuanian Supreme Soviet, candidates supported by Sajudis won 100 seats in the 136 districts in which they ran. A month later, the Chairman of Sajudis, Vytautas Landsbergis, was selected to replace the first secretary of the Lithuanian Communist Party, Algirdas Brazauskas, as chairman of the Supreme Soviet. Under Landsbergis' leadership, the parliament immediately voted to declare the independence of Lithuania. Although Moscow rejected Lithuania's assertion of independence, the situation changed abruptly with the hardliner's failed August 1991 coup against Gorbachev. Western nations began recognizing Lithuanian independence and on 6 September the Soviet State Council granted recognition as well.

In other republics, the development of popular front movements followed a few steps behind that in the Baltics. Although the popular front in Ukraine (*Rukh*) held its founding congress in September 1989, statements from the Congress were conciliatory and well within the limits proscribed by Gorbachev and the Communist Party. The Ukrainian Supreme Soviet did issue a declaration of sovereignty in July 1990, but only after a similar resolution had been adopted by the Supreme Soviet of the Russian union republic (RSFSR).

As late as March 1991, 70 per cent of Ukrainians voted with Gorbachev in support of a 'Union of Soviet Socialist Republics as a renewed federation of equal sovereign republics'. Yet, 80 per cent also agreed that 'Ukraine should be part of a union of Soviet sovereign states [based] on the principles of the declaration on the state sovereignty of the Ukraine' (Solchanyk, 1991, p. 26). Leonid Kravchuk, the chairman of the Ukrainian Supreme Soviet, had proposed the second question as a means of using public opinion to validate the independence movement. He interpreted the results as mass support for Ukrainian sovereignty. In a December 1991 referendum, 90 per cent of Ukrainian residents expressed support for independence, and Kravchuk was elected President with 62 per cent of the vote. Ukraine, too, became an independent state.

Most outside observers were rather sceptical about the probability of success for the popular front movements when they first took up the demand for fully independent states, but media reports provided mounting evidence, coming from within the Soviet Union itself, that the popular front movements did indeed have a very high probability of success. Evidence of widespread support for a radical transformation in the constitutional structure of the Union – as well as mounting evidence of increasing vulnerability of the old order – was being provided through the mass media in the form of reports by Soviet sociologists on the results of public opinion surveys. The regular publication of opinion poll after opinion poll, all showing a nearly unanimous desire among the people for independent statehood and freedom from the repressive clutches of the old Soviet Empire, served to increase the sense of solidarity among movement participants and boost their belief that their efforts would ultimately be successful. Thus, the information provided by sociologists on the extent and the depth of the desire among the masses of the people for regime change served to solidify support for the movements calling for independence in many of the republics.

Attitudes toward popular front movements were registered in several polls conducted during this period. For example, the Public Opinion Research Centre of the Lithuanian Academy of Sciences, Institute of Philosophy, Sociology, and Law, conducted surveys in May, August and October of 1989. The surveys demonstrated the lack of popularity of the Lithuanian Communist Party while simultaneously providing evidence of the increased popularity of the Popular Front Sajudis. A poll taken in May 1990 asked respondents if they thought the decision to restore the statehood of Lithuania should be revoked. This was two months after the Lithuanian Supreme Soviet's declaration of independence and one month after the initiation of an economic blockade of Lithuania by Moscow. Despite the difficulties caused by the economic blockade, 72 per cent agreed that the decision should stand, while only 19 per cent thought that it should be revoked.[11]

Sociologists were also reporting on survey results in Ukraine, although to a lesser extent. In September 1989, the All-Union Centre for Public Opinion Research surveyed delegates to Rukh's founding Congress and the Ukrainian population. At this time the public had limited knowledge of Rukh. Only 10 per cent of those surveyed knew about Rukh's entire programme, while 24 per cent knew about some parts of it, and 23 per cent knew nothing about it (Paniotto, 1990). By 1991, sociologists could demonstrate the growing popularity and familiarity of Rukh. Among respondents polled in February 1991, 54 per cent reported that they would vote for Rukh in elections to the Supreme Soviet. Furthermore, the poll showed that eight out of ten of the most well-known political activists (politicians) in Ukraine were Rukh members.[12]

The development of popular fronts in the RSFSR took a quite different path from those in the Baltics or Ukraine. Among those who did advocate the formation of an all-Russian popular front were Tatyana Zaslavskaya, Boris Kurashvili of the Institute of State and Law, and Boris Kagarlistsky, a leader of Moscow's informal group movement. Despite the call for an over-arching umbrella organization, no unified popular front emerged in the RSFSR. Instead, popular fronts sprung up in cities all over Russia. The largest fronts were located in the major cities – Leningrad's popular front claimed a million supporters. A bloc calling itself Democratic Russia formed and successfully united 50 groups for the March 1990 local and republic elections.

As in the other republics, the government recognized these budding political movements and they found electoral success. Concessions by the central authorities in 1990 included ending the Communist Party's monopoly on power and granting equal rights to all political parties.

The growing power of the democratic movements was demonstrated by the Russian Supreme Soviet's selection of Boris Yeltsin as its Chairman in May 1990. Only a month later, the Russian Supreme Soviet declared the sovereignty of the RSFSR and in August 1990 declared the supremacy of republic authority over all natural resources and enterprises on Russian territory. In June 1991, Yeltsin was elected President of the Russian Republic, this time in Russia's first free presidential elections. The ill-fated August coup dealt the final blow to the ailing central authority. Following the collapse of the centre, the Russian government absorbed what remained of Soviet institutions on Russian territory.

Social science and the state after Gorbachev

The high status enjoyed by science, particularly social science, during the *perestroika* period did not survive the disintegration of the Soviet state. In December 1991, the once powerful USSR Academy of Sciences was replaced in Russia by the Russian Academy of Sciences. During the early-1990s, both politically and financially, scientists found themselves becoming increasingly marginalized. According to Mirskaya (1995, p. 723), prominent scientists were eased off the President's Council, which had been envisioned as an independent consultative body, and were replaced with members of the President's administrative apparatus. Scientists felt that their expertise, valued as an essential element of reform during the 1980s, was now being ignored by politicians. The vice-president of the Russian Academy of Sciences (RAS), V. Kudriavtsev, bitterly complained in 1992 that government officials and politicians were no longer responding to scientists' proposals, questions or criticisms.

Mirskaya (ibid., pp. 707–9) argues that although the economic collapse of the country made cutbacks in science inevitable, the declining fortune of science was also due to the precarious position of science in Russian and Soviet society.[13] The fortunes of science depend to varying degrees on the priorities of the state. When the state was focused on modernization, science benefited from state support and scientists were invited to participate in politics, but when the priorities of the ruling elite changed, the attitude toward science also changed rapidly.

Probably the most significant blow to the scientific establishment has come from the disastrous state of the post-Soviet economy. In January 1992, the Yeltsin government implemented a programme of economic 'shock therapy' by relaxing or abolishing price controls on most goods. Even the prices of basic foodstuffs and energy were allowed to rise.

Without concomitant increases in their own funding, the previously favoured scientists became members of the lower paid strata of society. Salaries in industry ranged from two to five times greater than in the sciences and even in the state sector of the economy salaries averaged 38 per cent higher (ibid., p. 710).

Financial support for science has continued to decline. *Nezavisimaya gazeta* reported that in the first seven months of 1996, science received only half of its budgetary allocation (Morozov, 1996). Delays in the receipt of funds forced the Russian Academy of Science to disconnect the phones in its far eastern division and to recommend that staff members be placed on unpaid leave of absence (Leskov, 1996; Morozov, 1996). In response, scientists have engaged in rallies, walkouts and hunger strikes to protest about inadequate state funding of science.

Some scientists have left the profession for careers in business or have emigrated to the West. Although figures vary, it is clear that the level of employment in the sciences has dropped dramatically. ITAR-TASS reported that the number of scientific workers in all fields fell by two-thirds since 1992 (OMRI Daily Digest, 2/14/96). According to the Council of the Trade Union for Employees in Higher Schools of Education, the number of scientific and research personnel at institutions of higher education fell by 90 per cent between 1991 and 1995 (Leskov, 1996 in *Izvestia*). Thirty-thousand Soviet scientists are estimated to be working in the West (ibid.). Many scientists who have remained in the profession have been forced to find secondary sources of income.

In addition to the suffering caused by the lack of financial support from the government and the dire state of the economy, scientists were also being blamed for their failure to navigate the country through the turbulent waters of economic and political transformation. A survey conducted by the Institute of Sociology of the Russian Academy of Sciences showed that only medical and engineering sciences were regarded as useful by a majority of those polled (Mirskaya, 1995, p. 723). Kudriavtsev (1994, p. 6) laments the low prestige of social scientists within the Russian Academy of Sciences, noting that scientists are not judged by the quality of their work, but by the state of their area of research. Hence, if the economy is bad, economists are to blame.

The loss of status for science has generated disillusionment among scientists. A 1994 survey of 412 members of 13 institutes of the Russian Academy of Sciences (including four social science institutes) found that 70 per cent of respondents were unsatisfied with their activities. Among the chief causes of dissatisfaction were low pay (cited by 73 per cent), the impossibility of carrying out research of real value (52 per cent), the reduction in opportunities for publication (28 per cent) and the feeling of their work being useless (24 per cent) (Mirskaya, 1995, p. 714).

Russian science has also been shaken by attempts to introduce organizational reform. The Russian government has encouraged Western models of peer review and competitive funding as the basis for awarding research grants to scientists in place of the Soviet-era system of awarding block grants to be distributed by the Academy. Through the competitive awarding of grants the Ministry of Science and Technology Policy would be able to reward productive scientists, but it would also have the potential to institute a gradual transformation of science in the direction desired by the ministry. The leadership of the Russian Academy of Sciences has been opposed to these reforms. Gaponenko (1995, p. 686) notes that under the old system, influence was concentrated in the hands of institute directors and powerful academicians of the Academy. Although peer-reviewed funding has been introduced through the Foundation for Basic Research (founded by the Science Ministry in 1992), and by Western funding sources, the traditional 'power-brokers' of science have been largely successful at resisting reform (Allakhverdov, 1994, p. 1153).

Given the financial and organizational crises facing all fields of science following the collapse of the Soviet Union, the field of sociology has actually fared better than most. In part this is because their share of the Russian Academy of Science's resources was already quite small. The budget for the 62 humanities and social science institutions in the RAS made up only 10 per cent of the Academy's expenditure in 1992 and employed only 15 per cent of its personnel. More importantly, sociologists have been successful at finding alternative sources of financing through market research and political polling. Many of the financially successful sociological agencies stay in business by conducting market research. *Sevodnya* reported in 1996 that 100 new sociological centres had opened since 1986 and that 90 per cent do opinion polling (Yurevich, 1996). Other important sources of financial support are from abroad (foreign and international organizations) and from Russian funds and foundations.

Nonetheless, a number of social research projects are still initiated by the government. The preference is for applied research and for projects that directly tackle the major political, social and economic issues; although there have been cases where the Russian Scientific Foundation has funded more academically-oriented projects. For example, the State Committee on Higher Education of the Russian Federation granted funds to Russian authors to prepare textbooks on sociology (Zdravomyslov, 1994, p. 48).

It is impossible to know the exact proportions of government, private and foreign financial support for social science research in Russia today. The notable drop of foreign support to the Russian government from organizations such as the Soros Foundation has to some extent been compensated for by the continuation of bilateral projects between universities or associations (Prazauskas, 1997). Also, certain non-governmental organizations, such as cultural or religious associations, provide financial support for projects that fall within their realm of interest.

Certainly, the increasing popularity of political forecasting among parties and politicians has served to raise the profile and status of sociologists. Larisa Kosova, of the All-Russia Centre for Public Relations Study, reports with satisfaction that Boris Yeltsin took the recommendations of sociologists into account during the 1996 Russian presidential campaign. During the presidential campaign, as well as during the campaigns for the state Duma elections in December 1995, the press was filled with survey predictions from a variety of sociological institutes.[14]

The surge of interest in political polling has not come without controversy. External funding has provided much needed resources for the conduct of research, but the external funding does not come without certain drawbacks. The negative influences of foreign funding emerge from the fact that external parties set the parameters of research agendas and, thus, sometimes ignore issues which are believed by indigenous scholars to be important for Russia (Melville, 1997). Widely disparate results among polling agencies, as well as the low accuracy of many polls, have raised questions and criticism about the work of social scientists. An editorial in *Izvestia* questioned whether election polling is science or a political service performed by 'hired propagandists' (Vyzhutovich, 1996). There are, of course, a number of legitimate explanations for polling disparities and inaccuracies ranging from the instability of Russian public opinion, deceptiveness on the part of respondents (this is one of the main explanations for the failure to predict the success of the ultra-nationalist Zhironovsky), and confusion on the part of voters given the plethora of parties and electoral blocks. In addition, some researchers have limited empirical experience, surveys may be unrepresentative because rural areas are not adequately sampled, and surveys sometimes employ leading questions. These problems have attracted significant attention, and numerous articles have been written on how to improve survey techniques (examples include Radaev, 1995; Sevelyev, 1995; Yurevich, 1996; Vilchek, 1996 and Vyzhutovich, 1996).

Nevertheless, the lack of transparency in the process raises questions. Clearly the business of political opinion polling is a profitable enterprise. *Izvestia* reports that a 1500–person, 30–item survey costs $12,000 (Vyzhutovich, 1996). Considering that most researchers earn less than $100 per month, this is a sizable sum. Details of such transactions are scant since who paid how much for a survey is generally not a matter of public record.

Politicians are eager to secure high places on polling lists. Since parties must earn at least 5 per cent of the vote to enter the state Duma, party leaders are especially anxious to be seen as making this threshold, particularly when voters are being urged not to waste their ballot on a party that will not be able to get into parliament. This has fuelled accusations that clients can buy 'good numbers' or that polling institutes make special efforts to provide pleasing results to their clients. Vs. Vilchek, Director of the Foundation for the Defence of Glasnost's Monitoring Sociological Articles in the News Media Project, alleges that the Vox Populi service encouraged voters to select 'electable parties' and then gave prominent attention to Rybkin's Bloc, even though their own surveys had indicated only a 0.9 per cent level of support for the party (Vilchek, 1996). Adding to the confusion, several party leaders claimed to have been duped by polling organizations that delivered survey results assuring their parties of election to the Duma.

Melville (1997) describes the emergence of a 'criminal and corrupted system of olygarchic cartels (plutocracy in its ancient meaning) under the smoke screen of formal democratic institutions'. When politicians do refer to the results of research, it is most often to research projects which they themselves had commissioned. Melville sites examples of various politicians giving money to different public opinion firms to come up with results favourable to them.

Nonetheless, once a study is commissioned, the researchers do have the independence to interpret and write up their results as they see fit. Likewise, politicians and government officials have the leeway to use or not to use the results, as they see fit. An example is a study commissioned in 1993 by the Analytical Department of Yeltsin's administration to conduct a series of focus groups to predict the electoral activities and preferences of citizens. The results – although quite pessimistic for the ruling elite and optimistic for communists – were submitted to the Analytical Department prior to the elections, but acknowledged only after the elections, when the predictions were confirmed. This is indicative of a broader tendency, which arguably remains from the Soviet era, to use research results primarily to legitimize decisions that have already been made. Kosova (1997) concurs that some of the tendencies of the Soviet period, such as using research to validate a theoretical framework that has been given official recognition, do continue today. A well-known phrase attributed to a Soviet official of high rank is: 'Public opinion should be formed, not examined'.

Besides public opinion polls, other techniques are also used by social scientists. Focus groups, content analysis, model-building, and comparative case studies are a few examples. Focus groups are arguably the most frequently employed method after public opinion polls. Other forms of field research are also important. Postmodernism has not gained many adherents and, according to Prazauskus (1997), many social scientists continue to look in their work for 'major driving forces of history'.

The controversy surrounding the adoption of Western-style political polling in election campaigns signifies the moral dilemma facing Russian sociology today. What role should social scientists play? Sociologists are quite sensitive to the politicized nature of their discipline during the Soviet era, and many are anxious to remain 'outside of politics'. It is in this light that one must view arguments about whether or not political polling is science or propaganda. Few bother to raise these questions in the West. Political pollsters in the West are already seen as 'spin doctors', not scientists. No one questions that political pollsters work intimately with their respective clients or that polling institutions frequently operate according to their own agendas. It undoubtedly raises the question of whether Russia should wholeheartedly embrace every element of Western-style politics. Yeltsin's clandestine employment of 'hired guns' from the United States to advise his 1996 presidential campaign was not encouraging in this regard. In any event, sociologists once again occupy a potentially important political position.

The changing agenda of social science from Brezhnev to Gorbachev to Yeltsin

Shalin (1990) has written on the changes that occurred in sociological inquiry during the 1980s. In this section, we will expand this overview to include the 1990s. Shalin notes that the most distinguishing feature of the 1980s was the dramatic expansion in the range of topics that were being probed and subsequently studied. His review, however, is limited

Table 10.1   Percentage occurrence of primary topics in published articles, *Sociological Studies* 1976, 1986 and 1996

Topics/Years	1976	1986	1996
Social issues			
Critiques of bourgeois sociology/critiques of capitalist way of life	9%	3%	1%
Scientific and technical change/evolution		1	2
Quality of life	2	5	1
Leisure time	2	5	2
Housing		1	0
Ecological crisis			1
Alcoholism		5	
Education/training	9	7	7
Family relations/marital relations, (including rural)	5	8	0
Youth	2	6	6
Social relations/social policy/development			0
Demographic studies/population growth	2	6	4
Urbanization		2	
Morality/ethics	5	1	
Culture studies	2		4
Religion			
Inter-nationality relations	5	2	6
Media/communications/journalism			3
Methods/methodology/sociological theory/reform in the discipline	5	8	13
Critique of bourgeois society/capitalism			
Economic issues			
Management/organization/industry planning	7%	3%	8%
Economic problems/reform/economic development			
Workers' attitudes and behaviour/identity	5	7	4
Improving efficiency/productivity	7	9	
Manpower resources/mobility/migration	12	1	2
Employment/unemployment/retirement	2	1	4
Rural employment/production/collective farms	5	6	2
Occupational structures/social, stratification/classes	2	6	2
Satisfaction of workers' needs	5	2	1
World economics/regional economics/integration			
Commodity/money/investments/price accounting		1	0
Political issues			
Marxism Leninism/historical materialism/ dialectics (Hegel)			
Party congress reports/documents			
Party organization, training, leadership, (Communist Party Activities), socialist democracy	5%		
International Communism/Socialism			1%

International relations/Detente	2	0
Imperialism/conflict/war peace/security/ military affairs		5
Global problems		
Revolution		
Political attitudes and behaviour/political, culture	2%	7
Justice/injustice/law	2	3
Critique of bourgeois democracy		
Government reform/(liberal) democracy/leadership		5
Elections/legislatures		3
Decentralized decision-making/regional elites/feder- alism		1
Government bureaucracy		0

Category summaries

Social issues: total percentage	49%*	59%	50%
Economic issues: total percentage	44	36	23
Political issues: total percentage	7	5	25
Other issues: total percentage			2
Overall total number of topics for each year:	43	88	198**
	(100%)	(100%)	(100%)

* Individual percentages may not sum exactly to sub-section percentage totals because of rounding errors.

** The journal expanded from 4 issues in 1976 to 12 issues in 1996. This accounts in part for the increase in the number of primary topics covered.

to those publications that appeared in *Sotsiologicheskie Issledovaniia* (*Sociological Studies*), the official journal of the Soviet Sociological Association. Our overview, to be presented below, includes professional journals from disciplines closely associated with sociology, as disciplinary boundaries tend to be fluid. Of certain interest, however, is Shalin's (1990, p. 1027) observation that in the late-1980s, over half of all of the space in *Sotsiologicheskie Issledovaniia* was given to opinion polls – thus, questionnaires and interviews were the most common methods of sociological research in the Soviet Union at that time.

In order to determine the exact degree to which the range of topics being discussed in published articles did increase under Gorbachev, the content of articles published in the Gorbachev era must be systematically compared with a previous era. In addition, more than one journal should be evaluated. We have conducted such a comparison and the decade of the 1970s is used as our baseline. Specifically, we examine how the content of social science publications changed between the mid-1970s, the mid-1980s and the mid-1990s. For the journals *Sotsiologicheskie Issledovaniia*, *Kommunist* (later *Svobodnaia Mysl*) and *Voprosy Filosofi*, we compare the content of all articles written in each journal for the years 1976, 1986 and 1996.[15] These years were selected as representative of the political influences of the Brezhnev regime, the Gorbachev regime and the Yeltsin regime respectively. In comparing the three years, we answer three questions: (1) What new topics emerged?; (2) What topics, if any, disappeared from publication?; and (3) What topics, if any, showed primacy through all three periods?

Because the range of topics addressed by social scientists is broad, we have grouped the topics into four categories: social issues, economic issues, political issues, and other issues. For *Sotsiologicheskie Issledovaniia*, the last five rows of Table 10.1 show the percentage of the total number of topics covered that fall in each of the four major categories. As this is predominately a journal for sociologists, most of the articles focus on social issues in all three years.[16] Notably, the share of articles devoted to economic issues tends to decline over time, dropping from 44 per cent in 1976 to 23 per cent of primary topics in 1996. The focus on political issues increases significantly between 1986 and 1996, with 25 per cent of primary topics being related to political issues in 1996.

With regard to specific primary topics, the biggest share of new topics appears with regard to political issues. Although no articles in *Sotsiologicheskie Issledovaniia* were devoted to the topic of government reform in 1976 and 1986, by 1996, 5 per cent were about government reform, democracy or democratic leadership; and 3 per cent were devoted to elections or legislatures. Likewise, articles focusing on international conflict, war and the related issues of peace and security are published in 1996. Noteworthy is the finding that 7 per cent of all articles published in *Sotsiologicheskie Issledovaniia* in 1996 included discussions of political attitudes and behaviour – a subject that was simply not a topic for research in the 1970s. Under social issues, social scientific methods/methodology, theory-building, and reform of the discipline began to be discussed more frequently in 1996. Internationality relations and cross-cultural interactions also featured more prominently in 1996. Representative examples of such work include the following titles: 'Ethnopolitical Processes and the Dynamics of the Russian National Consciousness' (A. C. Zdravomislov), 'Political and Ethno-religious Aspects of the Yugoslavian Conflict' (Z. Izakovitch), 'The Ukrainian Language Situation' (V. G. Gorodianenko), and 'Migration Potential of the Russian Population in the Countries of the Near Abroad' (L. L. Ribakovskiy).

As can be seen by the list of primary topics covered in *Sotsiologicheskie Issledovaniia* in 1986 as compared with 1976 (Table 10.1), four social topics are addressed by journal contributors in 1986 that were not seen in 1976: scientific/technical change, housing, alcoholism and urbanization. This represents moderate growth in the range of topics covered. In 1996, the only new primary social topic is the ecological crisis. With regard to political issues, however, new topics emerge as primary subjects for study in both 1986 and 1996. Political attitudes and behaviour, along with questions of justice, emerge as primary topics in 1986. Government reform, security affairs, elections and decentralized decision-making are all primary topics in 1996, though these topics had not been addressed either in 1976 or 1986. Representative of the increased emphasis on public opinion polling are the articles published in 1996 by Andrushenko, Dmitriev and Toshenko as well as by Sosedskiy.

Topics which appeared less frequently in the published articles of *Sotsiologicheskie Issledovaniia* were, most notably, those dealing with improving efficiency and production, with party organization, and with family relations. Clearly, the stagnation associated with the late Brezhnev era and the early Gorbachev era provided the impetus behind studies of efficiency and productivity. In the mid-1990s, the emphasis had switched to the management and reorganization of both the economy and government. The problem of alcoholism was a hot topic in 1986 – as this time-frame corresponded with Andropov's and Gorbachev's government-sponsored anti-alcoholism campaigns, but the topic disappears again by 1996.

Several social topics show remarkable consistency in remaining primary topics of study over the three decades: education, the problems facing youth, demographic change (population growth) and methods/reform in the discipline. Under the category of economic issues, social scientists in all three years devote research and writing time to management and organizational questions, to the attitudes and behaviour of workers, to employment and, to a lesser degree, to the issues of social stratification and rural employment.

We also conducted a similar content analysis of articles published in the journal *Kommunist*. Although the title of this journal was changed to *Svobodnaia Msyl (Free Thought)* in 1990, the primary topics for research and writing also show some consistency over time (Table 10.2). Political issues are the primary focus of the majority of articles published in 1976, 1986 and 1996 (see the final rows of Table 10.2). The number of overtly political topics declines temporarily in 1986 to accommodate the increased emphasis on economic reform ('acceleration') and efficiency, but political topics again come to dominate in 1996. The focus of articles on political issues, however, has changed markedly between 1976 and 1996. In 1976, much of the space in *Kommunist* was devoted to reporting on CPSU Party Congresses and Central Committee

Table 10.2   Percentage occurrence of primary topics in published articles, *Kommunist/Svobodnaia Msyl* 1976, 1986 and 1996

Topics/Years	1976	1986	1996
Social issues			
Critiques of bourgeois sociology/critiques of capitalist way of life			
Scientific and technical change/evolution	6%	7%	2%
Quality of life			
Leisure time	1		
Housing			
Ecological crisis	1	1	
Alcoholism		1	
Education/training	1	3	2
Family relations/marital relations (including rural)			
Youth	1		4
Social relations/social policy/development	1	2	2
Demographic/population studies		1	
Urbanization			1
Morality/ethics		1	
Culture studies	1	1	
Religion	1	1	3
Inter-nationality relations	1	1	4
Media/communications/journalism		1	1
Methods/methodology/sociological theory/reform in the discipline	1	1	1
Economic issues			
Critique of bourgeois society/capitalism	1%	1%	
Management/organization/industry planning	10	5	5%
Economic problems/reform/economic development	4	8	8
Workers' attitudes and behaviour/identity	2	4	1
Improving efficiency/productivity	1	6	
Manpower resources/mobility/migration			
Employment/unemployment/retirement	1	1	1
Rural employment/production/collective farms	1		3
Occupational structures/social stratification/classes	2	1	
Satisfaction of workers' needs	2		2
World economics/regional economics/integration		5	
Commodity/money/investments/price accounting			
Political issues			
Marxism Leninism/historical materialism/dialectics (Hegel)	7%	7%	3%
Party Congress reports/documents	19	8	3
Party organization, training, leadership (Communist Party activities), socialist democracy	7	3	
International communism/socialism	10	6	2
International relations/detente	6	3	13

Imperialism/conflict/war peace/security/military affairs	5	12	15
Global problems		1	
Revolution			
Political attitudes and behaviour/political culture		1	10
Justice/injustice/law	2	3	1
Critique of bourgeois democracy	1		
Government reform/(liberal) democracy/leadership		2	2
Elections/legislatures			4
Decentralized decision-making/regional elites/federalism		1	5
Government bureaucracy		1	1
Category summaries			
Social issues: total	16%[*]	19%	19%
Economic issues: total	26	31	19
Political issues: total	57	47	57
Other issues: total	1	3	5
Overall total number of topics for each year:	100%	100%	100%
	(145)	(173)	(129)

[*] Individual percentages may not sum exactly to sub-section percentage totals because of rounding errors.

meetings and also to the publication of party documents. Party Congress reports and documents were the most frequently addressed primary topic in 1976. Even in 1996, some of this continues, as historical party documents are reviewed to a lesser degree on the pages of *Svobodnaia Msyl*. The primary political issues addressed in 1996 were international affairs including conflict and aggression. Numerous articles also addressed the challenge of building peace and security within the international system. The third most frequent primary topic in 1996 includes political attitudes and behaviour. Discussions of federalism and decentralized decision-making, elections and legislatures also appear in 1996. The last of these topics had not previously appeared on the pages of *Kommunist* in 1986 or 1976. The increased focus on political attitudes and behaviour speaks specifically to the proliferation of public opinion polling that has marked Russian social science in the late-1980s and the 1990s. The focus on security and military affairs, however, is a separate development, and one that also had begun under Gorbachev.

With regard to social issues, the range of topics addressed in *Kommunist/Svobodnaia Msyl* does increase between 1976 and 1986, but then narrows again in 1996. New topics which become primary foci of the articles published in 1986 but that are not tackled again in 1996 include alcoholism, population change, and morality/ethics. The social topics

Table 10.3   Percentage occurrence of primary topics in published articles, *Voprosy Filosofi* 1976, 1986 and 1996

Topics/Years	1976	1986	1996**
Social issues			
Critiques of bourgeois sociology/critiques of capitalist way of life	6%	4%	
Scientific and technical change/evolution	25	13	11%
Quality of life	3	2	
Leisure time			
Housing			
Ecological crisis	1	1	1
Alcoholism			
Education/training	2	1	
Family relations/marital relations (including rural)			
Youth			1
Social relations/social policy/development	2	4	1
Demographic studies/population growth			
Urbanization			
Morality/ethics		1	
Culture studies	4		10
Religion	3	3	12
Inter-nationality relations	3		2
Media/communications/journalism	1		
Methods/methodology/sociological theory/reform in the discipline	8	4	5
Economic issues			
Critique of bourgeois society/capitalism	5%	3%	
Management/organization/industry planning	5	2	
Economic problems/reform/economic development	1	5	
Workers' attitudes and behaviour/identity		2	
Improving efficiency/productivity	1	2	
Manpower resources/mobility/migration			
Employment/unemployment/retirement			
Rural employment/production/collective farms			
Occupational structures/social stratification/classes			
Satisfaction of workers' needs			
World economics/regional economics/integration	2		
Commodity/money/investments/price accounting			
Political issues			
Marxism Leninism/historical materialism/dialectics (Hegel)	11%	7%	5%
Party Congress reports/documents			
Party organization, training, leadership (Communist Party activities), socialist democracy		1	
International communism/socialism	2	3	
International relations/detente	2		5

Imperialism/conflict/war peace/security/military affairs		9	
Global problems		3	
Revolution	1		
Political attitudes and behaviour/political culture		2	5
Justice/injustice/law		1	5
Critique of bourgeois democracy		1	
Government reform/(liberal) democracy/leadership			6
Elections/legislatures			
Decentralized decision-making/regional elites/federalism			
Government bureaucracy			
Category summaries			
Social issues: total percentage	58%	32%	43%
Economic issues: total percentage	13	13	0
Political issues: total percentage	16	27	26
Other issues: total percentage	13	27	31
Overall total number of topics for each year:	100%	100%*	100%
	(107)	(106)	(83)

* Percentage do not sum to exactly 100% because of rounding errors.
** Issues numbered 7 and 8 are missing from the 1996 figures because these volumes could not be located.

that receive the greatest frequency of attention in 1996 are problems of young people, internationality relations and religion. The only primary topic that appears to have significantly fallen from favour in 1996 is the impact of scientific and technological change on society – a topic that had been addressed frequently in both 1976 and 1986.

As had been the case with *Sotsiologicheskie Issledovaniia*, the overall frequency with which economic issues are addressed in the pages of *Kommunist (Svobodnaia Msyl)*, does decrease significantly between 1986 and 1996. Notably absent in 1996 are articles which focus primarily on improving efficiency and productivity, on the satisfaction of workers' needs, and on the topics of money and investment. Remaining important topics for research in 1996 are questions of management, organization and planning; economic reform; and also social stratification (inequality).

For the journal *Voprosy Filosofi*, the overall number of different primary topics covered changes only slightly between 1976 and 1986. As to social issues, the most frequently tackled topic in both 1976 and 1986 is scientific and technical change and the ramifications of this change throughout society (Table 10.3). Critiques of bourgeois society and the capitalist way of life also appear prominently in both 1976 and 1986.

Table 10.4 Percentage occurrence of primary topics in published articles, for *Sociological Studies, Kommunist/Svobodnaia Msyl,* and *Voprosy Filosofi* combined for 1976, 1986 and 1996

Topics/Years	1976	1986	1996
Social issues			
Critiques of bourgeois sociology/critiques of capitalist way of life	3%	2%	0
Scientific and technical change/evolution	12	7	3%
Quality of life	1	2	0
Leisure time	1	1	1
Housing		0	0
Ecological crisis	1	1	1
Alcoholism		1	
Education/training	3	4	4
Family relations/marital relations (including rural)	1	2	0
Youth	1	1	4
Social relations/social policy/development	1	2	1
Demographic studies/population growth	0	2	2
Urbanization		1	0
Morality/ethics	1	1	
Culture studies	2	0	4
Religion	1	1	3
Inter-nationality relations	2	1	5
Media/communications/journalism		1	2
Methods/methodology/sociological theory/reform in the discipline	4	4	8
Economic issues			
Critique of bourgeois society/capitalism	2%	1%	
Management/organization/industry planning	7	4	5%
Economic problems/reform/economic development	2	5	2
Workers' attitudes and behaviour/identity	2	4	2
Improving efficiency/productivity	2	6	
Manpower resources/mobility/migration	2	0	1
Employment/unemployment/retirement	0	0	2
Rural employment/production/collective farms	1	2	1
Occupational structures/social stratification/classes	1	1	2
Satisfaction of workers' needs	2	1	1
World economics/regional economics/integration	2		1
Commodity/money/investments/price accounting		3	0
Political issues			
Marxism Leninism/historical materialism/dialectics (Hegel)	7%	5%	2%
Party Congress reports/documents	9	4	1
Party organization, training, leadership (Communist Party activities), socialist democracy	4	2	
International communism/socialism	5	4	1

International relations/detente	4	1	5
Imperialism/conflict/war peace/security/military affairs	2	8	7
Global problems		1	
Revolution	0		
Political attitudes and behaviour/political culture		1	8
Justice/injustice/law	1	2	3
Critique of bourgeois democracy	1	0	
Government reform/ (liberal) democracy/leadership		1	4
Elections/legislatures			2
Decentralized decision-making/regional elites/ federalism		1	2
Government bureaucracy		0	1
Category summaries			
Social issues: total percentage	36%	32%	39%[*]
Economic issues: total percentage	24	27	17
Political issues: total percentage	34	31	35
Other issues: total percentage	6	9	9
Overall total number of topics for each year:	295 (100%)	367 (100%)	410 (100%)

[*] Individual percentages may not sum exactly to sub-section percentage totals because of rounding errors.

Science in socialist society was understood to be progressive and to serve the needs of the people, while 'bourgeois' science was seen as being both anarchic and exploitative. Studies of culture and internationality relations did appear in 1976, but not in 1986. The appearance of such articles in the 1970s represents the expansion in the range of activities of the Institute of Ethnography in Moscow during the Brezhnev years (Lapidus, 1984). Andropov similarly encouraged research into ethnic processes, while the early Gorbachev years were marked by a return to an earlier orientation, similar to the optimism expressed by Khrushchev, that the nationality problem had been 'solved'. In contrast, the coverage of economic issues in *Voprosy Filosofi* appears remarkably stable between 1976 and 1986, although an increased emphasis on economic reform (restructuring) does occur in 1986.

Expansion in the range of topics covered by the scholarly articles in *Voprosy Filosofi* in 1986 occurs with regard to political issues. Several articles were written in 1986 about war, imperialism, peace and global problems. These primary topics had not been the chief focus of any of the articles published in 1976. Concerns are raised in 1986 about strengthening the defence capability of the Soviet Union (Kirshin and

Popov), about US aggressiveness (Kondratkov; Krasin), and about war-oriented research (Kulkin) – to give just a few examples.

The publication orientation for *Voprosy Filosofi* changes again when 1996 is compared with 1986. The most significant shift occurs with regard to the increased frequency of discussion of religious questions and culture in the 1996 issues. Particularly noteworthy are the discussions of Russian culture, including references to the old concepts of 'Slavophilism' (Shchukin), 'Eurasianism' (Luks) and the 'Third Rome' (Panarin). Among the several articles that have a primary focus on religion are Mitiugov's on cognition and faith, Trubnikova's on Buddhism, and Afanasiev on paganism and Christianity. These articles illustrate a rather pervasive tendency towards soul-searching which is occurring more widely in Russian society today. Scholars continue to debate the mysticism of the 'Russian idea (soul)' and the 'Eurasian essence' of the Russian national character – yet younger scholars tend to pick up methodology, plus theory and ideology, from the latest editions of the leading American academic journals (Prazauskus, 1997). The political issues that provide the primary subject for discourse in 1996 include several reflections on democracy (Stepin and Tolstykh; Gadjiev; Pantin; Alekseeva and Kantor).

When the percentages are combined for *Sotsiologicheskie Issledovaniia*, *Kommunist (Svobodnaia Msyl)*, and for *Voprosy Filosofi*, certain discernable patterns of change emerge (Table 10.4). With regard to social issues, the focus on scientific/technical change, which occurs in both 1976 and 1986, declines in 1996. The more frequently addressed social topics in 1996 are methods and reform in the discipline, internationality relations, culture studies, education and the problems of youth. But none of these are new topics for social scientists, and all had been previously addressed in the 1970s and the 1980s. For economic issues, the primary pattern is one of continuity rather than change. Although the overall frequency of articles devoted to economic issues does decline and discussions of improving efficiency and productivity disappear in 1996, social scientists have continued to research the questions of management/organization, economic reform, workers' attitudes and behaviour, employment and social inequality. With regard to political affairs, we see a decline in references to Marxism/Leninism, international socialism and to the documents and work of the Communist Party; and in place we see increased discussions of international relations, political attitudes and government reform.

The subject matter for study does shift from 1976 to 1986 and from 1986 to 1996, but not as thoroughly as one might have hypothesized. It is also noteworthy that the polemics that surround the presentation of the empirical studies do not shift completely. As expected, the words Marxism and socialism do appear frequently in the presentations published in 1976, but the deliberations are not by any means smothered in Marxist–Leninist terminology. Interestingly enough, such concepts as economic dialectics and historical materialism can still be seen in 1996 publications.

Nonetheless, Andrei Melville (1997), who has published the results of his research in both Russia and the West, observes that the most significant shift in social science has been from the use of Marxist references to legitimize scholarly work in the last decades of the Soviet Union to the methodological and theoretical vacuum that he says exists today. Melville affirms our own observations that there are still some groups of scholars who continue to use Marxist methodology in economics, philosophy and history; but that these scholars are in the minority.

According to Melville, the methodological chaos that characterizes Russian social science today has resulted in part from the importation and distortion of approaches/schools developed outside of the Russian setting. Zaslavskaya (1996, p. 9) also laments the lack of general theory about post-Soviet society that could serve as the methodological basis for the organization of sociological knowledge in the way that Marxism once did. She says that the formation of such a conception is the central task not only of sociology but also of the other social sciences. The uncritical adoption of Western methodologies (in some cases old and outdated approaches) are not helpful to the development of the Russian social science discipline.

The most dramatic change does not relate to ideology or jargon, but rather to substance. By 1996, social scientists had become very focused on the political orientations of Russia's own citizens and on the question of Russia's place in the world system. In 1976, Soviet social scientists appeared to believe that their country could accomplish their goals of socialist transformation without any help from most of the rest of the world. In fact, in 1976, frequent references were made to the multiple mistakes being made by capitalist systems. By 1996, however, Russian social scientists showed an acute awareness of how inextricably tied the future of Russia is with the rest of the world – most notably with Europe and the West. The vulnerability of Russia was openly acknowledged in numerous articles and a willingness to share the ideas and methods of Western scholars clearly emerged in the 1996 discussions.

Conclusions

Our content analysis suggests that Russian social scientists (and Soviet social scientists before them) show a heartfelt desire to improve their society. They investigate difficult problems and genuinely search for workable solutions. Although a few appear to be writing from an ivory tower and devote their energies to the more esoteric pursuits, most are tackling the very real problems facing Russian society in their day. For 1996, these include articles about minority violence, migrant labour, unemployment, the challenges of raising children, and the problems associated with military service.

Nonetheless, Tatyana Zaslavskaya, in the lead article of the third volume of *Sotsiologicheskie Issledovaniia (1996)*, continues to berate her colleagues for not taking an active enough part in Russia's social transformation. According to Zaslavskaya (1996, p. 6), contemporary Russian sociology should serve three main functions. The first is 'scientific' – to increase factual knowledge about the nature of society. The second function is political, and is directly related to the interaction between sociology and the organs of power. Sociology can assist in the development of effective governmental policies by providing information about the results of governmental programmes and initiatives and by advising the government about ways of improving the effectiveness of reforms. The third function of sociology is to inform the citizens about the social processes taking place within the society. In order for Russian social scientists to play a more direct role in the reform process, she says that government officials will have to become more receptive to the work of scientists; but scientists, for their part, must also learn to communicate more effectively with policy-makers.

Russian social scientists, thus, view their role in the tradition of Durkheim and Comte, who favour 'enlightened' social policy and reform. Similarly, this tradition is represented in the orientation of C. Wright Mills who states that 'we study the structural limits of human decision in an attempt to find points of effective intervention' (Mills, 1961, p. 174, quoted in Gray, 1994, p. 172). The tendency among Russian social scientists is to believe that 'social knowledge is relatively useless unless it leads to social reform' (Gray, 1994, p. 169).

Melville, like Zaslavshaya, believes that the link between the state and the discipline is actually quite weak. As during the *perestroika* period, however, there are numerous examples of social science research impacting upon society. Certain occupational and professional classes are attentive to the publication and dissemination of research. This includes marketing research for various companies, interest groups and associations.

Prazauskus (1997) goes one step further and argues that politicians, as well as significant sections of the more politically active citizenry, have developed a deeper awareness of certain issues as a result of the work of social scientists. New topics that have received increased attention are the transitions from authoritarian to democratic regimes taking place in other countries, the economic performance of other states, and human rights. Prazauskus notes that a number of legislators have employed social scientists as their regular assistants. Experts are invited to parliamentary hearings and to the preliminary discussions of legislation. Examples can also be found where scholarly proposals and ideas have led to policy change. E. G. Tishkov has written happily about how, due to his efforts, the 'civic' as opposed to the 'ethnic' idea of nation has been supported by President Yeltsin. However, the official rhetoric adopted by the political leaders is not always realized in the actual implementation of policy. Prazauskus concurs with the commentaries of Melville and Zaslavskaya that in some respects research is still used for 'propaganda' purposes – especially by the better financed parties and interest groups.

Shall we agree with Shalin's (1988, p. 1034) assertion that there is 'nothing inherently unsavory about the alliance between scholarship and politics, sociology and reform'? Certainly, social scientists have been aligned with policy-makers in other countries. Shalin gives the example of American social scientists who sought to legitimize their own discipline by promising to aid progressive reforms (Fine, 1976). The authors of this chapter might raise a similar example that is more current: the promotion by the United States National Science Foundation of research which focuses on 'democratization' and 'democratic transitions'. Thus, one can state that if indeed the endeavours of Russian social scientists do serve the needs of the state, they are certainly not alone. So long as governments control the allocation of resources within a society, they will surely influence research agendas.

Josephson (1992, p. 589) argues that, at least during the Soviet period, the relationship between science and the state has been uniquely tight: 'In perhaps no other country do external forces shape the face of research so visibly.... In a word, politics and ideology played a predominate role in the Soviet scientific enterprise'. In the Soviet Union, state involvement was open and professed: 'The boundaries of Soviet sociology [were] always...weak because the political leadership...insisted that sociology be tied to the "relevant" issues' (Jones, 1989, p. 319). But this is true to some degree in all countries. In the United States, the subject of the intimate relationship between policy-makers and researchers (and the potential loss of true academic freedom) has rarely been the subject of scrutiny. Possibly, 'the intrusions are more subtle' (ibid., p. 319). But how do we know how much other governments shape research programmes? Maybe the Soviet Union, and now the Russian Federation, could be used as a baseline from which to judge others. Arguably, it is only when the state becomes severely weakened, either through processes of internal decay and deterioration or as a result of the force of external change, that the state may lose its customarily pervasive influence over academia and social research. Under such circumstances, the tables do turn, and social scientists/'intellectuals' have the opportunity to set the agenda for reform.

Unsurprisingly, a plurality of views as to what shape reform should take has emerged in Russia. Zdravomyslov (1995) reports a fundamental split between the Institute of Sociopolitical Studies and the Institute of Sociology, both part of the Russian Academy of Sciences. According to Zdravomyslov (ibid.), the Institute of Sociopolitical Studies opposed the reform course taken by the Yeltsin government, arguing that the state has been responsible for political and economic dislocation in Russia. As a result, the Institute publishes studies/polls that emphasize the negative aspects of the government's initiatives. In some respects, the Russian Academy of Sciences lags behind the transformations that have occurred in other parts of society. Although the Academy is no longer an institute of the state, past scientific bosses do still command authority and do still use their positions to advance their own programmes and their own students (Josephson, 1992, pp. 608, 611). The Institute of Sociology can be considered an exception as it supports the government's efforts at reform, maintaining that such dislocations are inevitable parts of the transition process to a democratic, market-based economy. Despite these differences in orientation, both sides are interested in answers to the same question: how is society responding to reform efforts and how much dislocation can citizens endure in the name of democratization and market reform? Although political leaders still want social scientists to legitimate their efforts – as in the past – today they are no longer capable of demanding their compliance.

Sociology in Russia is moving through the gateway into a new era of scientific endeavour. The delegitimation of Marxist–Leninist ideology has brought a whole new range of theories and social problems to the table. The breadth and scope of research topics has never been more open. Arguably, the biggest change that has occurred in the Gorbachev and Yeltsin eras is the full participation of Russian scientists in the

international scientific arena through institutional and individual interactions. While social scientists are almost universally euphoric about
this turn of events, the abrupt disintegration of the Soviet state left a
vacuum in the discipline. The transition to a new paradigm remains
incomplete. For the foreseeable future, sociologists will be grappling
with the issues of what their role in society should be, what new
forms the discipline should take (for example, to what degree should
Western models be adopted) and how relations with the state will be
structured.

Notes

1 For surveys of such studies, see M. I. Kulichenko (ed.) (1979) *Osnovnye
napravleniia izucheniia national'nykh otnoshenii v SSSR*, Moscow: Nauka; and
Iu. V. Bromlie (1981) *Sovremennye Problemy Etnografii*, Moscow, Nauka.
2 Zaslavskaya's speech, later published as an article in *Pravda*, 6 Feb 1987, was
translated by *BBC Summary World Broadcast*, 10 Feb 1987, and reprinted in
Social Research, 1988.
3 Zaslavskaya also co-authored the 'Novosibirsk Report' in 1983 which circulated widely in both political and intellectual circles. Written as a memor-
andum for a very restricted readership, the document searched for answers to
the crisis of the times.
4 See Bestuzhev-Lada, 1988; Dzhrnazian, 1988; and Ionin, 1987.
5 *Mezano uc-kcnpecc*, 11 April 1991.
6 *Moscow News*, 22 September 1991.
7 *Moscow News*, 29 December 1991.
8 *Rossiiskaya Gazeta*, 3 September 1991.
9 *Rossiiskaya Gazeta*, 3 September 1991.
10 *Moscow News*, 22 September 1991.
11 Foreign Broadcast Information Service. *Daily Report on the Soviet Union* (30
May 1990): 80.
12 *Svoboda*, 30 June 1991.
13 Scientific societies emerged with an expressed goal to 'combat incipient anti-
science attitudes among the population' (Josephson, 1992: 612).
14 A listing of opinion polls has been published in the Russian press (contact the
authors for details).
15 Among the journals read by most researchers are *Voprosy Filosofii*, *Polis*
and *Svobodnaia Msyl*. *Voprosy filosofii* was the only uncensored journal
(except by the Propaganda Department of the Communist Party's Central
Committee). Although *Voprosy filosofii* and *Sotsiologicheskie issledovaniia*
continue to be the major social science journals, *perestroika* helped to
stimulate the publication of a plethora of new sociological periodicals,
including: *Filosofskaia i sotsiologicheskaia mysl'*, *Voprosy sotsiologii*, *Thesis –
Teoriia i Istoriia Ekonomicheskikh Sotsial'nykh Institutov i Sistem*, *Sotsiologiia:
4–M – Metodologiia, Metody, Matematicheskie Modeli*, and *Rubezh* (Zdravomyslov 1995, 48).

16   For the most part, the number of primary topics is the same as the number of articles in the journal for that year. In a few instances, an article covered more than one primary topic; then both primary topics were recorded.

References

Afanasiev, A. Iu. (1996) Evolution of Image: From Paganism to Christianity, *Voprosy Filosofii*, 10 (in Russian).

Alekseeva, T. A. (1996) Democracy as Idea and as Process, *Voprosy Filosofii*, 6 (in Russian).

Allakhverdov, A. (1994) Rivals for Power lay Down the Law, *Science*, vol. 266, p. 1153.

Andrushenko, E. G., Dmitriev, A. V. and Toshenko, J. T. (1996) Polls and Elections in 1995, *Sotsiologicheskie Issledovaniia*, 6, pp. 3–17 (in Russian).

Arutiunian, I. (1980) Natsional'no-regional'noe mnogoobrazie sovetskoi derevni, *Sotsiologicheskie issledovaniia*, 3, p. 73.

Arutiunian, I. V. (1969) Konkretno-sotsiologicheskoe issledovanie natsional'nykh otnoshenii, *Voprosy filosofii*, 12, pp. 129–39.

Bestuzhev-Lada, I. V. (1988) Why Stir Up the Past, *Sotsiologicheskie Issledovaniia*, 3, pp. 101–4.

Dzhrnazian, L. N. (1988) Cult and Servitude, *Sotsiologicheskie Issledovaniia*, 5, pp. 64–71.

Filimonov, E. G. (1974) Sotsiologicheskii issledovaniia protsessa preodoleniia religii v sel'skoi mestnosti itogi, problemy, perspektivy, *Voprosy nauchnogo ateizma*, 16, pp. 73–80.

Gadjiev, K. S. (1996) Is it Epoch of Democracy, *Voprosy Filosofii*, 9 (in Russian).

Gamson, W. A., Fireman, B. and Rytina, S. (1982) *Encounters with Unjust Authority*, Homewood. IL, Dorsey.

Gaponenko, N. (1995) Transformation of the Research System in a Transitional Society: the Case of Russia, *Social Studies of Science* vol. 25, pp. 685–703.

Girnius, S. (1989) 'Lithuania', *Report on the USSR* (Radio Free Europe/Radio Liberty), 29 December.

Girnius, S. (1989) Sociological Surveys in Lithuania, *Report on the USSR* (Radio Free Europe/Radio Liberty), 10 November.

Girnius, S. (1992) Lithuania, *RFE/RL Research Report* 1, pp. 70–3.

Gaponenko, N. (1995) Transformation of the Research System in a Transitional Society: the Case of Russia, *Social Studies of Science*, vol.25, pp. 685–703.

Gray, D. J. (1994) Russian Sociology: the Second Coming of August Comte, *American Journal of Economics and Sociology*, 53(2), pp. 163–74.

Ionin, L. G. (1987) The Conservative Syndrome, *Sotsiologicheskie Issledovaniia*, 5, pp. 19–30.

Jones, A. (1989) Soviet Sociology, Past and Present, *Contemporary Sociology*, 18, pp. 316–9.

Josephson, P. R. (1992) Soviet Scientists and the State: Politics, Ideology, and Fundamental Research from Stalin to Gorbachev, *Social Research*, 59(3), pp. 589–614.

Kantor, V. K. (1996) Democracy as a Historical Problem in Russia, *Voprosy Filosofii*, 5(in Russian).

Karklins, R. (1986) *Ethnic Relations in the USSR: the Perspective from Below*, Boston, Unwin Hyman.

Kholmogorov, I. (1970) I*nternatsional'nye cherty sovetskikh natsii*, Moscow, Mysl'.

Kirsmin, Yu. A. and Popov, V. M. (1986) Problems of War and Peace: Some Results of Studies, *Voprosy Filosofii*, 2 (in Russian).

Kondratkov, T. R. (1986) Anti-Nuclear Movement: the Ideological Problems, *Voprosy Filosofii*, 3 (in Russian).

Kosova, L. (1997) Personal communication with the authors.

Krasin, Yu. A. (1986) The XXVII Congress of the CPSU on the Dialectics of the World Revolutionary Process, *Voprosy Filosofii*, 8 (in Russian).

Kudriavtsev, V. (1994) The Social Sciences Today, *Russian Social Science Review*, 35(3), pp. 3–18.

Kulkin, A. M. (1986) The Political and Socio-Economic Roots and Process of the Militarization of Science in the U.S.A., *Voprosy Filosofii*, 10 (in Russian).

Lapidus G. W. (1984) Ethnonationalism and Political Stability: the Soviet Case, *World Politics*, 36(4), pp. 355–80.

Leskov, S. (1996) Science's Survival Method – an Indefinite Leave of Absence, *Current Digest of the Post-Soviet Press*, 48(7), pp. 13–4.

Luks, L. (1996) Eurasianism and Conservative Revolution, *Vorposy Filosofii*, 3 (in Russian).

Melville, A. (1997) Personal communication with the authors.

Mirskaya, E. Z. (1995) Russian Academic Science Today: its Societal Standing and the Situation within the Scientific Comunity, *Social Studies of Science*, vol. 25, pp. 705–25.

Mitiugov, V. V. (1996) Cognition and Faith, *Voprosy Filosofii*, 6 (in Russian).

Morozov, A. (1996) Science in Collapse, *Current Digest of the Post Soviet Press*, 48(40), p. 26.

OMRI Daily Digest (1996).

Panarin, A. S. (1996) 'The Second Europa' or 'The Third Rome', *Voprosy Filosofii*, 10 (in Russian).

Paniotto, V. (1991) The Ukrainian Movement for Perestroika – Rukh: a Sociological Survey, *Soviet Studies*, 43, pp. 177–81.

Pantin, I. K. (1996) Postcommunist Democracy in Russia: Foundations and Features, *Voprosy Filosofii*, 6 (in Russian).

Prazauskus, A. (1997) Personal communication with the authors.

Radaev, V. (1995) Can Sociological Work be Trusted?, *Russian Social Science Review*, 36(6), pp. 53–63.

Savelyev, O. (1995) Expert: a Few Recommendations to Devotees of Sociological Surveys, *Current Digest of the Post Soviet Press*, 47(48), pp. 4–5.

Schwartz, M. and Shuva, P. (1992) Resource Mobilization versus the Mobilization of People: Why Consensus Movements Cannot be Instruments of Social Change, in Morris and Mueller (eds), *Frontiers in Social Movement Theory*, New Haven, Yale University Press.

Shalin, D. N. (1990) Sociology for the Glasnost Era: Institutional and Substantive Changes in Recent Soviet Sociology, *Social Forces*, 68(4), pp. 1019–39.

Shchukin, V. G. (1996) House and Shelter in Slavophile Conception, *Voprosy Filosofii*, 1 (in Russian).

Shlapentokh, V. (1987) *The Politics of Sociology in the Soviet Union*, Delphic Monograph Series, Boulder, Westview.

Shmelev, G. I. (1985) Socioeconomic Potential of Contract Family Farming, *Sotsiologicheskie Issledovaniia*, 4, pp. 14–21.

Solchanyk, R. (1991) Ukraine: From Chernobyl to Sovereignty, *Report on the USSR* (Radio Free Europe/Radio Liberty), 2 August.

Sosedskiy, A. (1996) Polls and Public, *Sotsiologicheskie Issledovaniia*, 6, pp. 132–4 (in Russian).

Stepin, V. S. and Tolstykh, V. I. (1996) Democracy and Fortunes of Civilization, *Voprosy Filosofii*, 10 (in Russian).

Tolz, V. (1992) Russia, *RFE/RL Research Report*, 1, pp. 4–9.

Trubnikova, N. N. (1996) The Peculiarities of Buddhist Tradition of Thought in Works of Kukai, *Voprosy Filosofii*, 9 (in Russian).

Tsypko, A. C. (1986) Possibilities and Resources of Cooperatives, *Sotsiologicheskie Issledovaniia*, 2, pp. 47–58.

Vilchek, Vs. (1996) Crafty Sociologists in the Ashes of the 1995 Elections, *Current Digest of the Post Soviet Press*, 48(19), pp. 9–10.

Vyzhutovich, V. (1996) "Mass Hypnosis Sessions: Sociological Fortune-Telling in the Thick of the Campaign, *Current Digest of the Post Soviet Press*, 48(19), p. 6.

Yurevich, A. (1996) Methods: Why were the Predictions 'not quite' borne out?, *Current Digest of the Post Soviet Press*, 48(1), pp. 10–11.

Zaslavskaya, T. (1988) Perestroika and Sociology, *Social Research*, 55(1–2), pp. 267–76.

Zaslavskaya, T. (1996) The Role of Sociology in Russian Reforms, *Sotsiologicheskie Issledovaniya*, 3, pp. 3–9.

Zdravomyslov, A. (1995) Sociology in Russia, *Russian Social Science Review*, 36(6), pp. 33–52.

Zemtsov, I. (1985) *Soviet Sociology: a Study of Lost Illusions in Russia under Soviet Control of Society*, Hero Books, Fairfax, VA.

Index